Slaughter in the Sacramento Valley

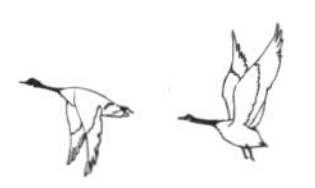

Other books by the author

Wildlife Wars
The Life and Times of a Fish and Game Warden

For Love of Wildness
Journal of a U.S. Game Management Agent

Defending Our Wildlife Heritage
The Life and Times of a Special Agent

A Sword for Mother Nature
The Further Adventures of a Fish and Game Warden

No Safe Refuge
Man as Predator in the World of Wildlife

The Thin Green Line
Outwitting Poachers, Smugglers and Market Hunters

Genesis of a Duck Cop
Memories & Milestones

SLAUGHTER

in the Sacramento Valley

Poaching and Commercial-Market Hunting—Stories and Conversations

Terry Grosz

Tom,
The Critters and I THANK YOU for dedicating your life to those in the world of wildlife who have no voice—

JOHNSON BOOKS
BOULDER

Published by Johnson Books, a Big Earth Publishing company.
3005 Center Green Drive, Suite 220, Boulder, Colorado 80301.
1-800-258-5830
E-mail: books@bigearthpublishing.com
www.bigearthpublishing.com

Cover design by Jake Ryan
Text design by Rebecca Finkel

9 8 7 6 5 4 3 2 1

Library of Congress Cataloging-in-Publication Data
Grosz, Terry.
Slaughter in the Sacramento Valley: poaching and commercial-market hunting—
stories and conversations / Terry Grosz.
p. cm.
ISBN 978-1-55566-426-8
1. Poaching—California—Sacramento Valley—Anecdotes.
2. Market hunting (Game hunting)—California—Sacramento Valley—Anecdotes.
3. Game protection—California—Sacramento Valley—Anecdotes. I. Title.
SK36.7.G746 2008
364.16'2859109794—dc22

2008029344

Printed in the United States of America

Contents

Preface

For decades as this country grew into the land it is today, its protein-starved peoples feasted on the abundant native wildlife. A twelve- to fourteen-hour work day, six days a week, on the farms, railroads, docks, mines, logging crews, or construction gangs took protein to replace the muscle lost. Citizens used the available wildlife resources because they were abundant, hunting was part of their culture, and laws did not exist against extreme use and misuse. In addition, alternative food sources were rare and expensive because the sheep-, cattle-, turkey-, chicken-, and hog-raising industries had not matured into the production giants they are today. Finally, the transportation and refrigeration infrastructure were lacking to supply such energy requirements in the outback. Accordingly, early Americans, like the residents of any developing nation, didn't have a choice but to live off the land in order to survive and flourish.

Commercial-market hunting soon became king, and many mammal, bird, and fisheries populations still feel the negative effects of these early-day slaughters. Barrels of buffalo tongues and squab passenger pigeons were salted and shipped to the major cities. Atlantic and Pacific salmon, sturgeon, cod, and every other finned and shellfish species moved in commerce to the ever-hungry people in the towns and cities. Ducks, geese, swans, loons, and shorebirds of every size, some weighing as little as an ounce, were gunned down where they lived and sent to the insatiable markets in the population centers. Wild turkey, elk, deer, bighorn sheep, moose, pronghorn, and what few bison were left fell to the market hunters' guns, beginning those populations' inevitable slides as they disappeared into the cooking pots of hungry citizens. The commercial markets even included such items as feathers, eggs, furs, hides, and other parts that were fashionable in the clothing markets or acceptable on the tables.

Soon this plundering and squandering of the nation's wildlife resources began to be felt (as early as the late 1600s in the Eastern United States) by those living on the land and an enlightened few informed and farsighted individuals in Washington, D.C. As commercially marketable species, especially the bird species, continued their slides into oblivion, those caring and in the know became more and more alarmed at what they were seeing. Soon powerful voices began to be heard and legal action taken regarding the slaughter of wildlife species for the markets. As a result, the long, slow process of species recovery from overharvest or the brink of extinction took its first few faltering steps. Those steps are protected by many laws and conservation practices today, but unfortunately, many species slid into extinction before those practices could be put into play. Others, such as the salmon and sturgeon, continue their slides into the dark holes of oblivion for many human-induced reasons. Species such as the tule elk, wild turkey, and striped bass slowly struggled back into the light of day and hopefully will continue to do so under the care of many state and federal land management agencies and concerned citizen conservation organizations.

America, especially during its early history, has always been blessed with wonderful animal populations, especially birds, both in numbers and in species. However, one group of winged creatures, those associated with wetland environments, found itself particularly susceptible to market gunning. During the heyday of commercial gunning, ducks, geese, swans, and shorebirds fell in the heaviest numbers to the demanding specialty appetites in the major cities. A rice-fed duck, stuffed white-fronted goose, or brace of plover was always welcome at almost anyone's table. Snipe, yellowlegs, avocets, godwits, curlews, plovers, and many other shorebirds fell in great numbers to the gunners for the few pennies they brought at the local markets as well. Soon they too felt the effects of decades of uncontrolled slaughter, and their numbers began declining.

In 1918, the United States and Great Britain signing for Canada (a like treaty was signed for Mexico in 1937) signed a treaty called the Migratory Bird Treaty Act. All three nations recognized the intrinsic values of migratory birds flying between their countries, not to mention the birds' importance in controlling insects for agricultural communities. The purpose of the treaty was to manage through good biology, land acquisition, and law enforcement the remaining migratory bird resources. In large part in those days, that meant controlling market hunting.

Many species were declared off-limits to any form of hunting, and commercial-market gunning was declared illegal, while many other species could be taken only under controlled seasons, bag limits, and methods of take. As in every law of this kind, there were loopholes, many of which were quickly discovered by those walking on the dark side. Just as quickly as those legal holes in the treaty were plugged up by state and federal laws, others were discovered and exploited. But after a few years, the conservation laws for the most part had righted themselves biologically, legally, and morally.

Major changes continued to be made right up through the 1930s because of excessive and unfair methods of take that were biologically unsound. Changes in the baiting laws (placing food grains in front of the guns to lure hungry waterfowl), banning the use of live decoys to lure cautious but unsuspecting waterfowl to the gun, restricting the gauge of shotguns and numbers of shells they could possess, and restricting the use of lead shot (in the 1980s) were implemented in order to emphasize conservation, wise use, fair chase, and sound biological practices.

However, as is the case in any law of the land, if it is not vigorously enforced, it doesn't work. In the early days of the treaty, the Bureau of Biological Survey, later renamed the U.S. Fish and Wildlife Service, was designated by Congress to be the lead agency in protecting the migratory birds because they were a national and international resource. This work was initially done by numbers of officers that were so limited that the effect of protection was basically nonexistent. Even today, some eighty-four years later, the number of federal officers designated to protect migratory birds is so low (less than 220 for the entire nation at the time of this writing) that it is considered a laughing matter by almost all the supporting state Fish and Game agencies, other federal resource departments, conservation groups, and many of the agency's officers themselves.

Due to this lack of federal on-the-ground enforcement presence, the continuing feeling that resources are there for the taking, the sometimes weak or limited supporting legal systems, the American people's general lack of interest in the plight of migratory birds, and the overall lack of Service in-depth understanding and leadership in the law enforcement field, the migratory bird resources continue to suffer.

Add to that mixture millions of miles of deadly transmission lines (bird strikes, electrocutions); oil development interests (uncovered oil pits representing death traps); illegal widespread use of poisons on sheep and cattle ranges to control avian predators (eagle and other migratory birds); illegal take with the use of rifles and traps for the unlawful feather trade (national and international in scope); illegal pumping of ships' bilges on the oceans and inland waterways (oil soaking birds, leading to death); wasteful taking by Alaskan Natives of nesting waterfowl, flightless birds, and their eggs for use as dog food; unwise and illegal drainage of the prairie pothole regions in the United States and

Canada, which reduces the nesting territories of many species of water-loving birds, heap-leech-mining operations in semiarid regions such as the state of Nevada (leading to death of species by cyanide poisoning); illegal scooping of eggs in Alaska by civilian waterfowl propagation interests (overharvest); illegal scooping of bird-of-prey nests by falconry interests; expansion of wind farms to generate electricity (mortality through bird strikes with the tower's whirling blades); losses through military programs in the name of national defense; and losses through construction projects—just to name a few things that continue to kill untold millions of migratory birds annually.

It is with this current sad picture of avian destruction that a historical element from the market hunting days in the Sacramento Valley of California is isolated in this book and presented as a central theme. The places are real, and many of the names are those of folks who were there. Those folks market hunting and killing hundreds of thousands of migratory waterfowl are a significant part of our American history; hence my interest. Their exploits and tales are as significant as those from the whaling industry, the buffalo hunters, the fur-seal and sea-otter hunters, and the mountain men trappers from this nation's past. That past was often smeared in blood and waste, but it is an integral part of this nation's growth and history just the same. With this in mind, I attempt to capture that small and unique part of history from the Sacramento Valley before it too disappeared quietly, never to be heard from again. Sadly, I started this project some thirty years too late. I missed my real chance to interview many of those old-time market gunners and "duck draggers" (so called, some say, for having to drag their heavy kills across the fields in burlap bags or tied in large bunches with baling twine) before they disappeared into the pages of history.

But I managed to find a few still alive to help me capture some of the essence of those days. For that I am thankful and only hope that the reader will be able to smell the damp of the rice fields, feel the winter's breezes, get a wisp of the smell of gunpowder from hammering shotguns, hear the thunderous roar of thousands of frantically beating wings, and feel the thrill of what it was like in the good old days when market hunting was king.

I had the honor of working with or against a number of the individuals in these stories. I even caught a few of them back in the day. However, in my recent associations with them as I conducted interviews in the summer of 2007, I began to sense a force that could not be overcome. Many of the gunners either refused to discuss their experiences openly or carefully provided only information guaranteed not to embarrass them or their living kinfolk. It soon became obvious that even after all the years since much of the illegal shooting had occurred, even though the statute of limitations had long since run out, there still existed a code of silence among them. For whatever reason, considerable information was shaded or outright eliminated from the interviews because of this code of silence. This was made all the more frustrating because many of those being interviewed were facing the inevitable march of time, as was the history they represented. With that "closed-shop" thread of reality, I sadly closed my books and made do with the information I had secured. It is enough to give the reader a sense of what occurred but unfortunately not the total heart and soul of the historical events now long past.

One thread of this heritage represents stories from the conservation officers and gunners who have long since stepped over the Great Divide. The second thread of this book represents stories from the days when I was young and on a vision quest in my beloved Sacramento Valley. The third thread represents information gleaned from those gunners still alive who would discuss their illegal adventures from a time when they and the country were younger and full of hope. The last thread represents my attempts to illuminate some of the little-known efforts of men involved in saving part of the world of wildlife.

All in all, the duck draggers, commercial-market hunters, officers, and involved civilians illustrated herein were a part of Americana seldom seen today. They did what they felt they had to do and then walked off into the pages of history like so many before them.

Enjoy the read for the tale it presents, for in the world of waterfowl, like so many other life histories, this story will be no more once today's resources are squandered and history stands in stark and sometimes mute testimony to our previous actions—or inactions.

Acknowledgments

Early in the genesis of this project, a set piece of unique American poaching, commercial-market hunting, and duck dragging histories, two dear friends were urging me to put pen to paper in this endeavor. It is those two men, Peter Grevie and So Han "Sonny" Park, whom I wish to especially thank for all the support and gifted counsel they provided.

I also wish to acknowledge those who became part of the pages of this book by stepping forth and providing their personal stamps on this piece of history. It came to life because of their foresight in providing their part of the puzzle as it related to the slaughter in the Sacramento Valley.

To the following men and women, I offer my sincerest appreciation for their parts in this work; Peter Grevie (Colusa), Bernadette "Bernie" Grevie (Colusa), Jess D. Turner (Williams), Fay Turner (Williams), Doug Turner (Williams), "Dutch" Bremer (Gridley), Vance Boyes (Colusa), Glenn Welborn (Colusa), Harold "Cocky" Myers (Arbuckle), Wallace "Ed" Dowell (Woodland), Ray "Pudge" Dowell (Woodland), and Charles Geyer (Arbuckle).

I also wish to acknowledge those living and dead officers whose stories were told to me and appear in this work: Glenn D. Ragon (deputy sheriff, Humboldt County, retired), Inspector Kenneth Hooker (California Department of Fish and Game, deceased), Warden Paul D. Kerhr (deceased), Warden Jim Hiller (deceased), Warden Bud Reynolds (deceased). I also thank several Colusa County residents whose information appears in this book but who did not want to be identified because of the concerns it would raise among their still living kinfolk in the valley.

Thanks to my publisher, Mira Perrizo, of Johnson Books in Boulder. She has always kept her eyes on the business end of things but in the process guided her authors to levels even they never thought possible. Her guidance and encouragement helped bring this project to fruition.

Finally, I would like to thank my long-suffering wife and cameraperson, Donna, who was dragged into this endeavor but, as expected, fully offered her support, as she always has throughout our married life.

My thanks to all of you once again for your contributions in bringing to print a small but unique piece of American history.

This book is dedicated to Peter Grevie and So Han "Sonny" Park,
quintessential visionary friends and great human beings;
men whose souls are in tune with the history of the times,
who are friends to all who truly see,
and whose wisdom and gifted counsel is before its time.
To these men possessing a true ethic of the land,
whom I respect as men for all seasons and love as the brothers they are,
I dedicate this book of unique Sacramento Valley histories
from one westering man to the great Americans they are.

CHAPTER 1

A "Sorehead" Gets His Due

This story is based on a conversation with Inspector Ken Hooker, California Department of Fish and Game, Colusa, California, during a station inspection in October 1967.

Captain Ken Hooker of the California Department of Fish and Game sat quietly in his patrol car in the cannery parking lot, from which he could watch the happenings on Fisherman's Wharf without being observed. The morning before, Hooker had received word from a reliable informant that a truckload of ducks slaughtered earlier in the week in the Willows area would be delivered the following morning to an Italian restaurant known to be frequented by members of the mafia. Since that informant had never been wrong, and he didn't want to share the information with anyone else for fear of exposing the identity of his source, Hooker sat alone and kept an eye on the delivery entrance of the restaurant in question.

About two in the morning, a dark van pulled into the back alley of Louie's restaurant, an area normally reserved for deliveries. After turning off its headlights, the occupants sat inside for a few minutes, as if they were on the alert for any signs of discovery. When they were satisfied that the coast was clear, three men quickly emerged from the darkened vehicle. One man walked around the van and with a set of keys opened the back door to Louie's. His two partners flung open the van's rear doors and began hurriedly unloading full gunnysacks with difficulty because of their weight. Soon all three men were moving the wet, heavy gunnysacks from the van into a darkened back room of the restaurant, unaware of Captain Hooker moving rapidly on foot from his patrol car in the parking lot toward their frantic activity. In the men's haste to move quickly, some of the sacks came open, and the broken bodies of unpicked ducks began spilling out onto the pavement.

As Anthony Carbone grabbed a sack of ducks from the rear of the van, he felt the cold steel of a pistol barrel being shoved gently against his neck and heard the words, "Don't move. Fish and Game warden; you are under arrest!" Startled and terrified by the pistol barrel being pressed hard against his neck, Carbone reacted by freezing as ordered and then wet himself.

Emerging from the darkened restaurant moments later, Gino Colleta, unaware of the drama taking place at the rear of the van, reached for a sack of ducks only to hear the quiet words, "Stand as you are! Fish and Game warden; you are under arrest!" Gino froze at hearing those words, standing dumbstruck by the commanding voice and the unexpected turn of events.

Dominic Carluchi emerged from the rear of the restaurant, strode over to the van, and hissed, "Get it in gear, youse guys; we don't have all night." Suddenly he became aware that there were now four of them standing at the rear of the van in the darkened alley, and in the same breath he exclaimed, "What the hell is going on?"

"Hold it right there; Fish and Game warden!" instructed Hooker as he turned on his flashlight, aiming its light into the men's faces so as to temporarily blind them.

"Run!" screamed Gino as he lunged for the end of the alley.

Dominic, realizing the serious trouble he was in—especially because he had recently been convicted for possessing illegal ducks—tried to break out of Hooker's firm hold on his collar. Unable to do so, he turned in his jacket and struck Hooker in the face with his fist. In quick response, Hooker smashed the barrel of his .38-caliber revolver across Dominic's head, sending him crashing to the ground in a haze of colorful stars just before everything turned to a soft gray and he passed out. Grabbing his wrists before he came to, Hooker quickly slipped on a pair of handcuffs.

Carbone stood absolutely still, as if his feet were frozen to the ground. His heart was beating frantically, causing him to hyperventilate as a roaring sound began to beat a drum-like tempo in his head. Gino had cleared the end of the alley in a sprint and disappeared among the parked cars in the parking lot and the foggy early-morning darkness on the docks of San Francisco.

Reaching into his back pants pocket, Hooker removed his spare set of handcuffs and placed them on Carbone's wrists. Directing Carbone to sit, Hooker took a look into the van with his flashlight. He opened one of the wet burlap bags, and his suspicions were confirmed as a dozen freshly killed pintail ducks tumbled out onto the floor of the van. His examination of the remaining five burlap sacks in the van revealed that all were full of freshly killed pintail and mallard ducks.

Taking his last spare set of cuffs from his coat pocket, Hooker handcuffed Carbone's cuffs to the back bumper of the van so he couldn't escape and then headed into the darkened restaurant to see what was in the burlap bags the men had already hauled into the back room. Again, Hooker's suspicions were confirmed. All six wet sacks on the floor inside contained dead ducks, and a quick look at the carcasses showed that the birds appeared to have been shot in the backs, a sign that they had been killed during an illegal "duck drag," or mass killing by commercial market hunters.

Dragging two of the heavy burlap bags out into the alley, Hooker checked to make sure his two suspects were still hooked up. Satisfied, he reentered the restaurant and hauled out the remaining sacks of dead ducks, which were now state's evidence. He removed the keys from the van in case the man who had escaped returned for the vehicle and the rest of the ducks, and then, walking Carbone in front and dragging Dominic, who was still out cold, by the collar, he moved the pair toward his patrol car.

When he reached his patrol car, Hooker used his Fish and Game radio to call the city's dispatcher and request backup. Soon a nearby San Francisco county sheriff's deputy rolled up, and Hooker transferred his prisoners to the other officer's vehicle for transport. He and the deputy drove their patrol cars to the van, and Hooker loaded all the sacks of ducks into his car, filling the back and passenger seats to the roof, with the remaining bags bulging out the back of his trunk. The deputy locked the restaurant's back door, and then the two vehicles made their way to the San Francisco county jail, where the two prisoners were booked for possession of an overlimit of ducks. Dominic was in urgent need of medical attention because Hooker's pistol barrel had left a six-inch-long gash on his head, so a visit to a nearby hospital for stitches was in order.

Hooker and the deputy then returned to the van and had it hauled to San Francisco's impound lot. It was never claimed and was later sold at auction, as was the policy of the city of San Francisco for any impounded vehicle that wasn't claimed by its owner within 90 days.

Three days afterward, Hooker was once again patrolling the docks of San Francisco, checking commercial fishing boats as they offloaded their catches. Approaching the cannery parking lot where he had parked three nights earlier, he was surprised to find a large black limousine slowly moving up alongside his driver's-side door. The back passenger window rolled down and a .45-caliber Thompson submachine-gun barrel was thrust out through the opening and aimed directly at Hooker. The gunman gestured with his free hand for Hooker to pull over to the side of the road, which he promptly did.

Another man emerged from the limo as Hooker looked down the barrel of the machine gun, opened the driver's-side door of the patrol car, and told him, "Get out; the boss wants to see you."

Hooker emerged from his car and quickly looked around for some kind of help. The men in the limo had done their work well because there was no one else in the area. He was outnumbered, outgunned, and on his own. He was forced into the backseat of the limo, where a bag was pulled over his head as the men quickly relieved him of his service revolver.

"What the hell is this all about?" Hooker asked in the strongest voice he could muster.

"Keep your yap shut," a gruff voice answered as the car roared off.

About five minutes later, they drove into a large warehouse somewhere along the docks. Hooker knew where they were because he could smell saltwater and hear the horns from the ships in the bay as they passed each other. The sounds echoed in what had to be a large building. The limo finally rolled to a stop, his hood was removed, and he was told to get out.

After Hooker's eyes had adjusted to the dim light of a warehouse full of new tires, he saw a group of men at the far end of the building in a glassed-in office. An abrupt shove on his shoulder forced him in that direction. As he got closer to that group of men, Hooker recognized one individual from the bandages on his head. It was Dominic Carluchi, reportedly a "made man" in the mafia, as Hooker had learned after the arrest he'd made three days earlier. One very well-dressed man was seated behind an old desk in the office. Everyone else stood at a respectful distance as if in deference to the power or position that man represented.

The seated man said, "Captain Hooker, my man Carluchi here says you pistol-whipped him without cause, in the tradition of San Francisco's finest. What do you have to say to that accusation?"

Ken Hooker, a slight, soft-spoken man, looked the seated one right in the eye and said, "Sir, your man started it by slugging me in the face after being arrested, and I finished the scuffle with a whip on his head with my gun barrel."

Carluchi started to object but was quickly silenced by a wave of the seated man's hand. Hooker thought Carluchi must have told his superior another version of the story and was now trying to make things right. The man at the desk had apparently come to that same conclusion after Hooker's short explanation but was giving everyone an opportunity to tell his side of the story before making any decision on the matter.

"What do you mean my man here struck you in the face? What did you do to force him to undertake such a rash action?" he quietly asked.

"I placed him under arrest for being in possession of illegal ducks, and he tried to get away from me. In the process, he struck me in the face before I hit him over the head with my gun barrel," Hooker quietly replied still not feeling overly confident about his chances of escaping the situation.

"Boss, that ain't true. He pistol-whipped me for no other reason than I was an Italian minding my own business in an alley and he hates Italians," screeched a wild-eyed Carluchi.

With another wave of his hand to silence Carluchi, the man asked, "Tell me again why you placed him under arrest, Captain Hooker?"

"I had received information that an illegal load of ducks would be dropped off that morning at Louie's restaurant. Since my informant had never been wrong before, I staked out the place. Mr. Carluchi and his friends arrived, just as the informant said would happen, driving a van with a large overlimit of ducks, and I made my arrest," replied Hooker.

"Captain Hooker, apparently we have made a grave mistake, and I owe you an apology. I will have my men take you back to your patrol car, and I hope you will let bygones be bygones," the man at the desk replied quietly. "Rest assured that I will take care of the problem on this end, and you won't be bothered in the future with such foolishness." He looked sternly at Carluchi.

"I have no problem with that, as long as your man pays his fine, as does his partner in crime. The one who fled the scene needs to appear and pay his fine as well," Hooker said in a matter-of-fact tone, now filled with a little more confidence.

"You can count on the right things being done, and please consider this matter closed," the seated man replied with a smile.

Hooker was driven back to his patrol car. After the men in the dark limo had returned his sidearm and left, he found himself noticeably shaken. He was a tough officer, but at that moment, he was a bit rattled.

One week later, all three men and their attorneys trooped before a state judge, pled guilty to possession of a large overlimit of ducks, and paid fines of $150 each.

One week later, Dominic Carluchi was found floating in San Pablo Bay. It appeared that the San Frisco mafia don who had sat at that desk to question Hooker did not want any adverse attention from any kind of law—even if it was over a piddling transaction involving a bunch of dead ducks and a whack over someone's head with a pistol barrel.

CHAPTER 2

The Drag, the Dump, and a Close Call

This story was told to me by Harold's son Dale in June 2007 in front of Linc Dennis's home in Maxwell as I waited for my longtime friend Mr. Dennis to return from the doctor's office. Dale and I were friends in the late 1960s, and he was a damned good informant on the goings-on in the Princeton area. During our opportune meeting in Maxwell, he shared this family story with me once he discovered I was working on Sacramento Valley market hunting stories for a new book. He asked that the true identity of the family be concealed because there are still many living relatives in the Norman-Princeton area of Colusa County whom he didn't want to embarrass. I did as he asked, and we are still good friends to this day.

Oscar looked at his pocket watch and said, "It's time. Lets get it in gear if we are going to get it done and leave without anyone being the wiser."

Harold nodded as his dad got up from the kitchen table, finished the dregs from his coffee cup, and headed for the back porch. He followed Oscar into the boot room off the porch, where the men grabbed their Model 11 Remington 12-gauge semiautomatic shotguns that were standing in the corner and headed out into the early-morning dampness of Colusa County. Both were dressed in long-sleeved shirts, tennis shoes, and bib overalls for the deadly task before them.

The Model T Ford growled to life as they settled into the hard seat. Flipping on the headlights, Oscar swung the truck out from his farm at the edge of Princeton and headed west on the Princeton Highway toward a friend's freshly harvested and recently burned rice field just northeast of the town of Maxwell. Ducks love to feed in burned-off rice fields because most of the chaff is removed, leaving the prized rice kernels readily exposed.

It was one A.M. in late November 1940, a good time for what they had in mind. There was no more than a quarter moon in the sky, the highway was deserted except for a few drunks coming home from the bars, and the wind was blowing softly out of the northwest. The slight moon and freshening breeze would be good for sneaking up on the feeding ducks, Harold thought with a grin and a shiver of anticipation.

Oscar said, "That's the farm trail we need to take," as he turned the truck south on a muddy, rutted, and partially overgrown dirt road, turning off his lights as he did so.

After motoring south for about half a mile in the dark, they finally bounced to a stop, using the emergency brake to eliminate the red glare of the brake lights. They were next to an old, abandoned farm shed, and Harold

A large kill of mallard and pintail ducks at the turn of the twentieth century in Sacramento Valley. The author counted over 400 ducks. (Courtesy Glenn Wellborn)

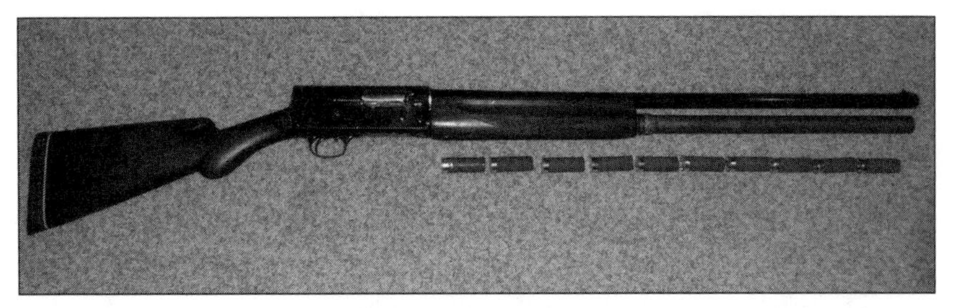

A classic example of a "Long Tom" or a market hunter's "killing machine." This is a model 11 Remington, 12-gauge shotgun with a magazine extender (see tube under the barrel), increasing the capacity of the shotgun from a legal three-shot firearm to one shooting 10 shells plus the one in the chamber. Some Long Toms were capable of firing 15 shots. Magazine extender courtesy of Ken Kagihiro. (Courtesy Rich Grosz, 2007)

bailed out of the truck and quickly ran to the building. Hurriedly unlatching and opening the front doors, he flung them wide open. Oscar drove the truck nose first into the maw of the shed, and Harold quickly shut the doors behind their truck. Then he fastened a wooden latch across the double doors from the inside. Peering through the crack between the doors, Harold carefully scanned the surrounding countryside for any signs of automobile lights or other telltale signs of discovery. Finding none, he slowly unlatched the shed doors, partly opened one, and walked out onto the muddy farm road. After a few more minutes of looking and listening in the inky blackness, he finally began to relax.

Hearing the shed door squeak open, Harold turned to see his father's darkened shape approaching.

"See or hear anything?" Oscar quietly asked.

"Not a thing, Dad," Harold replied in a low voice.

The two of them stood silent in the early-morning damp, intently looking and listening for the next twenty minutes.

"I suppose we best get ready," whispered Oscar as he turned and headed for the security and comfort of the shed.

The two men reentered the farm shed and shut and relocked the doors from the inside. Then they removed their shotguns, which had been hidden under a tarp in the back of the truck. They made sure they had an ample amount of precut sacking twine hung through and dangling down either side of the straps on their bib overalls; the twine would be used to tie up bunches of freshly shot ducks by their necks. Reaching into his toolbox, Oscar removed two long, homemade metal tubes that were the same diameter as a shotgun barrel and wrapped in oily burlap cloth for protection. Carefully removing the magazine cap and standard spring from his shotgun, he placed them on the floor. Then he replaced the magazine spring with a longer one and screwed the homemade extension onto the gun's existing magazine-cap threads. He now had a shotgun capable of firing eleven shots instead of the usual five. Harold followed suit, having been there and done the same thing many times before. Each man fed ten paper Remington Kleanbore number 6 shot, high-base shells into the magazine of his shotgun after indexing a single round into the chamber, for a total of eleven shots.

Unlocking and slightly opening one door to the shed, both men peered out once again to make sure all was clear. Being caught by the lowly "tule creepers," as local game wardens were called in those days, would garner a lot of ribbing and in some cases outright condemnation for stupidity from other locals in the business of market hunting. It would also cost them a fine in court and a loss of their evening's hard-won rewards in the forms of dozens of plump, freshly killed, rice-fed ducks.

They knew the devoted wardens would be out in those cold, damp rice fields. They were men as determined and strap-steel tough as the commercial market hunters whom they faced. Their only differences were in their numbers and dress. As was typical of any government organization, there were only a few of these dedicated officers in the whole Sacramento Valley. Facing them were dozens of dyed-in-the-wool market hunters and several hundred other farmers or men of the soil "dragging" or blowing up the ducks in organized mass shootings at night for their own uses. A good rice-fed duck dinner was a welcome addition to one's table or to the markets of the day, which sold ducks to many commercial eateries. Times were tough, and many families ate wild game at almost every meal because it was so readily available. Before all was said and done, many millions of ducks and geese fell to the outlaws' guns, destined for the marketplace and for tables in many homes before and after such takings were officially declared illegal in 1918 with the passage of the Migratory Bird Treaty Act.

The officers were at a disadvantage in the clothing department as well. In order to brave the long hours of damp cold in harvested rice fields at night, they had to dress warmly. After all, sitting or standing all night long protecting the feeding waterfowl would take a physical toll if one were unprepared. Heavy hip boots, gloves, warm hat, jeans with long handles underneath, and a sheepskin jacket usually were essentials of the officers' outfits. Such gear did not allow one to be fast on his feet when chasing market hunters or "duck draggers" trying to escape with their light clothing and tennis shoes, not to mention the fear of God in their souls. Plus, the market and drag gunners knew every inch of the land. Many times it seemed as if the ground just plain swallowed them up when they were being pursued by the clothing-encumbered, outnumbered officers. So stealth, closeness to one's prey, luck, and a hatful of guts were the officers' main keys to success if they were to win the battle at night in the rice fields against those illegally killing ducks.

Locking the shed doors behind them, the two men quietly walked south down the deserted, grass-covered farm road toward a familiar sound they both recognized—the noise of thousands of feeding ducks, which could be heard up to two miles away on a calm night. They also kept a sharp eye peeled for sign of other human activity, such as the law or other illegal gunning competition. They heard several long sequences of shots being fired into feeding ducks in other rice fields, some as far as a mile away. The sounds served to energize them for the task at hand as they hurried along, trying not to break a sweat.

"Sounds like the boys are busy again tonight," said Harold with a grin.

"Just as long as they're not busy in our field and keep the wardens on the run where they are, that's all I care about," said Oscar quietly.

After walking about three hundred yards, Oscar called a halt so he could listen again for the sound of feeding ducks. Cupping his hands behind his ears to enhance his hearing, Oscar turned his head and body 360 degrees until he was satisfied with what he heard. Harold did the same, listening to the water-flowing and grinding sounds made by the madly moving bills and grinding crops of thousands of feeding waterfowl picking up rice left after the harvest in the fields before them and one both sides of the road on which they stood.

"Mostly wigeon to the east," said Oscar in disgust.

Wigeon, a medium-sized duck not considered top-of-the-line table fare because of their frequent habit of feeding on grass, would produce only forty-five cents per duck in 1940 prices. *Hardly worth wasting shotgun shells on them,* Harold thought as he turned his cupped ears in an attempt to locate flocks of the bigger, or "money ducks," such as the heavy-bodied and much larger mallard and pintail. To the south, he could hear many thousands of mallard and pintail feeding in their greedy, noisy way. *Now, that's more like it,* he thought with a grin of anticipation.

His dad's teachings over the years ran through his mind as if he had heard them just yesterday. The mallard and pintail, being bigger ducks and needing more fuel to live, had a habit of forcing the smaller ducks out of the head of the chow line by flying over them and forcing them to the rear of frenzied feeding flocks of birds when it came to the rice-field fare. However, that was their downfall because to a commercial market hunter of ducks, there was gold in those species. Mallard, pintail, and canvasback (a large-bodied diving duck) were considered the best eating and brought the best returns for one's shooting efforts. In the markets of Sacramento, Los Angeles, Reno, Chicago, Oakland, and San Francisco, they would bring a dollar and a quarter to a dollar and a half each, unpicked. After a couple of shoots, one could have enough money to pay the banker on the farm loan and have some left over for other necessities.

Turning toward his dad in the dark, Harold said, "What do you think? Take that big bunch farther to the south?"

Overlimits of ducks taken over an illegally baited area by members of a private duck club in Sacramento Valley in the 1960s. Note the two bait scoop devises used by the arresting conservation officers to collect bait samples for courtroom use.

There was a long pause, and then Oscar slowly said, "Naw, the Feds like to sit on the big bunches, and that wouldn't do to blow them up and then have to fuss with running from those bastards the rest of the morning."

There was wisdom in his dad's thoughts, thought Harold; neither of them had been caught yet because of his dad's woods-wise thinking when it came to killing ducks from September to March in any given year. However, several of their family members had been caught selling ducks and had been sentenced to federal prison for their ill-judged efforts. If the Feds were sitting on the same bunch of birds you unwisely chose to shoot, then the race was on to avoid capture, and all your hard work would be for naught because the officers would pick up all your ducks—possibly as many as two or three hundred from one good shoot.

Finally, after another session of cupping his hands behind his ears, Oscar pointed toward a large flock noisily feeding to the southeast. Listening carefully, Harold could single out the bunch of birds his dad had located. As he did, he was amazed at the numbers of ducks feeding all around them in the harvested rice fields. There had to be at least fifty thousand feeding ducks within a quarter mile of where they now stood!

There was no way the game wardens could cover all of those bunches, Harold thought gleefully. Bringing his wandering mind back to the business at hand, he thought, *Not more than ten thousand ducks in the bunch we are listening to, and most sound like mallard and pintail.*

"Let's take that smaller bunch off to the southeast," said Oscar, pointing in that direction in the dark. "Just listen to that grind," he added, referring to the sound thousands of close-feeding ducks make as the grain's rough hulls get ground up in the bird's crops. "If we're successful and get into that bunch of birds, we can sneak down to where the A-Line Canal intersects our road and stack them there for an easy pickup with the truck. If the Zumwalts get cranky because we chose to blow up the ducks on their property, then we can give them a bunch or two of picked and cleaned mallards, and that should square it with them. Plus, that would make sure they won't squeal on us to the state or federal wardens," Oscar said smugly. "If they do, they might find that their barn gets burned," he added as a serious afterthought. Friend or no friend, no one squealed to the wardens on who was killing the ducks if they knew what was best for them. That feeling of fraternity persists to this day and age in some quarters, even though the halcyon days of gunning have long gone by. Many people felt that it was their God-given right to kill the ducks. After all, the ducks had fed in their fields and owed the landowner something in return. Those living on the land, like their grandfathers and great-grandfathers before them, had killed and sold ducks for many a year, so why all the fuss? Oscar considered it part of his and Harold's birthright.

The two men began walking toward the bunch of feeding ducks they had selected. Soon they were within a hundred yards of the birds, with the wind to their backs. Ducks usually feed into the wind so that, if alarmed, they can rise into the air more easily, especially if carrying a full crop of rice. The men began to sneak toward the birds, using the numerous rice checks for cover as they stayed low and out of sight. Soon they were just one rice check away from the madly feeding birds. Now moving slowly on their hands and knees, they crawled the last thirty yards to the cover the remaining rice check densely covered with water grass offered. Lying there for a few moments, they caught their breaths as the ducks rippled like a giant carpet ever closer to their hiding place as the mallard and pintail kept hopping over those in the front of the flock to get at the better eats of the leftover rice.

Having rested enough to be prepared in case they were surprised by the game wardens and had to run, the two men separated, taking positions about fifteen yards apart right in front of the large flock of birds from the back side of their protective rice check.

The sound of thousands of ducks' bills gobbling up the spilled rice grains continued for what seemed an eternity. Then there was a whistle from Oscar and instant silence on the part of ten thousand ducks as they raised their heads to look in the direction of the foreign sound for the danger it represented.

Boom-boom-boom-boom began the guns, with the shots in such rapid succession that they sounded like the ripping of a giant sheet. The first shots went into the upraised heads and necks of the ducks who had heard the whistle, killing and wounding dozens. As the ducks fled in panic, they lifted off the ground like a giant rug away from but still right in front of the blazing shotguns. In so doing, they presented their backs to the madly hammering shotguns, taking a lethal load of lead into their backs and vital organs—but not into their breast meat, the product the market hunters were hoping to sell! As they steadily lifted up off the ground in terror, the ducks constantly presented a new set of targets for each shot. Soon a mass of dead and crippled birds littered the ground in front of the two modified shotguns, or "Long Toms," as they were called in those days because of their long magazine extenders and excessive shell-holding capacity.

As the men shot, in order to keep the recoil from moving the shotgun barrels so that they pointed above the mass of escaping ducks, they each held a forearm over the barrel and pushed it down level with the fleeing flock as they sprayed the shots from side to side. After about the eighth shot, the barrel commenced to get pretty hot to the touch. By round eleven, any flesh touching the shotgun barrel could be burned; hence the wearing of long-sleeved shirts. Many an old-time commercial market hunter of ducks had numerous small burn scars on his forearms. Gunners such as Al Lawrence and Bill Murphy sometimes called those burns their "Badge of Courage" among other members of the market hunting fraternity. It was also a good tip-off to any sharp-eyed game warden!

Harold and Oscar finished emptying their shotguns into the mass of madly fleeing ducks, and then, except for the roar of other flocks of birds fleeing all around them, silence reigned. But the death and destruction in front of those shotgun barrels was unbelievable. About three hundred ducks lay dead to migrate no more as dozens of others that were crippled crawled off into the surrounding water grasses on the rice checks and ditch banks. Oscar had let the ducks approach to within twenty yards of him and Harold before firing, and at that range, a heavy kill was guaranteed, especially among those ducks shot across their heads and necks. His grandfather had taught him that trick of the trade, and it had worked well once again. Those dozens of birds that were injured and unable to fly would die a lingering death or be eaten by predators over the next several days.

After the drag, Oscar and Harold froze back into their rice check, moving only to reload their shotguns with several low-base 8s to shoot at any wardens who might be approaching or at anyone who might try to steal their kill. This was another trick of the trade practiced by the family, which had been market gunning ever since they had settled in the Sacramento Valley in the 1850s.

For the next few minutes, Harold and Oscar remained motionless, looking about from the protective cover of their rice check for the law. After that time had passed, seeing no one coming to investigate, the two men laid down their shotguns and commenced hurriedly picking up their birds. There would be no more shooting because that would give their position away to the now alerted law enforcement officers. Birds lay everywhere! Each man took a side of the killing field and began picking up the crippled birds first. In order to reduce the struggling birds' efforts at escape, they bit each one through the eyes once they had it in hand. This method crushed their skulls and killed them instantly. The shooters quickly worked their way to the center of where the feeding flock had been and placed the birds into several piles. Then they went to work to field-gut them all in order to reduce the weight to be carried. After gutting, they collected the birds into bunches of ten and tied them together with the precut pieces of butcher twine hanging from the straps of their overalls. Soon the ground was littered with tied bunches of mallards and pintail. The remaining cripples that had crawled off into the rice checks were left behind because it was too much bother to pursue and kill them.

After all the obvious birds killed and wounded close at hand in the shoot had been picked up, the two winded and heavily sweating men began struggling with their heavy loads toward the nearby, dried-up A-Line irrigation ditch, where they planned to deposit their birds. In less than an hour, all the birds were carefully hidden in the ditch as the two men stood in the field cooling off, continuing to look for any sign of human activity. Not seeing any, they began carrying bunches of ducks down the dry irrigation ditch to where it intersected the road they had walked down earlier. After throwing several cattails across the road at the point where the ditch ended so they would have a marker to let them know where to stop their vehicle, Harold returned to the piles of ducks to fetch more back to the road. Oscar walked back up the road toward the old farm shed and their truck. When he reaching the shed, after a careful look around, he opened both the doors and backed the truck out onto the dirt road. By now a light rain was beginning to fall, and he knew he had to hurry or the adobe-like Sacramento Valley mud would get sticky and almost impossible to drive on. Quietly clattering down the road in low gear to avoid detection in a morning now darker than the inside of a dead cow because of the heavy cloud cover, Oscar hurried as fast as he could. The previous four hours in the dark had accustomed his eyes to the low light levels, so he was able to spot the strip of cattails lying across the road. In addition, he knew every inch of the ground around him. If a man wanted to stay ahead of the law, he had to know the terrain, the roads, and where the gates were; possess keys to the locks; and know the landowner's attitude toward those illegally hunting waterfowl at night. As a third-generation market hunter, Oscar knew his way around quite well and made good use of those faculties during the five-month period of killing the ducks each year.

As Oscar loaded the bunches of ducks from the irrigation ditch into the back of his truck, he could hear Harold puffing as he carried another great load of carcasses down the dry ditch. Soon the two men had hauled all the ducks to the waiting truck. Hurriedly loading their shotguns into the cab, they boarded up, and soon Oscar had them rattling back down the muddy road toward the farm shed. They quickly opened the doors and once again drove their truck nose first into the cavernous tin shed, then shut and latched the doors from the inside.

Overlimit of ducks and geese hidden under the rear seat of an automobile to foil any field inspection by conservation officers. (Courtesy of the author)

Quickly they disassembled the shotguns, wiped them dry, oiled them down, reassembled them into a legal configuration, and placed them under the tarp in the bed of the truck. The Long Tom extensions were oiled down, rolled back into their oily burlap bags, and placed into the toolbox out of sight of the prying eyes of those wearing a badge if they happened onto the scene.

By now a hard rain was drumming on the tin roof, and both men smiled in the faint light of their flashlight at being out of the elements and among a pile of birds that would soon be converted into dollars. Shortly thereafter, all the birds had been hung in bunches from nails in the rafters and from hooks on the insides of the building to drain and cool out in the winter air. Both men urinated on their hands to wash off any remaining blood and then wiped them clean with a rag from a box left in the shed for that purpose.

Stretching his back, which was tired after their hard labors, Harold walked over to the doors of the farm shed, looked out through the cracks in the doors for any suspicious activity, and just about messed in his bib overalls. Quietly pulling up in front of their hiding place was a four-door Dodge sedan running without lights. It was a car just like the local game wardens were driving! Hissing quietly through clenched teeth, Harold got his dad's attention. Both men stared out the crack between the doors in disbelief. Sure as shootin', there sat the Dodge Sedan, and the glowing ends of cigarettes inside showed that it held two men. *Who the hell were these guys, and where had they come from in such silence?* thought Harold. Then the driver's door opened and out stepped a tall, thin man whom Oscar instantly recognized as Warden Jim Hiller from Willows, a city just to the north in Glenn County. Hiller had been after the two of them and many of their other family members for years, and now it seemed that he had them trapped with all the evidence he needed if he just looked in the shed where they were standing in disbelief.

"Paul, I have to take a dump. That dinner we had at the Maxwell Inn this evening is going through me like crap through a goose. I wonder if someone there recognized me and put some soap in my food? Damn bastards, that is the last time I ever eat in that place," said Jim Hiller as the other man in the car chuckled at his partner's obvious discomfort.

"I'll fix this damn dirt farmer who owns this shed. Just you watch. I will crawl in out of this cold damn rain and take a big dump right in the middle of it for him to find next time he uses it," said Hiller, obviously mad but still possessing a twisted sense of humor.

Harold and Oscar just about took their own dumps upon hearing Hiller's words and seeing him walking their way. They instantly had the same thought and quietly grabbed the latch holding the doors shut from the inside, hanging on with all their might. Hiller grabbed the outer handles and tried pulling open the doors as the rain's intensity began to increase.

"Damn, can you believe it, Paul? This door is locked from the inside. If that don't beat all," said Hiller, who continued to pull on the doors as Harold and Oscar frantically held on to the inside latch for dear life.

Just then divine providence played a card, and the men inside heard Hiller's suffering intestines give way with gas and then a loud squirting sound. "Goddamn it, I just crapped in my pants!" said an exasperated Hiller as he hurriedly pulled his pants down and finished his business in the grass in front of the doors.

It took all Harold's and Oscar's self-control not to roar out loud at Warden Hiller's predicament. Especially when Hiller wiped himself off, using some nearby weeds, and his howl of pain let them know he'd gotten one with some prickles.

Finally Hiller went to the trunk of his patrol car for the change of clothing that was routinely carried by most active game wardens in case they fell into a canal or a duck pond. By now the other warden had gotten out of the car, holding his two-cell flashlight to help Hiller change his soiled clothing—but not before teasing him about how he smelled.

About then another drag was heard nearby, and the officers jumped back into their patrol car, turned it around, and hastened north as fast as they could go without using any lights. Inside the shed, Harold and Oscar breathed a huge sigh of relief and then broke out laughing.

After waiting for about thirty minutes to make sure the coast was clear, Harold opened one door slightly and cautiously stepped out, careful to avoid the smelly mess lying in the grass just outside. Seeing nothing to arouse his concern, he returned to the shed and opened both doors. Oscar immediately started the truck and backed it out onto the farm road. Harold closed the shed doors and jumped into the cab, glad to be out of the rain, as the two of them headed north until they hit another muddy road that led directly to the Princeton Highway. Turning east, Oscar drove without using his headlights for about a mile. Then, sensing all was clear, they turned on their headlights and headed for home. As luck would have it, the heavy winter rains washed away all their tire tracks, leaving them with a perfect crime.

Oscar would let the Long brothers who owned and operated the Owl's Roost Bar on the main street of Princeton know of the kill and its whereabouts. The Long brothers, under the cover of darkness the next evening, would travel to the shed and load up and bag all the cooled-out ducks. Then they would return to their bar, placing the ducks in a back room where only they were allowed to go. They in turn would call a buyer from Chico named Wesley Doggett, who would come to the bar, pick up the ducks now in burlap bags, pay the brothers eighty-five cents per mallard and pintail (forty-five cents for other species), and take the illegal hoard to either Oakland or San Francisco for sale in the respective Chinatowns for $1.00 to $1.50 per duck. The Long brothers would keep $25 for their share of the risk, and Oscar would share the remaining take with Harold.

The Longs and their local bar would act as a central collection point for other trusted shooters in the Princeton area as well. They had acted as middlemen for many years and were well-respected businessmen who knew how to keep their mouths shut. During the bar's years of operation by that family, it is estimated that over twenty thousand ducks moved through it to various points west in the Bay area of San Francisco. But the Longs weren't the only game in town. Another bar in Princeton named the Duck Club was also a favored collection point for local shooters during this period, and as many as ten thousand ducks passed through the doors of that establishment as well.

The buyers would move the ducks to metropolitan areas with appetites for rice-fed duck dinners—no questions asked.

A similar operation from field to market was carried out with many minor variations among the 150 to 200 market hunters allegedly operating in the upper Sacramento Valley and Los Banos area of northern and central California from the 1930s through the late 1950s. This illegal killing and selling continued until it was mostly brought to an end by increasing pressure from the state and federal law enforcement communities; effective covert law enforcement programs such as those in the Los Banos area in 1934 and by such investigators as the "Peanut Farmer" (also known as Tony Stefano from the U.S. Fish and Wildlife Service) in the Sacramento Valley in the late 1940s and early '50s; changing attitudes of the general populace regarding the unlimited and unlawful killing of a limited resource; a loss of interest in greasy duck dinners; the general reduction in overall waterfowl population numbers because of droughts, loss of habitat, illegal and legal gunning pressures; more readily available work for the valley's residents so they didn't have to kill and sell ducks in order to make a living; and the courts finally taking the illegal killing and selling of waterfowl seriously.

Harold and Oscar would continue illegally gunning the duck until 1968, when Oscar died. The loss of his lifelong gunning partner and the advent of a new breed of game warden in the district forced Harold to hang up his worn-out shotgun, and he gave it to his nephew in Oregon as a piece of family history. Other members of the family were not so lucky, with some being apprehended by federal authorities and sent to prison for their duck-killing and -selling offenses. Harold's son Dale estimated from family discussions that his father had killed over thirty thousand ducks and geese with his favorite shotgun during its thirty-year heyday, before it became too dangerous to hunt with any further. Harold died in 1993.

Warden Jim Hiller, who long ago unknowingly had a digestive problem in front of his two worst duck-killing nemeses, has also stepped over the Great Divide after a long career in the Sacramento Valley as a Fish and Game warden. I wonder if the three of them ever talk about that night so long ago. Or is Jim Hiller still chasing Oscar and Harold across the clouds for killing too many ducks?

CHAPTER 3

The Devil Bats First, and the Local Priest Bats Cleanup

This story was told to me by George Bremer at his home in Gridley, California, while I interviewed him in June 2007 about the golden days of waterfowling in the Sacramento Valley and the duck slaughters that occurred during those times. George was ninety-three years old and just as sharp as he ever was. There was much more he wanted to say about the good old days, but he felt it was still not time to say much more than he did. I imagine George will have passed on to his reward by the time this book makes it to the presses. If so, the rest of his stories will just have to wait–especially the one dealing with a well-known local market hunter who shipped 100,000 ducks by train to San Francisco over his lifetime!

George Bremer paused to look skyward and check the weather, then stepped off his back porch and headed for his automobile. The November rains had come in all their fury, causing him to hurry toward the protection his car offered. Quickly sliding inside, he shut the door and hit the foot starter, and the old Dodge sedan engine roared to life. Sitting for a few moments to let the engine warm up, George noticed that the wind accompanying the winter rains was freshening as gusts rocked his car slightly. He slid the floor shift into low, let out the clutch, and inched out onto the rain-swept streets of Gridley, now covered with fallen elm leaves. Turning south on the main drag, George drove to his family's hardware store and parked in front. He ran to the front door of the store, hurriedly unlocked it, and quickly moved inside to avoid further soaking. As an afterthought, he turned, looked out into the weather, and let his eyes scan the early-morning gray skies. Off in the distance he observed several skeins of ducks and geese flying northward into the weather with difficulty. Standing quietly in the darkened store, he continued looking out at nature's fall spectacle of wind, flying leaves, gusts of rain, and skeins of waterfowl struggling in the air.

Weather only fit for the ducks and duck hunters crazy enough to venture out into it, he casually thought as he turned on the lights, letting the town of Gridley, California, know he was open for business.

Soon several of his clerks arrived, all complaining about the soaking they had received from the winter's rains as they had walked to work. Looking outside again, George saw that the rain was now coming down in sheets, and most of it horizontally because of the freshening northwesterly winds. As if on a whim, George stepped outside his store and stood under the protective storefront overhang, watching as the air continued to fill with more and more skeins of waterfowl struggling against the winds. A grin of anticipation slowly formed on his face as he hurried back inside his store as if on a mission.

Walking over to the telephone, he picked up the receiver, and the familiar voice of Mrs. Lundstrum, the switchboard operator, responded. "Good morning, George; may I have the phone number you wish to call?"

"'Morning, Alice. Hook me up with phone number 600 please."

"You calling Charlie Dean to see if he wants to go duck hunting this morning?" she asked. As the switchboard operator, she knew everyone in the small town.

"You got that right, Alice. This wind and rain are so fierce, the ducks and geese are almost walking instead of flying," he responded with a little excitement creeping into his voice.

"You men are all nuts," she responded good-naturedly. "You will catch your death of cold if you go out in this weather," she continued, admonishing George in her usual motherly way.

"You got that right, and if lucky, we will be able to hammer one heck of a slug of good-eating rice-fed ducks as well," proclaimed George.

"If you and Charlie get some extras, Richard and I would sure like to have a mess of those rice-fed devils for Saturday's dinner," she responded hopefully.

"Count on it, Alice. Now hurry and connect me with Charlie before he goes off and does something foolish like going to work on such a fine day," chided George.

Seconds later, George heard the phone ringing at his friend's house. "Charlie here," came the voice of his friend and longtime hunting partner.

"Charlie, George Bremer here. You got anything serious planned for today?"

"Naw, nothing except cleaning up Old Man Childer's blacksmith shop. What's up?" Charlie replied.

"Have you looked outside this morning?" asked George.

"No need to. The drumming of rain on my tin roof all night told me it has got to be raining cats and dogs," he replied.

"What say the two of us go up toward Richvale and hit those watered potholes to the south and west of the town?" asked George. "With weather like this, the mallard and pintail like to collect in those areas and ought to make for one hell of a good shoot."

"Sounds good to me," said Charlie. "Pick me up at the house, and bring me three boxes of Remington Kleanbore shot shells, number 6's, from your store if you would."

"You got it," said George. "It will take me a few minutes to get ready, but I will meet you shortly."

George hung up and informed Tom, his head clerk, that he would be gone for the day on a duck hunt with Charlie Dean. Then he headed over to the sporting-goods section of his store and picked up the three boxes of shot shells for Charlie. Thirty minutes later, he drove up to Charlie's small house and honked his horn impatiently.

Charlie erupted from the front door with his arms loaded with hunting gear and his mouth full of breakfast toast. He ran for George's car to avoid getting any wetter than he had to. Jumping into the car, he grunted, "Damn fine day for ducks and those crazy enough to get out into such weather with them."

"You got that right," said George with a grin. "There are the shot shells you requested." He pointed to a paper sack sitting on the front seat of his car.

"Great," said Charlie as he searched in his front shirt pocket until he dug out four silver dollars. He poured the silver dollars into the ashtray, saying, "There; we are even and then some."

George just grinned as he let out the clutch and the Dodge lurched out into the roadway, heading north of Gridley on State Highway 99 toward the historic town of Richvale. Some forty minutes later, the two men hurriedly dressed in their hip boots and oilcloth raingear inside an old tin farming shed on the Paul Grant farm. The wind and rain hadn't subsided one bit as they grabbed four empty gunnysacks and a full one loaded with hand-carved wooden decoys. Out they went into the howling elements with their heads bent down as they forged into the wind and rain. After a walk of several hundred yards, they came to an area of slightly rolling knolls with many watered basins in between. Glancing ahead into the pelting rain, they could see hundreds of resting waterfowl, with some reluctantly taking to wing from their watered havens upon spying the two walking men. Locating a small pothole with a lot of tall dead weeds at the south end of the pond, George hurriedly set out a dozen floating decoys as Charlie constructed a small blind from the vegetation at the shore's edge for the two of them to kneel behind.

They had no more than settled into their makeshift blind and loaded their model 11 Remington autoloading shotguns when a large flock of pintail fighting the wind struggled into their decoys. Ten shots later (they had removed the plugs from their shotguns), nine plump pintail bobbed dead in the water as the howling north winds blew them toward the concealed hunters at the south end of the pond. Almost immediately a flock of mallards winged into the decoys, hoping to find cover and get out of the winter winds as well, only to quickly find eternity at the hands of the shooters below! Both Charlie and George were excellent wing-shooters, and it wasn't long before they had over one hundred ducks down in the water, floating and bobbing toward their blind. Pausing to reload for the tenth time, the two men exchanged glances with grins reminiscent of the wing-shooting they had done as kids, when the Sacramento Valley had been flooded with millions of wintering waterfowl.

Still the birds came, and because of the high winds, they were bunching up in front of the decoys just before landing in such a manner that the two gunners were commonly killing two or three ducks with each shot. They continued to arrive regardless of the shooting, eager to get out of the weather and rest among their "brethren" sitting or bobbing dead on the water. They fell until George began to worry about the numbers of floating dead and stood up to signify that it was time to take a quick count. Twenty minutes later, they had gathered up fifty plump ducks each (the limit in those days), dumping them into their burlap bags.

An additional fifty-three ducks still floated in their little pond or were gathered along the shoreline by their blind! And the ducks kept winging into their small set of decoys as if hell were riding on their tails. After a long, careful look all around their shooting area for any sign of game wardens, the two men, with a mutual devilish look, settled back into their makeshift blind and continued wing-shooting the numerous flocks of willing waterfowl.

Standing up again, George took another long, careful look around for any sign of the dreaded and hated game wardens. The coast was clear, and within moments, the two friends had gathered up another ninety-one ducks from along the shore and floating in their little pond. Stashing the extra birds in some brush near a muddy farm road running close to their blind for later pickup with the Dodge sedan, the two returned to their blind and began reloading their hot-barreled shotguns. By now the devil had taken control of the two men if the looks on their faces had anything to do with the killing opportunity at hand. Fifty-four more birds soon graced the foaming waters of the pond, and by now the two friends were running low on ammunition.

"We can't quit now," said a gleeful Charlie Dean.

"I agree," exclaimed George. "I have never seen shooting like this, *ever!* I have two more boxes of shells in the car. I think I will go back and get them, and that'll give me a chance to make sure no one is around to see or hear our little duck shoot," he added with a devilish grin. "I'll take in a legal limit and hide them in the trunk at the same time. That way no one will be any wiser."

Standing up in the face of the howling winds and rain to leave for his car, George's grin quickly turned to chagrin. Abruptly sitting back down in their blind, George said, "That goddamned game warden Chet Ramsey is over by my car! I just saw that bastard looking our way with his binoculars as he stood on top of my sedan for a better look. Holy shit, he has us now!"

"How the hell did he find us?" asked an exasperated Charlie.

"I suppose he heard all our shooting and came over to investigate. He spotted my car, and that was that. He has been after me for years over all the illegal pheasants I have killed under his nose. In fact, I have kind of rubbed that in his face because he was too stupid to catch me, and now that may be just coming home to roost." George exclaimed through clenched teeth.

"How the hell did you do that?" asked Charlie, now worried.

"Well, I have several farms behind locked gates I routinely hunt for pheasant during the closed season. On both places I've noticed that Ramsey has a favorite hiding place to watch anyone opening up the hunting season early. So when I killed any pheasant, I would make a great show of throwing them into the trunk of my car, and then I would drive through a copse of trees along the canal banks, get out and remove the pheasants from the trunk when no one could see me, and put them into the hubcaps on my car. Then I would quickly clean any pheasant feathers out my trunk and drive out to where I knew that lazy Ramsey could check me. He would smugly go to the trunk of my car, open it up, and find nothing. Then he would tear my car apart, knowing I had killed those pheasants, but he could never find them. Since the local justice of the peace is my cousin, if Chet didn't have any evidence, my cuz would just throw out the case regardless of it being his word against mine. Then of course I would rub it in, and all that did was make Ramsey even more eager to catch me in a wildlife violation.

"Well, now I think he has that opportunity. All he has to do is walk over here, count our birds in the gunnysacks, and find those others we stashed by the road by following our muddy footprints, and he has us dead to rights. Damn, I wish I hadn't played with him so much on the pheasants," said George, exasperated.

About then the two men heard the grinding of a car's engine slowly coming their way along the muddy farm road from the west, the opposite side from where their own car was parked.

"Damn," said George. "They are coming at us from two different directions! Man, I am going to be the laughingstock in town once everyone finds out I was finally caught red-handed by my nemesis."

The sound of the engine stopped just out of sight of the two now very worried shooters. Moments later, from around the corner of a knoll, walking in a crouched position out of sight of the game warden, came a heavyset man dressed in hunting garb.

"Father Sabatini!" George said in surprise.

"Quick," said Father Sabatini, "bring your extra ducks over to my car parked just over the hill. We can hide them in my trunk."

Without any delay, George, Charlie, and Father Sabatini retrieved the piles of ducks representing their gross overlimits and hauled them down into the gully. From there, they ran in a stooped position to the priest's car and hurriedly lobbed the birds into his trunk. A second and third trip by the three men brought the remaining overlimits safely to the priest's car. After quickly placing their illegal ducks in the trunk, George and Charlie ran back to their concealed blind as the good father drove out of the hunting area to the main road by the tin shed and the waiting game warden.

George and Charlie crawled up to the lip of the knoll by their blind where they couldn't be seen and watched the events unfold. The good father's car slipped and slid its way on the muddy farm road over to the tin shed, and then its taillights came on. Father Sabatini stepped out and greeted the warden as Chet Ramsey walked out to the car from his hiding place by the shed. The two men talked for a while, and then Father Sabatini walked over to the passenger side of his car, opened the door, and dragged out his limit of ducks for the game warden to check. Satisfied that the priest was within his legal limit, the game warden sent the good father on his way with a wave of his hand, then turned and walked out to where George and Charlie had been shooting most of the morning. Climbing back down from their hiding place, George and Charlie quickly began to gut their legal limits of ducks, all the while appearing to be unaware of the game warden's approach.

"Hello," boomed out Warden Ramsey's voice over the still howling winds.

George and Charlie whirled as if they hadn't known he was there and then returned his greeting as they continued to act innocent.

"How is the hunting, lads?" asked Ramsey as he walked up to the two men.

"Fine," mumbled George, trying to appear calm as he gutted another duck.

"Care if I check your birds?" asked Ramsey.

"No, go ahead," mumbled Charlie and George as they stepped back and let the warden do his job.

"Need to check your licenses as well, lads," Ramsey said, obviously disappointed at not finding an overlimit.

George and Charlie dug around for their wallets and soon showed the game warden their hunting licenses, costing all of $1 in that day and age.

"Looks like you boys are legal," Ramsey said. "I will let you get back to your cuttin' and guttin' while I just take a look around, if you don't mind," he continued.

"No, don't mind a bit," said George as he and Charlie continued gutting their ducks in order to lighten their loads before carrying them back to the car.

With that, Ramsey, still not sure why they didn't have an overlimit, continued to look around, oblivious to the oddball sets of footprints going every which way. Realizing after a while that George had surely hoodwinked him once again, Ramsey wandered back to the tin shed and soon left the area in his patrol car.

Waiting a short while after Ramsey had left, Charlie and George finally hauled their gunnysacks of ducks back to their car. Loading them into the trunk, they headed for home—but not before George had dropped off four fat pintail for Alice, the telephone operator.

Later that afternoon, George and Charlie went to Father Sabatini's rectory in Gridley to retrieve their overlimits of ducks. They arrived just in time to see the good father hand over ten freshly gutted ducks to a man and his wife who were trailed by six little children. All appeared to be in dire need of a good meal and a bath.

"Good afternoon, Father. Charlie and I want to thank you for bailing us out of a real mess with that Ramsey fellow had he learned of our overlimits," said George after the poor family was out of earshot.

"Yeah, thanks a lot, Father," Charlie added.

"Well, seems like I bailed you two out from under the devil's work, to be sure," the priest said. "I knew Warden Ramsey would not check the trunk of a car belonging to a man of the cloth," he continued with a devilish smile and a twinkle in his eyes. "And it is a good thing he didn't check my trunk; otherwise I would be saying my Hail Marys and Our Fathers for a week." He chuckled, obviously pleased at his great escape.

George and Charlie joined in the laugh with relish. However, what followed erased their smiles of mirth at putting one over on the hated local game warden.

"If you don't mind, Father, Charlie and I will take those ducks off your hands and be on our way," said a still smiling George.

"You boys don't seem to understand," Father Sabatini said cheerfully. "Since I didn't think you wanted those illegal ducks by the way you hurried up and threw them into the trunk of my car, I have been using them for God's work. The way I figured it, since the devil made you kill so many of God's creatures over the limit, I couldn't think of a better way for you to atone for your sins than to repent of your illegal ways by using your ill-gotten gains for His work. Hence, I have been giving the ducks away to the poor from not only my parish but surrounding churches as well. And both of you will be happy to know that those ducks were happily accepted by everyone you benefited!"

George just looked at Charlie, and Charlie at George.

"Of course, if that is unacceptable, I can try to reclaim those ducks and let the two of you work it out with Warden Ramsey if you so desire," the Priest said quietly, still smiling. "And by the way, will I see you boys in church this coming Sunday? If so, each of you can put a box of shotgun shells, preferably 12-gauge, Remington Kleanbore, number 6's, in the offering plate so I can continue to provide for my table and those of my flock."

George and Charlie were happy to return to their legal limits of ducks, and it seemed that every time they had a duck dinner from that hunt, they had to smile at all the good they had done for those less fortunate then they were—however unintentionally.

Warden Ramsey never did figure out how he had observed two hunters kill a large overlimit of ducks and yet come out with only a legal limit. Hell, even the priest he had checked that day had only had a legal limit. Somehow Bremer had once again found a way to break the law in plain view and escape. *Someday he will be mine,* Ramsey thought. It never happened. Maybe it was because God was riding "top cover" for George Bremer. In fact, he still is because George is now in his ninety-third year.

The priest got his two boxes of shotgun shells in the offering plate that next Sunday and was happy to see his two duck-hunting buddies there to hear God's message.

CHAPTER 4

From Poacher to Law Enforcement Officer

This story is based on my experiences as a state and federal conservation officer in the Sacramento Valley of California from 1967 to 1974. Further information was provided by Doug Turner, the subject of the story, during my June 2007 interview of him for this book.

I was sitting in my U.S. game management agent's office in the basement of the U.S. Post Office in Colusa, typing out case reports on my typewriter in December 1971, when the phone rang. Irritated at being interrupted in the middle of my case report, I forced myself to be cordial when I answered the phone. On the other end of the line was the principal from Williams High School and the beginning of this story.

"Terry, I know you are busy with the problems of duck season and all, but would you have any time to talk to my high school seniors? More and more I am hearing that the boys are out blowing up the ducks at night now that the birds are all over in the valley. Maybe you could put the fear of God into some of them if you were to talk to them so they will cease and desist before they get caught," he said.

"Sure, why not? You are correct that many of your boys are blowing up ducks under cover of darkness. That kind of behavior is especially true over on the west side of the valley between Arbuckle and Maxwell now that the winter rains are here. Yeah, I can do that. Anything to cut down on the duck slaughter would be a help. When do you want me to be there, and what time?" I asked.

"How about this coming Thursday, ten o'clock in one of my classrooms? That isn't a shoot day in the valley and might be the best time to fit into your schedule," he responded.

"Count on it," I answered, and some small talk concluded our conversation. Little did I know the effect that talk would have down the road, along with the formation of a long-distance friendship that lingers to this day, some forty years later.

The problem the principal spoke of was not an unusual one. I was aware that many of the young men from the surrounding high schools in the five adjacent duck-rich Sacramento Valley counties routinely dabbled in illegal night hunting of the feeding waterfowl and just about every other kind of wildlife violation. Many were involved for the sport of it, the thrills and challenges of the activity, or the feeling that their kinfolk did it so why shouldn't they. They believed that killing ducks illegally was almost a God-given right because they had fed the birds all year on their farms, many liked eating the ducks, some killed for the money it offered, and sometimes their reasons were a little bit of all of the above. But no matter the reason, the illegal practices started early for many of the young in the valley communities and for some stayed with them all their lives or until they were caught and fined or jailed by the long arm of the justice system.

The appointed day found me standing in the small Williams High School classroom facing a group of senior-class students. They looked at me standing there in my hip boots still covered with rice-field mud from the night before and my worn hunting coat like a bunch of robins distastefully looking at an unappetizing worm. In turn, I saw about a dozen of the boys I recognized from previous run-ins or because I knew their family duck killing histories.

The principal made his introduction, and I launched off into a talk covering the natural history of the Sacramento Valley; the importance of the waterfowl resources; the laws of the land, particularly the Migratory Bird Treaty Act; a little bit on how I caught violators, including some of their local kinfolk (without giving away names and techniques); and some of the latest equipment I used in my duties. One piece of equipment, a military Starlight Scope being used in Vietnam at that time by our armed forces, particularly caught the eye of a student named Doug Turner. For the most part, his classmates remained silent, waiting for this obligatory time with the hated local federal wildlife officer to end—but not Doug. He was full of questions on the how and why of my profession and was particularly interested in my Starlight Scope. He was full of questions on how far I could see with it, did it really magnify the starlight or any other available light by a factor of fifty thousand, could those being looked at see it being used on them at night, did it work without any moon for light, and the like. Questions not for book-learnin' but for learning the limitations of the officer in the field chasing the bad guys at night, I thought with a knowing grin.

When I had finished my civic duty, the principal thanked me, and off I went back to the duck wars in the rice fields of the Sacramento Valley. But not before logging in the back of my mind Doug's many questions and my thoughts on possibly working the area north of Williams just a little more frequently in the future. Especially since that particular area was rumored to be the country in which Doug and some of his future kinfolk found the time to drag the feeding waterfowl in the wee hours of the night or early morning. I was aware of Doug's whole family's duck-killing history. His dad, Jess, had been a big poacher of ducks, especially since he had come home from the Korean War, and Doug's mother sometimes acted as the drop-off for his dad on such illegal shoots. In his parents' case, the illegal shoots came about because times were hard right after Jess came home from the war, and all he could find was a part-time job. So in order to make ends meet, he killed ducks illegally and sold them for a dollar each to folks in the surrounding area. I knew that Jess felt that poaching ducks was wrong, and that he had been forced into it because it was the only way he had to feed his family. In Doug's case, it was poaching for the sport of it, pure and simple, and Jess flat-out didn't condone such actions. However, knowing Doug would carry on in such illegal traditions anyway, Jess felt it best to pass on to his son the tips of the trade in order to avoid capture by the local wardens. However, that day in school, Doug had been sitting in the company of one of my best informants on the Williams kids and their illegal nighttime adventures and hadn't even known it! For all those reasons, I let Doug pump me for any and all information regarding my tactics and trade, all the while trying not to grin at his juvenile antics in interrogation.

By January 1971, the hordes of ducks in the Sacramento Valley had all but eaten themselves out of house and home in the harvested rice fields.

Lacking the life-giving grains of rice from the burned-off fields (ducks preferred the toasted rice kernels left after a field was burned off over almost any other kind of feed), the hungry ducks and geese now turned their attention to the less-desirable fields of milo as their grits of choice to ward off the winter cold. Soon almost every milo field had a flock of hungry ducks or lesser snow geese hungrily gobbling up every available grain left over from the harvesting process. With that knowledge in mind, I made sure my patrols took me through many of those milo-rich areas in Colusa and sometimes Glenn County as a matter of routine. However, I was glad to be nearing the end of waterfowl hunting season. That particular year, I had worked every day of the year except half a day on Thanksgiving and all of Christmas. I was averaging eighteen hours of work per day in an area of the Sacramento Valley that hardly ever seemed to sleep when the ducks were in town. Hundreds of commercial duck clubs, many more hundreds of hunting areas on private ranches, dozens of illegal shooters, and thousands of legal hunters on any given day was my battleground, and to be quite frank, I was fast wearing out. However, I felt it was a good fight, and one that had to be fought regardless of the challenges. Being young and having a very understanding wife, I gave it my all, especially when the hunting seasons were in full swing.

January 20, 1971, the last day of duck season, found me working the west side of my district just north of the town of Williams. It was just getting dark, and I had slipped my Dodge patrol truck alongside a parked harvester that had been left in a field after working a large milo field. Throwing a camouflage parachute over the vehicle, I took my binoculars and Starlight Scope and crawled up into the front seat of the harvester so I would be out of sight of the casual eye and have command of the high ground. A casual sweep of the area with my high-light-gathering binoculars revealed nothing more than numerous bunches of ducks swirling into several nearby harvested milo fields as daylight ebbed and the dark of night advanced. From their actions, they were pretty hungry because they swung over a landing area only once before dropping all caution in favor of a meal and landing to feed. This pattern was repeated many times as I continued watching this spectacle of nature instead of sweeping the area in the fast-disappearing light for any illegal gunners.

Then there they were, right in front of me! Two individuals were walking out into one of the harvested milo fields not far from Marengo's Shop about two hundred yards from Danley Road. Quickly putting down my binoculars and removing my Starlight Scope from its metal carrying case, I flipped off the lens covers and turned on the oscillator switch. Its faint whirring sound told me the scope was active and ready for use. Pressing my eye to the rubber eyepiece, I could clearly see the two figures walking stealthily into a harvested milo field before me. One man appeared to be carrying a model 11 Remington or a Browning autoloader and the other a Winchester model 12. I could also see in the faint lime-colored light of the scope that hundreds of ducks were still milling over the milo field. The ducks were so hungry for a meal that they dropped all caution and were landing all around the two men walking across the field, some only yards away from the danger the gunners represented. Both men paused and turned to look into the storm of ducks landing all around them, and when they did, they turned their faces toward me. One face clearly outlined in the magnification of the scope was that of the student at Williams High School who had been so full of questions some weeks earlier. Sure as shooting, it was young Mr. Doug Turner! I did not recognize the other man but found out later it was Bob, Doug's future brother-in-law. They walked on to a patch of cover and disappeared. In the meantime, the milo field continued to fill with hungry ducks. By now it was getting pretty dark, and without the Starlight Scope, I would have not been able to see the two men, much less recognize either of them.

A short time later, I saw a burst of flashes from the area where the two men had disappeared in the scope and clearly heard a long string of shots in rapid succession in the cool of the winter night. It was obvious that the shooters had pulled the plugs from their shotguns so they would fire five shells each. Many scattered bands of ducks rose up from the field and began to swirl away for the safety offered by other points of the compass. The two men stood up and openly surveyed their recent field of battle, believing the dark of the night would protect them from prying eyes. Apparently Doug had forgotten the man with the Starlight Scope! In the light of the scope, I could see one of the men lay down his shotgun and begin scrambling around one side of the area they had just shot over, picking up crippled and flopping ducks. The other did the same on the other side. Both appeared to be carrying duck straps and were putting the ducks just killed on them. Having seen enough, I bailed out of the harvester, threw off the camouflage parachute hiding my patrol vehicle, slammed my gear into the darkened front seat, and prepared to give chase and ruin those chaps' evening duck shoot. Then it dawned on me. One of my shooters was Doug Turner, and dollars to doughnuts, the other was a school buddy and a juvenile as well. It wouldn't do me a damn bit of good to give chase and catch them since I couldn't prosecute them in federal court until they were at least eighteen years of age. *Damn!* I thought. Then the devil rose up in me, and I got one hell of an idea. Suppose I just scared the living hell out of my two shooters without catching them? Suppose a little hellfire and damnation just brush-blocked them? Maybe a damned good scare would have some lasting effect, causing them to leave the field of battle to others of an age allowing prosecution. With those thoughts whirling around in my head, I put Plan A into action with a twinkle in my eyes and grin on my tired face.

In those days, I had one hell of a patrol truck. It was so distinctive that it was known to almost everyone, especially the outlaws, within a hundred miles of my hometown of Colusa. It was a Dodge three-quarter-ton truck, and that

Doug Turner (starting out young) standing by an overlimit of mallard, wigeon, and pintail ducks, probably shot by his dad, Jess Turner, and a friend, circa 1956. (Courtesy Jess Turner)

was where the normal description ended. It was painted a soft tan color that allowed it to blend into the golden-colored countryside, especially at night, and had a hood covered with black primer to cut down the glare from the sun. It had a 383-cubic-inch engine with a four-barrel carburetor that allowed the vehicle to reach speeds of over 115 miles per hour and still be accelerating! That configuration was rounded out with ten-ply tires, a double set of shocks all around, a 740-pound steel plate welded across the rear of the bed for additional traction, and an extra 75-gallon gasoline tank behind the cab. In short, I could cruise at over 90 miles per hour on gravel roads without losing control and never lost a chase in its five years of use (although it once took me seventeen miles on gravel roads in Bear Valley to catch a Porsche whose driver had been killing dove during the closed season). It also made a very distinctive sound when cruising down back and farm roads, which I routinely ran without the use of lights at night.

Cranking up my truck, I eased it out onto a small farm road to do battle and put Plan A into operation. Fortunately, my eyes were used to running in the dark of the night without lights. Thundering down the road with the engine howling and tires growling, my darkened truck hurtled toward where I had last seen my duck-shooting culprits. After about two hundred yards, I stopped the truck, jumped out, and turned on my Starlight Scope. There my two shooter were in the soft green light of the scope, running like hell. They had obviously heard and possibly seen the darkened shape of my pickup and, recognizing that the law was at hand, were hotfooting it across the milo field. Swinging from their shoulders were their full duck straps, and each hand carried his shotgun in one hand. Getting back into my truck, I headed down another farm road as if I were planning to cut off their escape route. Stopping after a short distance, I bailed out and turned on my scope again. My trick had worked! The two shooters were now running in another direction, with their ducks flopping wildly. Getting back into the truck, I headed off in another direction, seemingly in another attempt to cut them off. After running loudly in that direction for a few moments, I stopped and hopped out yet again. Turning on my scope, I could that see my chaps were now running for their lives in another direction in an attempt to evade the hated federal agent's patrol truck. I repeated this assumed cut-off procedure several more times until it seemed that I had forced the exhausted shooters to run through the fields in every direction of the compass.

During one of those times when I had stopped to view the culprits through my scope, I saw one of the lads throw his ducks at his partner, as if to say, *Damn you for getting me into this mess!*

On we went with this merry chase until my lads got the bright idea to cross a shallow canal. Watching them jump into this canal in the dead of winter had me laughing until tears ran down my cheeks. But I quickly turned sober when it became apparent that one of the men had gotten hung up in an unseen barbed-wire fence in the middle of the canal and could possibly drown. However, his partner returned to the struggling young man's aid and freed him from the entangling wire. By now they had tossed their ducks and, unencumbered by that flopping weight, were really moving out. I changed positions and turned on my headlights so that my new direction forced the two fleeing lads to change theirs as well. Into another canal they went, and this time they both appeared to be hung up in some underwater wire. Finally escaping that challenge, they came up out of the canal at a quickly tiring dead run. Determined to keep up the heat of the chase, I bored in from another cut-off position. Again the lads changed their escape route, and this time I noticed they were running without their shotguns!

Damn, I thought, *they have ditched their shotguns to lighten their loads!*

Sweeping the field they had just come through with my trusty Starlight Scope, I spotted the stocks of the two shotguns sticking up into the air. In their desperate attempt to escape, they had shoved the guns barrel-down into the mud to lighten their loads, and possibly to frustrate any seizure of their weapons if I caught them. Again I had to laugh at the antics of the two young men, who now probably wished they had never ventured into that field that evening. Changing position one more time, as if still trying to intercept them, I finally shut down the chase and watched them struggle out of sight. Both men appeared to be somewhat worse for wear. Their clothes, in addition to being wet from crossing the canals, appeared to be somewhat tattered from their run-in with the barbed wire.

When the two men had first entered the milo field, it had been about six-thirty in the evening. When I finally backed off from my part of the fun and games, it was about ten-thirty P.M., and the lads were a long way from where the chase had started. I imagined that they had about two more hours of walking in the dark of the night in cold, wet clothing before they reached home. I later discovered they made it to their homes, wet, tired, and tattered, about twelve-thirty P.M.! And, of course, without any of their illegally killed ducks or their shotguns.

I found out later from my Williams High School informant that I was correct in identifying one of my two shooters that evening as Doug Turner. I never said anything to Doug about my little plan but let him draw his own conclusions. He said nothing to me about the escapade until more than thirty years later, when, as a sheriff's lieutenant, he was providing vehicle control near Ladoga, where I was doing a movie for the Discovery Channel based on some of the stories from my books. The rest of this story came out in June 2007 when I interviewed Doug about his days as a young duck poacher for this book.

He informed me that my little ruse had scared the hell out of him to the extent that from that day forward, he had gone straight when it came to the wildlife laws of the land. He told me that he had in fact thrown the dead ducks from his duck strap at his future brother-in-law in frustration at having been goaded into going out that evening so long ago to blow up the ducks. As for the birds and shotguns they had discarded, Doug had gone out the next morning and recovered everything. One of the shotguns shoved barrel-down in the

Doug Turner (left), Bruce Rolen (center), and Jim Keegan (right) with a large overlimit of ducks, possibly from a "drag," circa 1960s. (Courtesy Jess Turner)

mud had been his dad's pride and joy, and to leave it would probably have earned him a fate worse than death. I had thought of retrieving those shotguns myself and just letting the two boys sweat out the consequences the next day, but I was happy to see Doug do so from my hidden position in the harvester early the next morning.

Today (as this story was written) Doug Turner is a highly respected lieutenant with the Colusa County sheriff's office. He is a model citizen in the community and, as a result of that night in 1971, a very ethical sportsman. Even better, he has shared this story with his son, whom he has taught the same quality ethics.

When I asked him during the 2007 interview about his role as a young man poaching wildlife, Doug became quiet and introspective. It soon became apparent that he was sorry for his actions as a kid and that he felt some responsibility for the demise of waterfowl in the Pacific Flyway. He talked about the millions of birds that were everywhere in his younger days and the comparative scarcity of the waterfowl resources today. He realizes there are other factors causing the tremendous decline in waterfowl populations, such as drought, loss of habitat, legal overharvesting, disease, parasites, weather, and accidents, but he was also frank about the loss of ducks through the many years of illegal slaughter that occurred in the Sacramento Valley. Today Doug and his son are mindful of the remaining resources of the land and take only their fair share.

CHAPTER 5

A New Sheriff Comes to Town—and Gets Schooled!

In September 1967, I transferred as a California State Fish and Game warden from Eureka in northwestern California to the small town of Colusa in the northern Sacramento Valley. The transfer took me from the quiet of the redwoods and the many salmon streams to the lands of the duck and the related waterfowl slaughter in the Sacramento Valley. Over the next seven years, I would experience firsthand the good, the bad, and the ugly of what the valley and some of its people had to offer. During that period, I would also move from being a state Fish and Game warden to being a U.S. game management agent and ultimately a special agent, or criminal investigator, for the U.S. Fish and Wildlife Service. Over the course of my career, I would exercise my wildlife protection credentials in many places on the North American continent, one country in Europe, and seven countries in Asia.

No matter where my travels took me, my heart was never far from those early experiences in the Sacramento Valley. My waterfowl law enforcement experiences during that seven-year period didn't hold a candle to the tempestuous times from 1918 until the mid-1950s, the heyday of the waterfowl slaughter in the Sacramento Valley. But, late as my time was in a historical sense, the ducks and geese illegally taken were just as dead.

Upon my arrival in August 1967, I had been forewarned by other officers about the vast wildlife resources in the valley and the subsequent illegal and legal killing I would experience. My mother suffered no fool, but little did I realize how paltry a sword for Mother Nature I would swing during the next seven years, despite my best efforts. The valley and a good many of its people were steeped in a history based on raiding Mother Nature's pantry. Since the birds were already migrating into the valley by the thousands in late August, I discovered that my learning curve, of necessity, would have to be almost vertical!

First and foremost, I had to learn Colusa County's roads, dirt as well as paved, within its 1,200-square-mile area. Then I had to learn the locations of over three hundred commercial-duck-club boundaries, including those in the Butte Sink, and the many farms whose owners routinely allowed hunting on their properties. I had to meet the county's people on the land, in the courts, and in the local law enforcement communities and get to know my brother Fish and Game wardens in the districts adjacent to mine. I noticed right away that the local folks seemed for the most part to be distant and unenthusiastic when meeting their new local game warden. Some of them were local outlaws who had little or no use for me because of their nefarious activities and our differing philosophies. A goodly number of those remaining had other axes to grind. Some had duck-depredation problems in their rice fields and felt the government was not doing enough to keep the ducks at bay. Others' reasons seemed to be more deeply rooted, and I had to do a little digging to mine information regarding their unspoken issues from among my few trusted friends. Soon I discovered that my immediate predecessor had had a reputation, real or imagined, as being a loudmouthed, overbearing lout. Then I learned that the local game warden before him had allegedly been a drunk and womanizer. Local legend had it that a common sport among the folks when they discovered him drunk out in the sticks was to dump him out on the ground in a drunken stupor, take his patrol car, and hide it. It was said that the game warden before the drunk used to seize the locals' birds for minor Fish and Game violations and then eat them himself. On and on went the stories and gripes.

Coupled with all that, my early deer season was in full swing in the western mountainous region of the county, and I was expected to work the problems associated with that season at the same time as I was learning my way around! Trespassing, loaded rifles in a motor vehicle, shooting from a county road, taking game with the use and aid of a motor vehicle, hunting accidents, hunting without a lawful hunting license, untagged deer, killing the wrong sex of deer, and wanton waste were just a few of the immediate problems I confronted in that arena. There were also those who enjoyed killing deer illegally at night with the use and aid of a spotlight. Suffice it to say, I kept busy seven days a week, sixteen to eighteen hours a day, and into the night. And the advent of duck season, with its thousands of hunters, was just a month away! Thank heaven and my lucky stars for a forgiving and understanding wife, who, in addition to running our home and raising two hell-bent-for-leather young sons, had a full-time job as a schoolteacher in the nearby town of Williams to keep her busy as well.

The important learning began with information gathered from all points of the compass about the complex scenario I faced with the hordes of arriving waterfowl. By 1967, the heyday of the market gunner had mostly passed, for many reasons. Tougher courts, more federal officers in the valley applying the historical flying-squad concept (officers brought in from all over the country and concentrated in a problem area), people's changing attitudes regarding the slaughter and sale of ducks, use of state and federal undercover officers in greater numbers to infiltrate the illegal "duck-legging" rings, more and more locals being prosecuted and paying higher fines or being sent off to jail or prison, the taste for greasy duck dinners beginning to wane in the commercial eating establishments of the day, and a variety of other reasons rang what was almost the death knell (but not entirely) of the commercial-market gunner in the Sacramento Valley. However, illegal "dragging," or night shooting of feeding waterfowl, by the locals and others for their own freezers continued to flourish. As a result, I learned from a few informants, local law enforcement officers, and some trusting landowners where many of the remaining historical market hunting and duck-dragging hot spots would be located once the birds arrived. During those information-gleaning activities, I spent hundreds of hours talking to the locals, including bartenders, hunters, duck-club operators, old market gunners now out of the trade, concerned sportsmen, and rice farmers, picking up every bit of intelligence that might help me with my enforcement responsibilities. I spent many more hours scouting out the locations of bars, restaurants, and any other place of business alleged to be collecting or selling ducks, along with the names of the locals and their families said to be involved in illegal dragging. I also spent time in the Sacramento Valley, learning the life-history information and the habits of the ducks and geese so I would understand where to be when they needed protection the most.

In a short time, I learned a great deal about the waning illegal market hunting trade and the thriving local duck dragging activities. I learned that a drag was the illegal organized shooting of waterfowl, primarily ducks (mostly mallards and pintail because they are the largest) at night. However, if the weather was right and the ducks were out in force, some duck dragging went on in the daylight hours as well. Those market gunners still in operation in the Sacramento Valley rarely made use anymore of the Remington Model 11 semiautomatic shotgun with a magazine extension increasing the shooting capacities anywhere from six to eleven shots. Not only was it hard to hide such a weapon, but the extensive number of shots from such firearms was a dead giveaway to law enforcement officers regarding a shooting location. In its day, this modified shotgun was called a "Long Tom" by its users. However, the remaining commercial shooters and the numerous local duck draggers were using the standard pump and autoloading shotguns of the day with their plugs removed. Most of these illegal gunners operated about six months of the year (October through March), when the ducks were on their wintering grounds in their best body (eating) condition. Many of the serious illegal gunners would wait until several weeks after the regular duck season had closed. In that space of time, the ducks would relax because they weren't being shot at every day, which made it easier to sneak up on them, be it in daylight or the dark of the night.

The author holding a "Long Tom" shotgun like the kind used by many market hunters. This firearm was favored by Herb Murphy, Bill Murphy (no relation to Herb), and Al Lawrence, all local Sacramento Valley market hunters. Magazine extender was given to the author by Ken Kagihiro, a long-time close friend. (Courtesy Rich Grosz, 2007)

Once the ducks left the rice fields to feed on the green grass in the spring, usually March, the night shooting stopped because the birds' flesh was considered undesirable. There were still a few market hunters who allegedly operated year-round, supplying trout, pheasants, sturgeon, quail, frogs, ducks, geese, and deer to the commercial markets mostly in the Oakland and San Francisco Bay areas. These were the tough ones to capture because they kept their illegal activities close to their breasts and were as quiet as a mouse pissin' on a ball of cotton.

I learned that the best eating ducks (pintail), and easiest to bag because of their feeding habits, began arriving in the Sacramento Valley at the end of

A forty-five minute White-fronted goose shoot, killing 106 geese, near Williams in 1916. Standing at left is Frank Wallace and seated in the automobile and standing to the right of the car are the Rogers brothers. (Courtesy Ed Wallace)

August and usually peaked in numbers by November, as did the other species of marketable ducks, most notably the mallard and canvasback. Ducks were the main targets of the few remaining market hunters, and most were sold in the markets in Oakland, San Francisco, and Sacramento. But a few went to such faraway places as Reno, Las Vegas, and Los Angeles (allegedly the Brown Derby restaurant), and some were sent as far as Chicago. Of lesser commercial interest were the various species of geese, but given a chance, many thousands of those fell to the gunners as well. Colusa, Willows, Maxwell, Princeton, Delevan, Grimes, Williams, Olivehurst, Gridley, Arbuckle, Oroville, Woodland, Knights Landing, Live Oak, Oakland, San Francisco, Alameda, Butte City, Marysville, and Yuba City, along with many other little towns in between, harbored many of the main groups and families of illegal night shooters. Drawn and cooled ducks in the market during its early heyday had sold for as little as

45 cents for the smaller ducks and as much as $1.50 to $1.75 for each of the larger ducks such as the mallard, canvasback, and pintail.

I learned that a drag was many times organized around three to four individuals, one of whom was usually a driver whose job it was to drop off and pick up the shooters and be on the lookout for any game wardens in the designated area. The ducks would leave their areas of protection, such as national wildlife refuges strategically located in the Sacramento Valley along with flooded areas in the Butte Sink, and head out into the harvested rice fields to feed around four in the afternoon, or earlier if the weather was adverse. The birds would often advertise their feeding locations by coming down into a field like a huge living tornado. Such phenomena, comprising thousands of hungry ducks, could be witnessed from long distances. Most ducks preferred rice fields that had been harvested and burned so they had ready access to the toasted rice kernel and didn't have to plow through the chaff. Market gunners or other night shooters on the prowl during those times would lock on to the feeding, swirling masses of birds, plan their attack, and move in under the cover of darkness for the kill. Other gunners would come out after dark, when the possibility of detection was at its lowest, and listen for the masses of feeding birds. A man would stand on the road or on top of a truck, cupping his ears and making a 360-degree turn with his body. If there were any feeding ducks nearby, a flowing-water sound of thousands of moving bills picking up spilled rice grains would be the listener's reward. This sound could be heard from as far away as two miles on a calm night. He also listened for what many of the locals described as a "grind"—a sound made from many close-at-hand ducks as their collective gizzards ground up the rough-hulled rice grains.

Standard shooting procedure was to sneak out into fields occupied by thousands of feeding ducks, creep up behind a rice check, and let the swarm of feeding waterfowl make its approach. When the shooters deemed the ducks to be close enough for a shot–usually just a few yards away, when the more experienced gunners could hear the ducks' crops grinding—someone in the group would whistle or make a sound, instantly alerting the ducks to the danger at hand. The ducks would raise their heads to listen quietly for the sound that had alerted them, and that was when the gunners would shoot into the raised heads en masse, killing many instantly. Then they would quickly empty their shotguns, swinging them from side to side as they shot into the now rapidly fleeing horde of flapping ducks. After the shooting ended, the gunners would work quickly from the sides of the shoot inward, gathering up the cripples (with the more experienced shooters biting through the wounded ducks' heads to still them), and would throw them into several piles. The ducks would be gutted to lighten the load and stacked in the field under a row of rice straw or hauled out to a place where a driver was to meet the gunners. I learned that most serious gunners would pull a shoot, gut their kill, and be out of the area in an hour or less. If the situation safely allowed it, the ducks were often hauled to a nearby barn or shed and hung to cool out for later pickup, or left in the field to be retrieved the next day. The gunners would clean up with rags and water left in the barn for that purpose, stash their shotguns, and calmly walk out to be picked up or stroll back to their parked vehicles with no evidence in hand of their recent illegal activity.

I learned that on nights when the weather was bad, the ducks would feed and then leave right away to return to their safe resting areas such as the valley's refuges or a large naturally watered area such as the Butte Sink. They would also feed more quietly on rainy nights, making it harder to locate the feeding masses. Many gunners would not go out on rainy nights and fight the cold, mud, and wet. They would wait for a better night because good weather made the killing and hauling of carcasses easier. The feeding ducks were at their quietest when it was foggy. It was also tougher in fog to determine where the center of a mass of ducks was located; hence, many gunners passed up the foggy nights to wait for one with some moonlight so they could see better. However, during a foggy day, wing-shooting could be fast and furious because the birds' confusion made it easy for a gunner to shoot large overlimits. It was also tougher for the game wardens to echo-locate a serious shoot because the fog tended to deaden the sounds and provide cover for the shooters.

When the birds fed in a rice field, they were so tightly packed together that it was hard for all of them to get airborne instantly in the face of danger. Only the ones on the edges of the feeding masses could lift off quickly once alarmed. The rest had to wait their turn because if they all tried to rise at once, they would knock each other back down. The ducks generally always fed into the wind so that if danger presented itself, they could get into the air more easily and escape danger. Plus, when a bird was packing a full gut of rice or milo, it was easier to take wing if it lifted off into the wind. In mixed flocks that included smaller ducks, the larger ducks such as pintail and mallard were always short-hopping over the leaders of the feeding masses because they were greedy and needed more fuel to keep going. That pushed the smaller ducks to the rear of the feeding flocks. It also gave the illegal gunners the advantage that when they fired into the feeding flocks, their kills of mallards and pintails would be proportionately higher, and thus so would their rewards, either from selling the most desirable ducks or for the filling of their freezers.

I discovered that historically, the heaviest numbers of ducks were moving in the markets around the Christmas and New Year holidays because of the increased demand from the clubs, night spots, and restaurants for specialty dinners. I also learned that a buyer had to look out when purchasing ducks because some sellers would try to give them domestic (picked and cleaned) or "Toller" ducks (tame and trained ducks used to lure wild ducks to the gun over a watered shooting area), and that the best way to tell was to look at their feet. Domestic ducks had calluses on their feet, and wild ducks did not! The crippling rate in a drag ran from 30 to 40 percent. On and on my learning curve went as I tried to level the playing field with those who, in some cases, had been involved in the trade of illegal killing for over fifty years!

However, my learning curve was soon going to be put to use, resulting in my executing over ten thousand arrests or citations in a little over ten years as a state and federal officer. As a result of those arrests or citations came the seizure of over thirteen thousand illegal ducks, geese, dove, striped bass, mule

Goose shoot (probably for the market) in Sacramento Valley, March 21, 1892. Claud Kagee is second from right, sitting. Note the "gut wagon" in the left rear of photo. Careful examination reveals several heads of live geese used as decoys sticking up over the wagon box. The author, with the use of a magnifying glass, stopped counting the dead Canada geese hanging on the fence at 400. (Courtesy Glenn Wellborn)

Snow geese settling into a harvested rice field to feed, with the Sutter Buttes of Sacramento Valley in the background. (Courtesy Peter Grevie)

deer, salmon, shorebirds, black bass, sturgeon, steelhead trout, rainbow trout, rabbits, hawks, owls, chukars, other migratory nongame birds, feral hogs, tule elk, black bear, Rocky Mountain elk, pronghorn, white-tailed deer, moose, abalone, and frogs! Over $1 million in fines was collected during those years, and those were in the days when, unlike today, a $500 fine per offense was considered a really good case!

The local folks and outlaw gunners soon learned that a new sheriff was in town. And he didn't mind the long days, crappy weather, muddy rice fields, and a little hard work.

CHAPTER 6

Cement Anchors

My first day of duck season in the Sacramento Valley in 1967 was a swirling mess! On that day, over twenty-five thousand duck and goose hunters piled into the valley with blood in their eyes. With that much human activity, it didn't take long for several million confused ducks and geese to scramble into the air. There was a gentle breeze from the northwest that fine day, and soon the sky was filled with thousands of skeins, flocks, singles, and doubles of confused birds flying every which way trying to find a quiet place to land. The hordes of sportsmen literally filled the skies with lead and the sounds of popping shotguns and many off-color duck calls. In fact, for the first two hours of the duck season, it sounded like it must have when General Pickett fielded his men in a mile-long line in front of the Union guns at the battle of Gettysburg! Never in my life had I heard so much shooting and seen so many ducks falling from the sky for the last time.

The limit was eight ducks and six geese per hunter per day that year, and if one wanted to kill eight pintail, it was legal to do so. Many hundreds of sportsmen did, and I remember I checked 108 full limits of ducks that day before I found someone who did not have a full daily bag limit—and most of the ducks killed were the graceful little pintail.

Today this nation's pintail populations are in a world of hurt. Not just because we overshot them in 1967 but because of large bag limits over many of the following years. In fact, their numbers are so low today that many states allow only one pintail a day in the bag limit.

Soon I was busy doing what game wardens do best, and by noon on that first day, I had written thirteen citations (among the thirty or so for other violations) to shooters who had exceeded their daily bag limit of eight ducks. If my memory serves me correctly, the lowest overlimit that day was eight over, and the largest overlimit was by one fellow who was a terrific wing-shot—he had killed thirty-three over and was still going strong when I approached him on the White Mallard Duck Club to shut him down for the day! By the end of the next day, I had cited a total of thirty-four individuals for killing or possessing overlimits of ducks and had gotten my welcome to just a part of what I called "Slaughter in the Sacramento Valley."

As that duck season progressed (it was 107 days long in those days), my apprehension rate for those killing overlimits grew. Soon Inspector Hooker paid me a visit to congratulate me for being the first officer in his Region II squad to apprehend over two hundred individuals that hunting season for taking overlimits of ducks or geese (that number did not include all my other citations, just those for overlimits). To me, it was no big deal. I had over three hundred duck clubs in my area of responsibility and waterfowl galore everywhere else as well. All it took were a lot of long hours of hard work, and many times a wet ass from going in over my hip boots to catch those who'd had problems in Mrs. Wilson's third grade math class. I spent several days working with Hooker, who was one hell of a man and had many tales to tell of the early years of wildlife law enforcement in California during his time as a younger officer.

The numbers of ducks continued to increase throughout the winter, but now the birds were much wiser because they had been shot at all along their migration route, and overlimit cases were harder to come by. But they were still there to be made, especially on the big private duck clubs and in the Butte Sink; I just had to work for them. The hunting public's numbers remained steady, as did its appetite for a duck or goose dinner, and it seemed to an overwhelmed game warden (remember, other hunting seasons were now open as well) that so did the problems it brought. With the advance of the season came the winter storms, and in such fury that they began to make themselves felt on my now tiring carcass. It seemed I was always wet, cold, or stuck in the adobe mud on the valley's many farm roads. However, I was young and full of piss and vinegar, the hunting for humans breaking the laws of the land was good, my wife was letting me fulfill my vision quest, and my two guardian angels were keeping me out of harm's way. So with those green lights, I sailed off into one of the weirdest cases I ever made involving the hunting of migratory waterfowl and the gunner's desire to cheat.

Working just off Four Mile Road to the north and west of Delevan National Wildlife Refuge one morning, I heard fairly constant shooting by two guns farther north on a duck club in the Lambertville area of the county. Nothing crazy, mind you, but enough that a good game warden would lodge the event in the back of his mind for later inspection if he had the time. The wind and rain had picked up by that time of the day, as had the numbers of low-flying flocks of waterfowl, and I had just worked my way into a second group of hunters on Newhall Farms. In that group I had located four gunners hiding behind a densely weeded rice check who were really shooting the hell out of the northward flow of low-flying ducks as they crossed over their place of ambush.

By the time they had killed thirty ducks according to my count (remember, the daily bag limit was eight), and I knew they had been shooting long before I had located them, I thought a visit from their local happy game warden was called for. Creeping (yes, a guy my size can creep!) out to their place of concealment in the middle of a large rice field by using another rice check for cover, I finally got within stomping distance. Another flock of mallards went over them, so low they might as well as have been walking because of the howling winds and pellets of rain (ducks fly into the rain with their eyes open), and the lads opened up. The flock of ducks, upon seeing the kneeling hunters rise up to shoot, quickly lifted skyward with the aid of the winds. Alas, it was too late, and nine fell stone-cold dead to the popping sounds of the shotguns below.

That's enough! I said to myself as I rose out of my hiding place to walk over and check out my errant lads.

"Morning; how is the hunting?" I asked a heavy-set man sitting with his back to me, hastily trying to reload his shotgun from a sitting position. *Damn!* I thought. *I've never seen such a fat man jump like a bug on a hot rock!* Sure as God made little green apples, he jumped straight up from a sitting position without even coming to a kneeling position first.

"Holy Christ!" he exclaimed. "You scared the crap out of me."

I saw another three heads pop up out of the wind-blown water grass lining the rice check as they looked in surprise at the large, grinning man standing beside one of their own.

"Morning, gentlemen," I said loudly enough to overcome the howling wind. "State Fish and Game warden. I would like to check your licenses, birds, duck stamps, and shotguns for plugs, if you please."

Before anyone could comply, the now worrying sound of those two shotguns to the north firing six times rapidly grabbed my attention again. At the sounds of that last barrage, I had seen four geese tumble out of the remainder of a flock hurriedly trying to put some space between it and the shooters below.

However, a quick scurrying by one of my four lads in the rice check caught my eye, and I turned my attention back to the detail at hand, putting my goose shooters on the back burner for later. I noticed as one of the lads stood up that he had pulled his empty decoy bag slyly over something beside him on the rice check, as if trying to hide something.

That is all right, I thought. *Whether you realize it or not, that will be one of the first places I will check.*

All four men quietly crowded around me as if wanting to meet my requests with as little fuss as possible so that I would soon be on my way. *Fat chance,* I thought. *Not until I have checked the rice check around you guys to my satisfaction.*

The men all checked out as legal with their licenses and duck stamps. I then checked the plugs on their shotguns, and those were in order as well.

BOOM-boom-boom-boom, went the guns to the north once again. *They have to be on the Sheriff's Gun Club,* I thought as I began to hurry with the chaps at hand so I could go check out my troublesome shooters to the north. By now my sixth sense was kicking in, telling me to get with it and get up there to see what was going on. …

Checking my four lads' piles of ducks located in their shooting positions, I could see they each had a limit. However, a check farther along the rice check and under the hastily thrown empty decoy sack revealed another fifty-nine freshly killed ducks, which placed them far over the daily bag limit.

"Gentlemen, what have we here?" I asked with a grin. For a moment, the men just looked at one another and then at their feet.

"I think we got carried away with the good shooting and forgot to keep a closer count," finally said the fat one.

"I would think fifty-nine over the limit is more than just getting a little carried away," I retorted as I continued to sternly look at anyone in the group who would look back at me. With no takers for additional discussion, I said, "All right, lads, let's gather up all your gear and head for that gray pickup sitting over there on Four Mile Road."

I filled their decoy bag with the overlimit and made the men carry all the rest of their gear, including their individual limits of ducks. Arriving at my truck out of breath from packing the heavy decoy bag, I threw the ducks into the bed of the pickup. I then had the men do the same with all the other ducks they were carrying since they were now part of the overlimit as well. That produced some howls of anguish once they realized they were losing all of their ducks as part of the overlimit for state's evidence. (The birds I collected went to the Colusa County jail to feed the prisoners.) Sitting inside the cab, I wrote each man a citation for possession of an overlimit of ducks while the rain and wind rocked the truck gently and provided a constant drumming sound on the roof. When I was finished with the paperwork, I gave each shooter a copy of the citation and an evidence tag for his share of the overlimit bag.

As they walked dejectedly off toward where they had parked, I turned my face into the wind and rain. It was now quiet where I had seen the geese fall out of the flock on what I supposed was the Sheriff's Gun Club in the Lambertville duck-club complex (an area comprising about thirty separate duck clubs). Hoping against hope, I began gutting my evidence ducks and throwing the entrails into the ditch for the critters to eat. I listened for the suspicious shooting to the north to resume but was rewarded only with the sounds of the wind and rain hitting my raingear. Finishing with the gutting, I washed my bloody hands on the wet grass alongside the road, got back into my truck, and headed toward the area in question.

I found a place to park out of sight on the Gunner's Field property, then stood up in the back of the truck and used my binoculars to search the area where I had heard the shooting. Nothing of note met my eyes, either in the area where the shooting had occurred or where the hunters might have parked their vehicle. Getting back into my truck, I boldly drove to the place where I thought my suspect shooters must have parked earlier and walked out to their duck blind. There I discovered a lot of freshly fired shotgun shells, goose feathers, and fresh guts galore in a fifty-gallon trash barrel, but little else to speak to the morning's events. It had taken me too long to get there, and as a result my shooters were long gone. Still, my sixth sense told me something was wrong, so I took a walkabout, looking for any signs of bait, wanton waste of game birds, or the like. Finding nothing, I walked back to my truck and then spied a wooden shot shell box behind some bamboo thickets where the hunters would have parked. Looking into the wooden box, I saw nine concrete anchors weighing about ten pounds each. A nail had been inserted into the concrete of each anchor while it was wet and then bent over when dried. Attached to each bent nail was a short piece of heavy-duty fishing line.

What the hell? I thought. *What would anyone want with a contraption like this near a duck blind?*

Leaving everything as I found it, I climbed back into my truck and headed for the Norman area to investigate more heavy shooting (windy days made for good overlimit opportunities). However, all the way over to the new area, I continued to ponder the concrete anchors.

Now, a standard game warden maxim if you suspect someone is doing something wrong and hasn't yet been bothered by the law is that he or she will return at a later date and most likely an identical time to do the same thing again. With that in mind, I bided my time. For the next two shoot days (shoot days were Wednesdays, Saturdays, Sundays, and holidays in those days), we had bluebird weather patterns with no wind. But come the third shoot day, the winter wind was once again howling out of the northwest, and the rain was coming down so hard the ducks almost had to walk to get where they wanted to go. Well, almost … Sure as shooting, your friendly game warden was once again sitting in the driveway of Gunner's Field, out of sight behind the main gate's stone facade, watching the Sheriff's Gun Club. And sure as cow slobbers, there right on time were my two shooters! I later discovered that they had gotten into their blind way before sunrise and before my arrival. However, I was now set up and began to watch. Soon a pair of mallards winged into their decoy area, and two quick shots brought them down.

But that wasn't what caught my eye. When the shooters had shot at the ducks, I had seen other movement at the edge of the pond by their decoys, and what was moving there were not the usual coots! Walking on the edge of the duck pond near the shooters' decoys, were what appeared to be three dark geese! A closer look revealed a fourth one swimming in the water among the decoys. Yet they hadn't flown when those shots had been fired just over their heads at the two mallards.

What the hell? I thought, trying to crawl into my binoculars for a closer look.

Then the clarion calls of Canada geese could be heard coming from the south. Whirling from my vantage point, I observed a small flock of large Canadas coming my way. Fighting the howling winds, they dipped low and then rose higher to the lessening wind gusts as they continued plowing their way through the headwinds toward the Sheriff's Gun Club as if on a string. Then the calls of other Canada geese could be heard coming from the duck blind holding the two hunters and from the bank by the Canada geese in and around the shooter's duck decoys! By now fascinated at the birds' flight against the elements and their impending doom if they continued their ill-fated direction, I watched in fascination. The four live Canada geese, now all in the pond, were calling their heads off, and in response, the free-flying geese were homing right in on their brethrens' siren calls!

The shooters had to be using live decoys, but why hadn't they flown when shot over? I pondered. Finally the sun shone on the manure pile behind the barn! *Damn,* I thought, *now I see why the government outlawed the use of live decoys! They are so deadly and effective when used, the wild birds being drawn to their calls have no chance in hell.*

On the flock came, and when it passed over the blind, the two men rose in unison and killed five of the flock of eight deader than a box of rocks. However, that was not what got my attention. The four live geese on the duck pond tried to rise off the water at the sounds of shooting, only to be jerked back down by something holding their feet!

"Son of a buck!" I yelled into the wind. "Those bastards are using live decoys that are somehow tied down!" Having seen enough, I jumped back into my truck, roared out of the Gunner's Field driveway, and hurtled toward the driveway of the Sheriff's Gun Club. The two men stared in surprise when they saw me hammering into their driveway. Then, realizing this might just be the law, one of them sprinted from the blind toward the live goose decoys. Skidding to a stop at one frantically flapping goose, he began slashing at something on its feet. Sliding to a stop, I jumped out of my truck and, with a whistle to Shadow, my Labrador retriever riding in the back, took off at a dead run for the culprit messing with the wildly flapping Canada geese in the pond.

Running past the first shooter in the blind, who was standing transfixed at the turn of events, I yelled at Shadow, "Get the duck" as I gave her a hand signal toward a flopping goose just released by the shooter at the edge of the pond. She sped by me as if I was standing still.

"Touch another bird and you are going to jail!" I thundered at the man with the knife at the edge of the pond as he grabbed another live goose. Ignoring my command, he cut the line tied to the foot of that Canada goose as I yelled, "State Fish and Game warden; you are under arrest!"

That was followed by a rather large thud as I put one of my best football tackles on his miserable carcass just as he grabbed another live and tethered goose by the neck. Down the two of us went, all eyeballs, hind ends, and false teeth into ten thousand years' worth of mud, tule roots, and goose crap at the edge of the pond.

"Don't hit me; don't hit me!" screamed the man with the knife as I jumped up, jerking him to his feet so violently that several fountain pens came flying out of his shirt pocket.

"Next time you had better do what you are told or you will wish you had!" I roared, still upset over the fact that he had tried to destroy the evidence I needed to make a case for using live decoys to illegally take migratory waterfowl.

The man cowered in my grip as I jerked the knife out of his hand and tossed it into the grass at his feet. About then, here came Shadow, my faithful dog, with a live Canada goose in her mouth. Reaching into my back pocket, I removed a set of handcuffs, and before the cowering lad knew it, he was wearing a set of well-used Smith and Wesson bracelets. ...

"What are you doing?" he asked in a scared voice.

"I told you to put down that knife and not cut the line on that goose's foot, and you chose not to listen, so now you will pay the piper. Plain and simply, my friend, you are going to jail for taking migratory waterfowl over live decoys and failure to show upon demand," I explained, still coming down from the emotion of my flying-tackle arrest.

I removed the goose from Shadow's mouth and then sent her hightailing after the other one my shooter had released, which was still trying to hide in the grass at the edge of the duck pond. Looking down at the goose Shadow had just brought me, I could see the fishing line still tied to its leg. A closer look revealed that the bird had been wounded earlier in the tip of the wing and was unable to fly. A closer look at the two geese still tied to the concrete anchors in the pond revealed that both of them had also been wing-shot before being used as live decoys. Trotting back with her second goose, Shadow presented me with another wing-tipped goose with fishing line still tied to its leg.

The man with the knife was booked into the Colusa County Jail for violation of the Fish and Game Code by taking migratory waterfowl with the use and aid of live decoys and by failure to show upon demand. Since his partner had not attempted anything foolish upon my surprise arrival, he was merely issued a state citation for taking migratory waterfowl with the use and aid of live decoys. Since he hadn't cut any of the lines holding the geese to their cement anchors, he was spared a citation for failure to show upon demand. In addition, both men were cited for possessing an overlimit of dark geese—to wit, twelve over the limit!

Both appeared in the Williams Justice Court some time later, where they were found guilty and fined $500 each for their offenses ($1,500 for one violator and $1,000 for the other) and forfeited their two new Browning AL-5 shotguns to the state of California. As I discovered later, their wives had gotten together just three days before I had caught the shooters and had purchased the shotguns for the men's birthdays (this was before all those crazy guns laws went into effect with their long waiting periods before ownership). This case was even more unusual because the men were twin brothers and deputy sheriffs from San Francisco.

That was the only live decoy case I ever made during my thirty-two-year career, and before the cold, wet day was over, Shadow was rewarded with an extra-large can of Alpo for her part in bringing back the evidence.

CHAPTER 7

A Close Call, but No Cigar

For a week in late December 1968, the ducks had been streaming off Delevan National Wildlife Refuge and winging their way over many large rice fields just west of Two Mile Road. Once over their rice field of choice, the numerous flocks of ducks began a lazy, wide circle that tightened into a tornado of living feathered bodies of all species as they descended into the freshly burned fields to feed. Seeing such a spectacle always made me nervous. If I could see that living tornado descending into a rice field to feed, so could mean-spirited sets of other eyes with less-than-noble thoughts about what would come next.

Hidden in a large clump of brush beside the railroad track to the west of a monster harvested rice field, I scanned the area before me with my binoculars. Slowly moving south just to the east on Two Mile Road under the high-flying ducks streaming off the refuge was a pickup containing two men I recognized as duck-killing outlaws from the nearby town of Maxwell. Farther to the north, I spotted another pickup pulling off Interstate 5 and driving into the field just north of the swirling mass of ducks. Soon I could see Tony Valente Jr., who was rumored to be somewhat of an illegal duck killer, quietly surveying the living tornado.

Then the unexpected happened. My two Maxwell chaps disappeared down Two Mile Road, only to reappear a short time later on the road leading to the farm shed where I had hidden my state patrol truck. One of the chaps jumped out of the pickup as it approached my shed, threw open the doors, and stood to one side as his partner tried to drive hurriedly into the building before anyone saw them. Then on came his brake lights as his truck lurched to a stop. The man who had opened the doors realized at the same moment that the shed was already occupied by the hated local game warden's patrol vehicle! Tires madly throwing gravel told me the pickup was rapidly backing up as the passenger quickly reloaded his carcass into the front seat. A quick turn, and my culprits were winging their way out of the area at a high rate of speed. Hell, they didn't even bother to shut the shed doors! You should have seen the game warden rolling around in the mud under the brush in which he was hiding as he laughed at the frenzied event that had just taken place. That was the last time I saw those two chaps anywhere near my living tornado of ducks.

Getting over my fit of laughter and looking back north to where Tony Valente Jr. had been standing earlier, I noticed that his pickup was now gone as well.

Where the hell did he go? I asked myself as I quickly swung my binoculars from point to point, trying to locate his pickup around the increasingly larger swirl of ducks moving into the rice fields to feed. *Damn,* I thought, *looks like I might have my hands full this evening if this collection of knotheads continues to gather like the vultures they can be.*

For the rest of the afternoon, I continued watching my swirl of ducks until it got too dark to see. Several other vehicles had stopped to watch my swirling bunches of ducks, but none had made any suspicious moves. Finally it got dark enough that I could get up and change my position in order to provide better protection for the ducks. Gathering up my gear, which included my Starlight Scope, I began walking in the direction where I had last seen the densest portion of the huge flock of feeding waterfowl, figuring I would stay with the ducks until they returned to the safety of the refuge. Soon the sound of twenty thousand hungrily feeding ducks became music to my ears. Changing direction slightly, I continued slowly moving north toward the ducks in such a manner so as not to spook them. Then I became aware that I had even more company than I had thought. I now had another large flock of feeding ducks swirling in to the south not one hundred yards away. Finding a spot where I could be more or less in the center of all this feeding activity, I set up shop. Locating a good high rice check to sit on, I burrowed into the covering water grasses, turned on my Starlight Scope, and took a 360-degree look around.

What a sight! I must have had sixty thousand feeding ducks all around me and as far as I could see to the north and south with the night-vision scope. The air was full of speeding ducks moving from flock to flock, hoping the grass was greener than where they had just come from. Small bunches continued swirling all around me and then quickly dropping to the ground when they spied some of their kind wolfing down the grits. Singles and doubles steamed over the rice checks like cannon shot as they looked for places to feed with their necks and heads pointed downward, searching for company. The flocks near me looked like large waves of ducks rolling ever forward over the leaders of the feeding flocks, hoping for better feed in front, and now the feeding ducks were walking right by my place of concealment. They were so close that I could have reached out and wrung their necks had I wanted. Any conservation officer who is blessed with such a living sight finds that it acts as a recharge of one's tired batteries and makes all one's sacrifices for the world of wildlife worthwhile! And yet, it saddened me deeply when I remembered that my kind were so few in number that I was the only one within five counties in the Sacramento Valley that evening out doing what I was doing.

About midnight, the December cold set in as frost began forming on everything, and I began shaking uncontrollably. Then I realized that part of the problem was that I hadn't eaten anything since five that morning. Reaching into my coat pocket, I took out a stick of salami and, taking a bite out of the hardened sausage, let the fat juices swirl comfortably around in my mouth. By now my entire area was alive with happily feeding ducks. They had flowed over the rice check on which I was sitting and into the next field in their eagerness to feed and ward off the winter cold. I had ducks walking so close to me that several had bumped into my legs and feet. As the ducks walked by, they looked up at me in the soft moonlight as if to say, "Who the hell are you?" and then moved on in their eagerness to feed.

About three in the morning, as I was beginning to nod off in the intense cold, my little world blew up! To the north, about half a mile away, I heard what sounded like a loudly tearing sheet as twenty shots from unplugged shotguns rent the cold morning air. Jumping off my rice check in surprise, I fell flat on my face in the rice stubble as my cold legs failed to work. Unbeknownst to me, they had gone numb sitting for those many hours on the cold, muddy rice check and for the moment failed to work properly. I had been unable to move much for all those long hours because I had feeding ducks all around me, and to do so would have sent them off in a panic. The entire feeding frenzy could have turned to a fleeing frenzy and emptied out my rice fields from stem to stern, as the flocks were wont to do when disturbed at night. However, there was no reason to worry now. That ragged string of shots had alerted everyone in my neck of the woods, and the air was now full of the sounds of many thousands of fleeing ducks. I quickly turned on my night-vision scope and found that the lime-green view was full of flying ducks and many thousands of others quickly rising from the ground. Almost all were rapidly fleeing to the east and the safety offered by the Delevan National Wildlife Refuge.

Quickly turning my scope northward toward the shooting, all I could make out were thousands of ducks fleeing those particular feeding grounds for the refuge as well. Getting up and staggering on fast-thawing legs, I headed north as quickly as I could safely navigate the rutted field. Shuffling in a ground-eating dog trot, I ran a hundred steps and stopped. I looked north once more through the scope and could faintly make out the hurried movement of four people running around in a rice field picking up what appeared to be ducks. Turning off the scope to save my limited battery life, I again shuffled northward another hundred steps and stopped to rest and look once again. Breathing heavily out of exertion and the emotion of the moment, I turned on my scope. There they were! Four men clearly gathering up dead and crippled ducks and throwing them into piles in the rice field where they were frantically working.

I was still a good three hundred yards to the south. But with a little luck their duck shoot would soon be spoiled, I thought gleefully.

Doing my old-time fur-trapper's run of another hundred yards and resting, I threw the night-vision scope up and turned on the switch. Sure as hell, there were my four individuals still picking up ducks and biting the heads of the cripples in order to kill them. Then my little world turned to crap! I could hear the faint whirring sound of my scope oscillator slowing down as my screen went from lime green to purple, a splash of bright yellow, and then darkness! *Damn,* I thought as I shook the scope in the hope that a good shaking would bring it back to life. Nope, nothing, *nada, nyet*—the scope was down for the count with a dead oscillator! Swearing under my breath, I grabbed the binoculars swinging from my neck and, using the fast-setting moon for light, could just barely make out my shooters. Pretty well crippled without my night scope at that distance, I continued walking toward them in the hope that I could get close enough to do some damage without being detected. Ten minutes of quiet walking brought me into pitch darkness as the moon set behind the mountains to the west, and now I was walking very slowly, trying to get close to my shooters without spooking them. However, I was having problems. I couldn't see the rows of rice stubble so I could walk between them, so my feet were making loud crunching sounds. It was also hard to walk silently on the frosted field. Realizing I was not winning, I stopped and just listened for any sounds of talking or walking from my shooters. For the longest time I saw or heard nothing.

Then to the west near the interstate, I saw two sets of vehicle lights come on as the rigs left the edge of the rice field about a quarter mile away, turned north on the highway, and hurriedly left the area. I waited through more abject darkness, quiet, and frustration, figuring those lights represented my duck draggers leaving the field of battle with their ducks—and in the process leaving the game warden holding a handful of nothing.

Come the dawn several cold hours later, I swept the area to the north with my binoculars. Nothing out of the ordinary came into view. Continuing to walk northward, I began to look for the rice field that earlier in the evening had held ducks but would now hold only spent shotgun shells, footprints, maybe a few dead ducks left behind, and lots of feathers near splotches of bright-red blood.

Then I came upon the killing field. Feathers everywhere, along with lots of human tracks and duck poop in the soft, muddy rice field. It was a rice field that had not yet been burned, and rice straw had been kicked everywhere as the four men had pursued their kill. I saw few ducks either crippled or dead, and I sat down on the nearest rice check and tried to reconstruct the event so I might learn from my misadventure. After a few minutes I walked onto a muddy farm road to the west of the killing field, where I spied four sets of tracks departing from the area. I tracked them to where two vehicles had sat at the edge of the field among some abandoned buildings on another farm road near the interstate. I could see where the men had gotten into their trucks and, leaving muddy tire tracks on the asphalt, entered the highway and traveled north.

Walking back to my killing field, I stood on top of the nearest rice check to survey the area for any more clues that might help me find the shooters or do a better job the next time something like this happened. Nothing out of the ordinary greeted my eyes, but just as I started to leave, I spotted something unusual. When a harvester harvests rice, the kernels are deposited into a holding tank on the machine and the rice straw is dumped out the back in long dense rows. Looking down two of those rows near the edge of the field, I noticed that they were emitting steaming spirals in the morning cold in several places!

What the dickens? I thought as I stepped off the rice check and headed in that direction. Arriving at a still steaming rice-straw pile, I noticed that all the rice straw leading up to the piles still had morning frost on it. The areas over the steaming straw piles had none! With the toe of my hip boot, I kicked some of the straw off the first steaming pile and damned nearly fell over. There at the toe of my boot were dozens of freshly killed and gutted ducks! Walking over to another steaming straw pile, I kicked off the straw and was rewarded with many more freshly killed and steaming ducks in a pile. Their still-warm bodies had kept the frost from forming over their bodies, and in the morning's cold, those bodies were emitting steam! Quickly walking over to the remaining steaming rice-straw pile, I kicked that straw aside too. Sure as God made little green apples, there lay another fifty or so freshly killed mallard and pintail!

Those bastards left these ducks behind because they killed too many and couldn't carry all of them out in one trip, I thought. *So they are going to come back today and retrieve these!*

With that realization, remembering that I was standing out in the middle of the rice field like some damn stork, I quickly dropped to my knees and grabbed my binoculars. Swinging them upward toward the place where I suspected my shooters had parked earlier, I was met with the view of a black Ford or Chevy pickup I did not recognize hastily leaving the area by the old farm sheds and thundering out onto the interstate. From there, it headed north like the devil was on its tail!

Striking my fist into the soft mud of the rice field in frustration, I let God know in my best logging-camp speak that I was not a happy camper. Watching the pickup drive out of sight, I rose and, knowing that was an opportunity lost since they had spotted me in their rice field, began gathering up all the ducks from the steaming piles. Moments later, I had my own steaming pile of drawn ducks in the cold December morning waiting for their ultimate collection and disposal.

Walking back to my patrol truck in disgust, I drove out of the farm shed and headed north to my suspects' parking area near the farm sheds. Four trips later, with two full duck straps thrown over my shoulders and my hands as well, I had all the ducks in the back of my truck. I had picked up 136 dead ducks from the previous evening's drag and wondered how many more had actually been killed and hauled out by my four shooters. It had to be a bunch, probably numbering in excess of two hundred ducks.

That particular day just happened to be a shoot day in the Sacramento Valley, and the state-run shooting areas on the national wildlife refuges were in full swing. Taking my ducks up to the state shooting area on the Sacramento National Wildlife Refuge, I handed out limits of ducks to the little kids in the parking lot whose dads were out hunting until they were all gone. Then I headed for home, a shower, a couple hours of sleep, and then back into the fields.

I wonder how many other piles of steaming ducks lying in the rice fields I had walked by during my tenure in the valley? No two ways about it, it was one slick idea. It was winter cold, the ducks were gutted and not going to spoil, and it was a surefire way to hide what one couldn't pack out. Then all one had to do was make sure the coast was clear before returning to gather up Mother Nature's bounty. Pretty damn slick.

Someday God will let me know just how poor a job I did protecting his critters. I doubt He will give me a cigar for my good efforts on this one. …

CHAPTER 8

Lions Six, Christians Nothing

Walking out of my home at five in the morning, I was met with fierce winds from out of the northwest and the smell of rain in the air. Looking skyward, I could see only light from the streetlights instead of the stars from the heavens as the last leaves of the season from the elm trees in Colusa whipped around on the deserted street by my home like small tornadoes.

Best use the county patrol truck today, I thought, grimacing at the specter of trying to get around in the Colusa County mud with only my two-wheel-drive state patrol truck.

Leaving my state patrol truck parked at the Colusa County sheriff's office and picking up my county four-wheel drive, I headed across the bridge over the Sacramento River and into the east side of my law enforcement district. The lesser snow geese had been piling into the rice fields on the whole east side of my district over the past few days, and I wanted to give them some relief from the shooting public. I thought about the problem as I headed for the Colusa-Gridley Highway that cut across the northern boundary of my district.

By then, sheets of rain heralding this latest winter storm had arrived, along with some pretty stiff winds that rocked my pickup gently as I sat off Putnam Road out of sight in some cottonwoods, waiting for it to get light enough for the duck and goose hunters to shoot. *Shooting time will be later today because of the cloudy and rainy weather,* I casually thought as I lit up one of my Toscanni cigars and let the strong tobacco smell permeate the cab of the truck and then drift lazily out a crack in my driver's-side window.

Soon dawn drifted in, along with more scudding rain clouds—and so did the hunting public. Vehicle after vehicle turned off the Colusa-Gridley

Highway and thundered through the potholed Putnam Road with a vengeance, throwing water every which way as they headed for a favorite spot on the Terrill Sartain Ranch and hunting club. To the east lay what is known as the Butte Sink, an ancient watered depression in the land holding many wealthy, top-of-the-line duck clubs and hundreds of thousands of resting ducks and geese.

Soon small groups of the beautiful little wood duck began to grace the airways as they whistled off the Butte Sink and darted around looking for a choice spot for breakfast in the harvested rice fields to the west. Then came the hordes of pintail and mallard as they literally began blanketing the harvested rice lands west of the Butte Sink with their presence. Last to arrive on the rice-field feeding grounds were the snow geese, followed by the lordly Canada geese. Soon the airways were filled not only with the sounds of the winds and pattering of winter rains but with the staccato popping of shotguns. Then my day began as I moved out of my hiding place and into the swirling maelstrom of winged creatures and the chaps pursuing them.

My method of operation was simple. I either moved to the sound of the guns or to the lure of the massive swirls of ducks and geese alighting on rice fields to eat. Either way was a surefire formula for finding trouble of the kind I was paid to control and correct. On that particular day, my job was easy. The evening before, tens of thousands of snow geese had fed in the middle of one of Terrill's big rice fields. Geese are creatures of habit who will return to almost the same spot where they fed the evening before if not disturbed. This day's behavioral pattern for the geese was no different. Thousands of snow geese began to wing over Terrill's fields, forming into large, slowly moving white swirls as they began their descent into the rice fields. Soon the ground was covered with about ten thousand geese, and still they came in huge numbers, winging over the mass of feeders on the ground now eagerly loading up with leftover rice.

With that aerial display of biomass visible for miles, others would come, and soon, I thought with straight-lipped certainty over the slaughter that was to come if I wasn't on the top of my game.

Soon over fifty thousand snow geese graced Terrill's rice fields, and still they came—but now from all points of the compass. Humankind just can't leave well enough alone under such circumstances, and didn't in this case either. From my vantage point on the levee near the White Mallard Duck Club, I watched six men getting out of two vehicles parked on the edge of Putnam Road. Looking all around as if to make sure the coast was clear, they drifted silently into the many rice checks adorning Terrill's land, moving toward the mass of feeding and still circling birds in a crouched position. Soon they disappeared into the weedy rice fields and noisy mass of geese as if on a mission.

Slipping quickly into my raingear and grabbing my binoculars, I started out into the same field the six hunters had just entered. As an afterthought, I returned to my vehicle and put a second pair of handcuffs into my "possibles" bag. I don't know why I did that, but I guess my guardian angels were awake and suggested the precaution in case the six hunters became a problem.

Working my way out into the wet rice fields, I became aware of just how many snow geese were really on the ground and in the air. In the process of sneaking out into that field, I was hit by goose poop from the thousands of birds flying overhead five different times! Soon I was at the edge of a huge flock

Thousands of snow geese feeding in a harvested rice field in Colusa County in Sacramento Valley. A view of what the commercial gunners or "draggers" would have seen and shot into. (Courtesy Peter Grevie)

of feeding geese and decided I would just dig into the nearest rice check, make myself comfortable, and watch Mother Nature in all her glory. As for my six hunters who had entered the field earlier, they were nowhere to be seen. For the next forty minutes or so, I had the privilege of watching probably twenty thousand snow geese fly into the area, land, and feed across the harvested rice fields like a moving white carpet. The constant happy din they created with their calls was indescribable, especially when new flocks arrived overhead.

Then this loud, happy din went instantly silent as the birds snapped into a heads-up position of alertness. Peering over the rice check to see better, I was met with a tremendous clattering of shooting and the stinging sensation of a number 4 pellet striking and sticking just under the skin on my bare right wrist! For the next few moments, hell and all its handbaskets reigned. Ground-sluiced, head-shot geese were flopping everywhere, brought down by the numerous shotgun blasts. Crippled geese began moving across the rice field toward me and away from the shooting after they tried once or twice to lift off and couldn't. The remaining thousands of geese rose up en masse and headed right at me and away from the shooting as if hell was on their tails. There was another outburst of shooting, and this time I was rewarded with a number 4 pellet in the lower lip as I peered into the maelstrom. As the huge flock of birds got the hell out of Dodge, dozens that had been hit in the first barrage and not killed outright were now dying in the air and dropping right and left like maggots off a deer carcass being dragged away for disposal. The carnage was unreal as many more single and double volleys of shooting took place directly before me. My six culprits advanced from their hiding places in the rice check and started shooting flopping cripples. For the next ten minutes or so, this killing and the wringing of necks was carried on with a fury of urgency. Being just forty yards away and directly across from my shooters, I knew if I started across the open field in plain view, they would scatter like quail and I would have six of them to chase down. However, I had one ace in the hole: I was between my goose killers and their vehicles! With that realization, I just held my position and figured I would let them come to me when they got good and ready.

After picking up all their geese and stacking them behind the rice check where they had been hiding, my six shooters quickly disappeared. Except for the noisy geese, who had moved one huge rice field down from the shooting and were commencing the gathering all over again, nothing moved. Edging down my rice check to where I would be more in the shooters' line of retreat from the killing field to their vehicles, I dug in and recommenced waiting. About thirty minutes later, I saw two men peering through the water grass on top of the rice check as if looking to see if the coast was clear. They saw nothing out of the ordinary, so here they came, carrying a limit of six snow geese apiece. As they slogged through the muddy field toward my rice check, I continually changed my position, crawling along in order to intercept the lads once they had crossed over and were out of sight of their remaining four buddies. Soon I could hear them walking across the muddy rice field and talking to each other in low tones.

Letting both men step over the rice check within feet of where I was hiding, I quietly hissed to get their attention and, when they turned, held my finger up to my swollen lip in a signal for silence and motioned for them to sit down. That motion was reinforced by my badge in the gesturing hand in plain view. Standing there in surprise, both men looked like someone had just taken a large bite out of their last part over the fence. I gave another wave for them to sit down, and they both did as if they had been poleaxed.

"Gentlemen, you need to listen and listen well because I am only going to say this one time! I am a state Fish and Game warden, and both of you are under arrest for taking and possessing an overlimit of snow geese. If either of you tries to warn your buddies about the fact that I am here, that person will find himself heading for the federal lockup in Sacramento faster than he can imagine. Do we have an understanding?" I asked in my sternest voice.

Both men nodded vigorously as if they were scared out of their socks.

"Good," I said. "Hand both of your shotguns to me butt first, and make sure their barrels are not pointing at either of you." The men were so scared that they disregarded my instructions and handed their shotguns to me with the barrels pointing directly at each other!

Taking and unloading their shotguns, I said, "Hand me your hunting licenses and driver's licenses, please." They complied, and I put those items in my shirt pocket and fastened down the button so I wouldn't lose them. Then I took one pair of handcuffs out of my back pocket. I thought for a moment the two men were going to pass out when they saw what I was holding.

"Here," I said, "take these, and each man put one of the cuffs on his right wrist." Both men clumsily complied; I knew that if they tried to escape, it would be difficult for them to run while handcuffed in such a manner.

By then I could hear more men coming, and with a finger to my swollen lip for silence, I turned and peered through the tall water grasses on the rice check behind which I was hiding.

Good, I thought. *Here come two more men with limits of geese, and they are going to cross close to where my first two culprits crossed the rice check.*

Crawling just a few feet away from where my first two lads were sitting in order to get closer to their approaching companions, I waited to spring my trap. When the next pair crossed the rice check, I did the same thing I had done with the first two. These fellows responded just like their friends, only with even more terrified emotion. I instructed them to sit in the mud behind the rice check and tossed one of them my second set of handcuffs. The man who caught the cuffs looked at them for a moment, and for a second the unusual look on his face made me think I might have a fight on my hands. Then he dropped the cuffs, slumped forward, and promptly passed out! For a moment I just knelt there in shock. Then I asked the other guy what his partner's problem was.

"I don't know," he replied. "Perhaps he is just as scared of you as I am."

"You," I said, pointing to him, "put one of the cuffs on your right wrist and then do the same for your buddy." I thought, *Man, I have caught some real cowards in this bunch.* Then I asked, "Why didn't all of you come out of the field at the same time instead of in twos?"

"Well," said a tall, thin chap named John Golba, "we thought we would arouse less suspicion if we came out in pairs with legal limits each time. That way, if checked, we would always be legal and could eventually bring out the huge numbers of geese we killed and hid by that rice check over yonder."

"Why the hell did you guys blow up the geese in the first place? As many as there were flying around, you guys could've had a great wing-shoot," I said.

"We paid a lot for this lease," said Golba, "and have little to show for it this year. It seemed every time we came up to hunt, the weather was nice and the birds were not flying. So when we had the chance, we made up for all those days we never fired a shot." He gave a halfhearted grin of justification.

Shaking my head in disbelief, I looked over the rice check. Coming across the field were the last of my gunners, and they did the same thing the previous four had done. They walked right to me, and the final round of the trap was closed.

Gathering up all their shotguns, along with their hunting and driver's licenses, I headed the crew of rather forlorn-looking chaps across the rice field toward my truck. The chap who had passed out was now awake, but I wouldn't have bet a month's paycheck he could have made it to my truck under his own power.

Once there, I called the Colusa County sheriff's office on my radio and asked the dispatcher if they had a deputy on patrol on the east side near Putnam Road. The dispatcher, whose name was Billie, a great gal and grandmother to one of the subjects of an earlier story in this book (see Chapter 4), advised me to wait, and after a short interval indicated that Deputy Del Garrison was just south of my location on the Boggs Ranch. Did I need him to come my way?

I responded, "Affirmative," and added that I would meet Garrison at the bottom of the road near the south turn on the levee near the White Mallard Duck Club and Butte Creek with six prisoners needing transport to the jail.

I turned my attention to my now really unhappy shooters, who were sitting on the ground and getting even wetter as the winter storm appeared to take it out on them for blowing up God's critters. "Gentlemen, in a short while Officer Del Garrison will be arriving, and he will be taking you to the Colusa County Jail for booking. At that time, the bailiff will explain your options to you," I informed them.

About fifteen minutes later, Del Garrison, a bear of a man (and a dear friend who has since passed away), arrived. "What do you have for me, my little friend?" he boomed as he slid his massive, bear-like frame out from under the steering wheel of the patrol car. Before I could reply, he added, "What the hell happened to you?"

"What the hell you talking about? I look just like I always have, ugly as a water buffalo," I responded with a grin that was twisted due to my sore-as-hell lip.

"You'd better take a look in my outside mirror," he responded with a worried look.

Not sure what all the fuss was about, I looked into his patrol-car mirror and then realized why one man had passed out earlier. I was covered with blood from my swollen lip, down my chin and across my throat and the front of my coat. Apparently when the shotgun pellet had hit me, I had bled like a stuck hog, but I hadn't felt it because of the rain running down my face. Taking some

A large flock of snow geese on the rise from a flooded and harvested rice field in Colusa County in Sacramento Valley. This would have been the view facing market hunters and "draggers" as they began their shooting. (Courtesy Peter Grevie)

wet grass from the side of the road, I wiped off my face, careful not to hit my sore lip, and then dug my Buck knife out of my "possibles" bag. Using Del's mirror, I used the tip of my knife to dig out the lead pellet still sticking in the meat of my lip. If I had bled a lot before, you should have seen it then! Holding my handkerchief to my lip, I continued with the business at hand.

Grinning as best I could and speaking a bit unclearly through my goofy lip, I said, "I have these six chaps who just ground-sluiced a ton of snow geese. Four are already in irons, and the remaining two are loose and need coupling up. All have been searched and are clean and ready for transport."

"Good," said Del. "You want me to wait until you get all your evidence collected, since I doubt you arrested all these lads for just that little amount of geese you have in the back of the truck?"

"If you don't mind, that would be great. Besides, I can follow you in, and if you have any trouble, I can give you a hand," I said.

"Got you covered, little buddy," he replied with his signature knowing grin.

With that, we loaded all six of my shooters into Del's patrol car. It was a little crowded, but Del couldn't have cared less. With the gang under Del's care, I put my truck into four-wheel drive and began working my way slowly around the back side of Terrill's rice field on a muddy farm access road where the goose shoot had occurred. I was not prepared for what I discovered! After slipping and sliding my way around to the back of the rice field, I stopped the truck at the edge of the check. Walking out to where my six had launched their shoot on the unsuspecting snow geese, I discovered a huge pile of birds. It took me eighteen trips across the field to my truck carrying double handfuls of evidence birds, to collect them all. In addition to the 36 geese my six had brought out with them earlier, there were 171 dead geese in the pile, for a grand total of 207. That did not take into account the geese scattered to hell and back that had fallen from the flock as they tried to escape after the shoot, which was another 32 by the count I had taken from my place of hiding as the flock had flown off! In short, my six scofflaws, using unplugged shotguns shooting five shots apiece, had killed at least 239 snow geese in their daylight "drag."

When I returned to Del, he clucked his tongue and shook his head at the mound of dead birds in the back of my truck. We drove back to the Colusa County sheriff's office, arriving without any problems, and I booked my suspects for taking and possessing an overlimit of snow geese (the legal limit in those days was six white geese per person) and the use of unplugged shotguns.

As the booking process began, I got the surprise of my life for that day. Every man I had arrested was *a man of the cloth!* Four were full-fledged ministers, and two were lay ministers. As it turned out, five of them pooled their money and made bail. John Golba had to wait for a family member to come from the nearby town of Yuba City to post his bail.

Later that afternoon, I was once again in the jail booking two duck hunters who had slain a nice four-point buck during the closed season in the Butte Sink, shooting it with their shotguns as the animal had swum through the decoys on their duck club. As it happened, they had done so just as I had paddled into their hunting area in my canoe to conduct a normal field inspection on their hunting activities.

Standing in the booking area was a tiny lady no bigger than a small duck. She was very neat and trim and, from the look on her face, pissed off beyond belief. She turned out to be John Golba's sister, and what a hornet she was when finally able to confront her brother. I don't think I ever saw a man get such a dressing down for breaking the law. As it turned out, Carolyn Golba was a conservationist and did not cotton to wildlife violations. I could just imagine the hind-end chewing John got on that ride home with his sister.

For their slaughter in the Sacramento Valley, each of the six pled guilty and paid a fine of $1,150. As for the snow geese in the back of my truck, I left fifty for the prisoners in the Colusa County Jail to pick and clean for some of their meals. Then I headed for Delevan National Wildlife Refuge and let unsuccessful duck hunters on the state-run shooting area take what they could use up to a legal limit. Again, the birds were put to good use and not wasted.

This case was truly one in which it was "lions six and Christians nothing!"

CHAPTER 9

The Depredation Wars

Since time began, the Sacramento Valley has been a major wintering ground for all manner of ducks and geese. They occupy every river, slough, and splash of water in between, feasting on the available grasses and weed seeds. By 1880, thousands of acres of wheat, oats, rye, and barley festooned much of the valley, and those crops provided another food source for the increasing millions of wintering waterfowl. In those days, in order to save their livelihood, the farmers openly herded or shot these unwanted flying guests feasting in their fields to prevent the destruction of their crops. In fact, the damage was so extensive in some areas that a few of the surrounding Sacramento Valley counties paid 2 cents bounty per goose killed while committing depredations on a farmer's crops.

Aiding the farmers with their depredation problems in part, though their contributions were made in secret, were the commercial-market hunters who worked the area around 1890. They operated without the restrictions of state or federal wildlife regulations prohibiting such activities (regulation of the sale of wild ducks and geese along with other migratory game and nongame birds would not come until 1918 with the passage of the Migratory Bird Treaty Act). However, night hunting of waterfowl became illegal in 1907 under the state of California's hunting regulations. Commercial-market hunters quickly realized there was a market not only for goose feathers (50 to 75 cents per pound for use in pillows and bedding) but also for their meat, predominantly in the big cities nearby. Prices ran from $2 to $2.50 per dozen for white-fronted geese, 85 cents to $1 a dozen for lesser snow geese, $1 to $1.50 per dozen for Canada geese, and from 50 cents to $1 each for plump ducks in such markets as San Francisco, especially in that city's Chinatown.

Shortly after 1910, rice as a crop was introduced into the Sacramento Valley. Given the valley's well-watered areas and favorable terrain, soon there was a rice-growing boom taking place. However, with the boom came another problem, namely, increased duck depredation. The rice farmers created a natural buffet, and the ducks came to dinner. As the numbers of acres planted in rice increased, so did the wintering waterfowl populations. Now that there was a man-made food source of the highest nutritional value expanding its acreage in the valley, waterfowl populations reacted accordingly. Soon millions of ducks descended into the valley during their annual migration, arriving usually before the rice was harvested and safely tucked away in the silos or storage bins. If winter storms blew a hole into the head-heavy rice stalks, and the ducks discovered such a natural landing place in the middle of a buffet table, in they came. Great hordes would rain into a rice field and expand the opening through their aggressive feeding, and many a farmer would lose acres of unharvested rice per night! That problem was exacerbated by the poor harvesting technology of the early days. As late as the 1930s, the rice farmers would drain their rice fields when the rice was close to ready for harvest. When the field was dry enough, in they would come with their horses or a primitive tractor pulling a swather. The swather would lay down a five-foot row of unharvested rice to dry. When it was sufficiently dry, the farmer would return and pick up the rice with a harvester. Much overripe rice would be left on the ground, which created another feeding boon for the ducks.

During this process, several problems arose, one of which was bad for the farmer and the other not good for the ducks. First, after the swaths of rice were cut and were lying in the fields to dry prior to harvest, the ducks would alight on the rows and trample the rice into the soft mud as they fed. In addition, sandhill cranes arrived in the Sacramento Valley in large numbers about 1910. They, like the ducks, preferred to walk on the rows of swathed rice, kicking the straw every which way like a bunch of oversized chickens as they leisurely fed. This created havoc when it came time to harvest the now scattered rice and generated a lot of anger among the farmers toward the ducks. However, this behavior was also bad for the ducks. Since they liked to walk along the swathed rows of rice while feeding at night, a natural concentration of bodies strolling along en masse made a perfect target for the commercial-market hunters' guns. With living bodies so compacted, and the streams of shot from shotguns focused as well, thousands of ducks died a quick death. As a result, a market hunting trade was encouraged, legally at first and then illegally after the passage of the Migratory Bird Treaty Act in 1918. This illegal trade continued to flourish for many decades after passage of the act, even as late as the 1960s.

Soon in addition to being killed in large numbers by angry rice farmers trying to protect their livelihood, many hundreds of thousands of the ever-hungry ducks and geese were slaughtered by market hunters following the smell of money and excitement. In fact, by 1911, it was rumored that over one hundred commercial-market hunters were operating in the Sacramento Valley. Their business became even easier as modes of transportation advanced and spread. Soon it seemed that hardly anyone was immune to the thrill of the chase and the resulting riches from the sale of thousands of carcasses to the hungry public. Even those entrusted with protection of the critters sometimes fell prey to the siren call of the market hunting business. In 1918, Game Warden E. S. Catton was caught with three hundred illegal ducks in his possession after taking them illegally the night before in violation of state and federal regulations. ...

I arrived in the middle of this historical, economic, and social mess in the late summer of 1967. Dumb as a box of rocks and unaware of the depth of the problems caused by duck depredations and the illegal harvesting of waterfowl on the large duck clubs or in the fields at night, I happily sailed into the maelstrom that I would soon come to know as slaughter in the Sacramento Valley.

One of my numerous duties as a state Fish and Game warden was the issuing of duck-depredation herding permits to harried rice farmers suffering crop depredations. If a rice farmer was suffering depredations, I would investigate the damage and then issue him a permit that allowed him to legally herd (not kill) the offending ducks from his fields. I soon found myself up to my eyeballs in duck problems on the local rice fields. From daylight until dark, in addition to all my other duties, I was constantly on the go responding to the rice farmers' urgent pleas for help. The U.S. Fish and Wildlife Service had a depot on the Sacramento National Wildlife Refuge near Willows where they cached hundreds of cases and boxes of M-80 and cherry-bomb firecrackers for scaring ducks. In addition, they had hundreds of cases of SCRAM rockets that, once the fuse was lit, would go out like hell on wheels for about a thousand feet and then blow up with a loud bang. They also stocked cases of shell crackers (shot shells with a cannon cracker inside), which when fired would go about forty yards and blow up. Last but not least, they had a program to lend Zon Guns and propane tanks (propane cannons that could be set to go off at different times to scare away feeding waterfowl) to the harried farmers. I carried so many explosives in my patrol truck in those early days that if I'd had a wreck and the truck had caught fire, there would have been nothing left but a crater from the massive explosion!

As far as the farmers were concerned, they were under siege, and they had the mean-assed tempers that went with that feeling! Just about every farmer I met over depredation issues blamed the state and federal governments for the problems the ducks were causing. They all wanted instant relief, and most wanted the federal government to pay for damages!

At first I was sympathetic and did everything I could to help. Then I began to notice that lazy or shoddy farming practices led to many duck-depredation situations. Oftentimes no one was really staying after the ducks and moving them off their rice, or they were doing nothing but griping about their inflated losses. And then I became aware of something even more sinister going on in the duck-depredation business.

People forget that a good, hardworking game warden is constantly out and about in his district. In those travels he discovers not only the married town leaders in compromising positions with other men's wives, or gay relationships among the rich and powerful, but also the illegal killing of bird species allegedly eating one's crops. Soon I began finding piles of dead coots (a water bird) and many resident ducks, and later on migrating ducks, lying dead and hidden away in culverts or scattered dead around the rice fields where depredations were occurring. At first those finds were few and far between. But as I became more skilled in learning what was going on around me from informants and my own discoveries, I began to find dozens of freshly killed birds. Most commonly, folks were shooting depredating ducks with .22s (light-caliber rifles) or shotguns; I knew this from the shot shells I would find ditched in the brush around a field. On the east side of my district, I discovered live traps to catch the offending birds, and off to one side in a tule ditch, seventy-nine dead ducks with their necks wrung! That surprised me because I had assumed that those catching or killing the ducks would be eating them. However, they were undesirable during that time of their lives because of their lousy shape after migration and gobs of pinfeathers.

With those revelations, it didn't take me long to harden my opinions and closely examine what a farmer was telling me regarding his waterfowl-depredation woes. With a gutful of being lied to by some of my clients and deceived by others, I began putting out the word that if I caught anyone illegally killing depredating ducks, there would be a price to pay. As a follow-up to my threat, I met with my Colusa and Williams judges and filled them in on what was happening out in the rice fields. I got their support to initiate a law enforcement program to put a stop to such illegal killing practices, especially in light of all my efforts and the free explosives provided to the rice farmers to ward off their problems. To put my efforts into perspective, I issued over three hundred depredation permits my first year, distributed over $50,000 in depredation supplies, and many times myself herded ducks off a farmer's rice when I found them eating unharvested crops.

One evening just south and east of the Garvin Boggs place, I quietly sat in my patrol vehicle listening to the sounds around me. The heat in and around the adjacent rice fields was intense, exceeded only by the humidity. All around me were the beautiful green rice fields, the booming sounds of Zon Guns warding off the ducks, and the constant hum of a million mosquitoes. Lighting up one of my noxious Toscanni cigars and gleefully watching the mosquitoes head for the windshield, buzz frantically while trying to get away, and then fall dead on the dusty dash, I sat back in my seat, aware of the oppressive heat but with a happy heart.

As dusk came, I cast my eyes eastward toward the Butte Sink. Soon the air began to fill with small black dots, which soon turned into tens of thousands of hungry ducks flying around the unharvested rice fields looking for their evening's grits. Getting out of my patrol truck, I took the ever-present can of mosquito repellent from the dash and liberally spread its contents all over my sweating carcass. Lighting up another strong cigar, I let the smoke lazily curl up around my forehead, as I listened for anything out of place. Earlier in the week, whispers from several farm-laborer informants had led me to this place. Soon the air was filled with graceful little wood ducks with their trilling calls as they circled the rice field before me, looking for a safe place to land and feed. They were soon followed by the whistling wings of the graceful greyhound of the skies, the pintail. Then the large, shallow-flapping mallards graced the darkening skies, and soon the entire duck world followed. It seemed that every winged critter was looking for a place to land and feed at the hardworking farmers' expense. To the northeast, I could hear the popping of shotguns and cannon crackers going off in an effort to ward off the feeding ducks now filling the skies like a living blanket. Or was that what the sounds meant?

Those last shots from a shotgun sounded suspicious, I thought as I listened intently. There was the sound again … and again, only in a different location for the second series of shots. The shooting pattern didn't appear to be random shots fired into the air to move ducks off the unharvested rice. They almost sounded spaced out, as if someone were wing-shooting ducks! Scrambling into the back of my patrol truck and then up on top of the cab so I could hear better, I strained my ears for more telltale sounds of something wrong.

There it was again, only this time I clearly heard at least three shotguns sounding like they were wing-shooting ducks as they poured out of the Butte Sink and into Terrill Sartain's rice fields. With that, I scrambled off my truck and into the cab. Cranking up the engine, I quietly drifted down and across the various farm roads and trails toward my suspected shooters. Soon my travels brought me onto the south side of Terrill's properties, the area where I thought I'd find the suspicious-sounding shotguns. Parking on top of a nearby levee, I once again scrambled out of the cab and into the bed of my truck to listen.

Sure as God makes green apples, there that suspicious shooting was once again to the north. *And guess what? I would bet my last silver dollar those shooters don't have any notion I am even in the country,* I gleefully thought, scrambling back down. I had just started the engine when, out of the corner of my eye, I saw the overhead light in the cab of a pickup parked forty yards away at the base of Putnam Road come on as if someone had just opened the door! Grabbing my binoculars, I used the bottom of the fast-rising moon in the top of my lenses to provide enough light for me to see a pickup quietly sitting on the road blocking my way.

Damn, I thought with a frustrated grimace. *Someone has blocked off the road as if to intercept anyone wanting to interfere with the illegal shoot.*

And what a shoot it was! The air was by now full of low-flying, swirling ducks, and the shotguns, now numbering at least four, were having a moonlight shoot of a lifetime! Grabbing my flashlight, an extra set of handcuffs, and my binoculars, I began trotting down the levee toward the now darkened pickup. Crossing from my levee up onto the levee that ran by the White Mallard Duck Club, I escaped being seen by those in the pickup as I scurried like a land crab behind it in the fading evening light.

That will break him from sucking eggs, I thought, grinning as I continued dog-trotting north on the White Mallard levee. Working in behind the shooters and using my binoculars, I could see I had four of them strung out along Putnam Road. Every now and then I could see the flame shoot from the ends of their shotguns and see the birds flare overhead or drop when shot. For a moment, I watched in fascination. These shooters were spaced out along one of Terrill's huge rice fields. They were using duck calls to lure the ducks even closer and were having the shoot of a lifetime. In the short period during which I watched these lads shoot, they dropped about twenty ducks either on the road or into the rice field before them.

I began stalking the closest shooter, moving through the tall weeds on the levee behind him. Snaking through the dry weeds, trying to remain soundless, I was soon within ten feet of my first shooter. He was a short man, but what a shot! It seemed as if, even in the poor light, every time his shotgun barrel went up, a bird came down! I waited until he knelt to reload his shotgun before I made my move. Since his back was to me, I crept across the road, reached over his shoulder, and jerked the shotgun from his hands. Before he could say anything, I grabbed him by the shoulder and said, "State Fish and Game warden; you are under arrest! Keep your mouth shut and don't warn your buddies, or else!" I surprised him so much that he just sat down in the road and started gasping for air.

"Get up," I commanded, grabbing him by the scruff of the neck and lifting him to his feet.

"Don't hit me, Mister, please don't hit me!" he wheezed.

"Do as you are told and nothing will happen," I growled, trying to scare him badly enough that he would not warn his compatriots. If he did, they would be gone like black-tailed jackrabbits in front of the hounds!

"Yes, sir, yes, sir," he bleated.

"Let's go," I commanded as I shoved the hapless chap down the road toward my next-in-line night shooter.

I always had a maxim that if the lads aren't expecting you, they won't see you. Believe me, it works like a charm, and in this case, it did as well. My second shooter was having such a grand time in his early-season duck shoot and was so fixated on what he was doing that he never saw us approaching in the dark until it was too late. I handcuffed the two men together by their right wrists, and then I and my two stooges started down the road toward shooter number three. I guess he couldn't count, since he didn't notice the extra man approaching with his buddies, and we were upon him before he could even pass gas in the wind. Alas, the same fate befell shooter number three that had befallen my previous two. The four of us continued walking north on Putnam Road until we got to shooter number four, who was a little sharper than the previous three.

He could count and instantly asked, "Wally, who is that with you?"

Before Wally could respond, I tried a ruse that always seemed to work in the field when I confronted a culprit in the dark of the night. I would blurt any name while continuing to walk toward my subject. By the time he had processed that name and realizing it meant nothing to him, I had gained another step or two before he could decide to bolt. This time, I had a stroke of pure genius. I blurted out the name of the landowner, figuring he had given them the okay.

"It's Terrill Sartain," I said.

"Damn, Terrill, don't sneak up on me like that. You looked almost like that bastard Grosz when you loomed up out of the dark," he answered with obvious relief (Terrill was just a little smaller than I was).

By now within grabbing distance, I said, "Well, it is too bad you didn't go with your instincts. Sorry to say, it is that bastard Grosz, and you are under arrest for killing ducks during the closed season." I snatched the shotgun from the man's surprised hands, and that was the end of all the fluff and ferocity. I used my second set of handcuffs to fasten my last two shooters together by their right wrists. Then I concealed all their shotguns alongside the edge of the road so my hands would be free. With no further ado, the five of us began the long walk back to my hidden patrol truck. As we walked by the man in the pickup still guarding the south end of Putnam Road, I greeted him nicely and kept walking. You should have seen the shock on his face when he saw all his buddies shackled in irons.

Loading my prisoners into the bed of my patrol truck, I fired her up, and we headed back down the levee toward Putnam Road. I noticed the sentry and his pickup were long gone. *Probably on his way to tell Terrill,* I thought with a grin, knowing the likely outcome based on Terrill's temper. Continuing up the road, I stopped where my first shooter, one Wally Opum, had been shooting and after a bit of a look found a pile of freshly killed ducks numbering fifty-seven! As I said, he was a good shooter. Proceeding to where my second shooter had been standing, I gathered up his ducks, which were lying all over in the darkened road. My second shooter, Albert Givings from Chico, had thirty-one ducks. Shooter number three, Tim Duncan, was a bit of a poor shot and had only twenty-eight ducks to his credit. But this was Tim's first trip to jail, especially in the back of a game warden's pickup and I bet he wished he had never pulled a trigger this evening. My last stop was where Wes Dollar, also from

Chico, had been shooting, and he was a killer. Eighty-three ducks graced his pile—mostly wood ducks!

I stopped to pick up the men's shotguns, and we headed to the Colusa County lockup, where I booked all four of the men for taking migratory waterfowl prior to the hunting season.

I ran across Wally and Wes many times over my career in the valley after that. Every time I did, it was for shooting over bait, possessing overlimits of ducks and doves, closed-season shooting, and the like. They were not really friends of the world of wildlife.

The arrest of those four men, reportedly for herding ducks off a poor farmer's rice fields, stirred up a real nest of hornets! Especially with the landowner on whose lands I had caught my four outlaws. The next day, while out working on the west side of my district by a little town called Sites, I received a call from the Colusa County sheriff's office. The call informed me that Terrill Sartain wanted to talk to me—*pronto*. Since things were pretty quiet in the Sites area, especially with Deputy Carter Bowman on the prowl, I headed east.

I was ushered into Terrill's farm office, and man, did I walk into a bandsaw! I was facing the maddest damn dirt farmer you ever saw. He screamed and shouted about trying to feed the world while *my* damn ducks were eating him out of house and home. On it went at such a volume that his office staff got up and left the building.

I let him rant and rave until I thought he might break a gut and then yelled right back. I informed him that as long as his duck herders continued to kill *my* ducks under the guise of depredation control, *I would throw every one of their hind ends in the can every time I caught them!*

It got really loud just as a tall woman walked in and quickly leveled the two of us. She made it abundantly clear that the yelling had to stop, or else. Terrill ignored her, and then she told him in terms that even I could understand. "Terrill, if you don't stop yelling this instant, it will be a cold day in hell before you sleep in my bed again!"

That seemed to cool things down just a tad, and the three of us spent another hour discussing the duck-depredation issue and then went to lunch. Terrill was still a little hot over having to eat with the hated game warden, but the tall woman, one Helen Sartain, his wife, kept a lid on things.

After seeing that I was not easily buffaloed, Terrill eventually settled down, and he, Helen, and I over the succeeding years, went on to become good friends. There were still many times when Terrill would run on the edge of the law, but he knew I would pinch not only him but his influential hunting friends as well, so an uneasy truce ensued. After that run-in, Terrill became a supporter of my wildlife programs, which helped because he was a major farmer in the valley. Helen and Terrill have since gone on to their rewards, but both are still in my heart as friends.

As a result of that case and all four of my shooters being found guilty in the Colusa Justice Court, the whining about duck depredations continued, but it seemed that the illegal killing abated a bit. The change became especially apparent after I apprehended another eighteen alleged duck-depredation herders actually killing ducks over the following month and prosecuted them all. The number of ducks those twenty-two shooters collectively killed was relatively small, totaling only 636, but those birds were dead just the same. How many ducks were slaughtered during the depredation wars only God will ever know. But it was a massive slaughter before the closed-season killing slowed and eventually came to a halt.

By the way, my informants who had put me onto the tails of the shooters at Terrill's always seemed to receive a lot of seized game from the local game warden from then on. … Maybe it was because between the two of them, they had thirteen children!

CHAPTER 10

Botulism

One little-known aspect of the slaughter of ducks and geese in the Sacramento Valley was the involvement of a government entity—an entity whose mission from Congress was to preserve, protect, and enhance those waterfowl and others in the migratory-bird world.

Ducks were the major problem when it came to crop depredation because of their arrival in the valley in the late summer before the rice was harvested. The problem became so bad that Congress allocated funding for the purchase of lands in the form of national wildlife refuges in order to draw the depredating ducks off private lands. The U.S. Fish and Wildlife Service purchased thousands of acres of prime farming lands central to the Sacramento Valley and the problem of rice-crop destruction. Those lands were used to create four major national wildlife refuges stringing south from Willows to Yuba City. Once flooded, these refuge lands became a haven for millions of resting and loafing ducks and geese—and in some instances, their death traps as well. Literally hundreds of thousands of ducks and geese were killed annually on these havens before the mysterious problem was rectified!

After their migration from Alaska and Canada, the migratory waterfowl resting in the natural marshes of the Tule Lake Refuge complex would mysteriously begin dying in large numbers. Thousands died annually for dozens of years. Service scientists began investigating the mysterious losses because the dead and dying numbered in the tens of thousands. After a period of time, the killer was identified: *Clostridium botulinum,* Type C, avian strain, was discovered to be the culprit in all the water-bird deaths. Botulism, as it is commonly called, is a bacterial toxin found in warm, anaerobic conditions involving shallow alkali waters that are high in organic matter. Scientists discovered that the *Clostridium* bacterium produced a metabolic by-product that is highly toxic to animals. The Type C avian strain is extremely deadly to birds.

The problem spread south with the establishment of the Sacramento Valley refuges. Once the flooding began to attract the ducks off the private lands' rice crops, the dying began. Those birds healthy enough to migrate from the Tule Lake complex to the Sacramento Valley refuges carried the bacteria on their feet, on their feathers, or inside their already sickening bodies. Or perhaps the bacteria were inherent in the valley's alkaline soils and, once the waters and temperatures were right, began generating deadly levels of the toxic by-product. Either way, Sacramento, Delevan, Colusa, and Sutter National Wildlife Refuges soon became killing fields for the unsuspecting waterfowl and shorebirds.

Refuge managers began flooding their refuges early in the summer, preparing for the fall migration with the idea of holding the migrants on site and preventing their settling in the nearby farmers' unharvested rice fields. Once that water was turned onto the refuge lands, the toxic problem reared its ugly head. Soon shallow pans of warm alkali, organic, and rich anaerobic waters spread across the Sacramento Valley refuge lands. Weeded areas were flooded, attracting thousands of teal and pintail, all big seed eaters, almost immediately. Soon the birds were waxing fat with all the seed production from the refuges' shallow waters. And they continued flocking to newly wetted areas holding these abundant seed crops.

Soon, just as at the Tule Lake Refuge complex, Sacramento Valley birds sickened and began dying. Many fearful of avian predators crawled off into the dense vegetation, only to fall prey to the foxes, raccoons, skunks, and muskrats. Birds could be seen flopping across the shallow water pans, unable to fly, as they tried to escape from danger. Many could only swim around in circles, trying to hold their limber necks up to keep their heads from dropping into the water. Others, unable to swim because of paralyzed legs, sat in the water and eventually drowned. Being deathly sick, many could not feed and began starving, and those found dead showed extensive keels from starving, green-stained vents, and mucous-coated eyes. Soon those lying dead in the warm waters began to putrefy, attracting flies. Then the carcasses in the warm environments became loaded with maggots, which passing ducks saw as more grub on the hoof and quickly ate off their brethren. The maggots supercharged with the botulism toxin soon poisoned those ducks eating the maggots, and the deadly cycle continued.

Arriving in 1967 as the Colusa game warden, I saw the sick and dead ducks on Delevan and Sacramento National Wildlife Refuges because they were in my law enforcement district. Ducks were dead or dying by the thousands in every body of water on those two refuges! Come hunting season on the state-run shooting areas on my refuges, I saw more than one sick flopper unable to get airborne, shot by a happy hunter thinking he had bagged a good meal.

I knew what was causing the problem because of my college wildlife management background, but because I was so busy with my law enforcement issues, I let the refuge managers, who were at least as well-educated, worry about their excessive duck mortality and botulism problems. I figured they had the answers and were responsible for managing such issues, so I went my way, just trying to hold all the lawlessness in my neck of the woods in check.

In 1970, I traded in my state Fish and Game warden's commission for a federal commission as a game management agent for the U.S. Fish and Wildlife Service. After I got through the check-in and completed all my paperwork for this new position, my agent-in-charge, Jack Downs, assigned me to airboat duties on Delevan National Wildlife Refuge. I was to run an airboat over that particular refuge, picking up and sacking all the ducks that had died or were dying from botulism. In two weeks of such duties, I picked up *over thirty-four thousand* ducks, or parts of ducks, that had died from botulism on that refuge! Most of them were teal or pintail. The refuge folks had a deep ditch dug on site, where the plastic bags filled with the carcasses we picked up were buried. Mine was only one of three airboats that picked up similar numbers of duck carcasses on that refuge in that two-week period that year! Because of other, more pressing duties, I never ran the airboat on Sacramento National Wildlife Refuge that summer, nor did anyone else from my squad. But I heard from other officers or refuge staff that duck losses were also extremely high that year on Colusa and Sutter National Wildlife Refuges.

This kind of more-or-less government-sponsored slaughter continued to take place for the next couple of years until Ed Collins became the manager of the entire complex of the Sacramento Valley's four refuges. Realizing that shallow-water ponds were in part responsible for the terrible losses, he changed the flooding policies. Ed saw to it that ponds on the refuges were flooded only if they could be rapidly and deeply filled with fresh water, thereby severely reducing any chance of botulism rearing its ugly head. As a result of those policies, I began to see fewer and fewer birds that had died from botulism on the valley's refuges. Today, because of wiser water management policies, the Sacramento Valley refuges no longer suffer the dreadful losses they once did—and, if the truth be known, suffered for years!

In 1970, I was all over Sacramento National Wildlife Refuge working the duck hunters on the state-run shooting area. I had to do much if not all of the work on foot. During that period, I don't remember going anywhere on that refuge where I did not see the skeletons of ducks underfoot. If I had to estimate the number of dead from botulism based solely on the number of duck skeletons I saw, I would say at least 100,000 ducks had died that summer on Sacramento National Wildlife Refuge.

On Delevan National Wildlife Refuge that summer in 1970, three airboats collectively picked up approximately another 100,000 dead ducks. The numbers picked up on Colusa and Sutter National Wildlife Refuges that year exceeded ten thousand for each refuge. That means 150,000 dead ducks (and many others crawled off into the weeds to die so that their remains were never found) were picked up that year on three of the four Sacramento Valley Refuges. I have often wondered just how many ducks died on Fish and Wildlife Service lands set aside to protect them over the many years that the Sacramento Valley's refuges operated with the botulism problem. At least a million would be my educated guess.

As you can see, the slaughter in the Sacramento Valley came from more than just the end of a shotgun barrel.

CHAPTER 11

A State and Federal Flying Squad

This story is based on a conversation with Warden Jim Hiller, who was in my Fish and Game squad in 1969, as the two of us staked out a popular alfalfa field in the Sites area for deer poachers and spotlighters. Hiller had a lot of stories about bygone times to tell an eagerly listening rookie officer. Hiller's stories were rounded out and validated later the same year by retired warden Paul Kerhr when I worked in his old district checking deer hunters as a newly minted Fish and Game warden. Hiller and Kerhr, along with their federal counterparts from the old flying squad, have long since stepped over the Great Divide.

The story about Charlie Dennis was told to me by Charlie himself one day in 1970. He mentioned it in a relaxed moment between an old gunner and a law enforcement officer as I helped him with his rice farming during my vacation while living in Colusa as a U.S. game management agent. Charlie, a great friend and source of history, stepped over the Great Divide after living well into his nineties.

Jim Hiller, game warden from Willows, and Paul Kerhr, game warden on loan from his mountain district in Quincy, sat quietly due west of the Sacramento National Wildlife Refuge, located just south of Willows, California. To the north were about thirty thousand feeding ducks that had been pouring off the refuge all day and loading into several of the harvested rice fields the officers were now quietly watching.

It was a cloudy, cold, blustery day in 1948, and the ducks must have suspected the coming of worse weather; hence their mad frenzy to load up on the rice grains from the harvested field. By their very numbers and closeness to Willows, a historical market hunters' haven, the ducks were just asking for trouble.

With that thought of impending doom in mind, Jim and Paul swept the field with their binoculars one more time, looking for any sign of human activity. They were rewarded with the sight of dozens of flocks of ducks flying across their lenses as the birds eagerly sought out the life-giving rice grains left on the ground after the harvest. It was a spectacle that at any other time of the year or in any other place would have brought smiles to the faces of those witnessing it. But dark would fall any minute, and both men were hoping that if someone showed up with evil intentions, it would be soon. It would be easier to spot them before it got much darker.

Federal agents Fairchild, Savage, and Gerow watched the same harvested rice fields from their hidden position just to the west. Even though they were experienced waterfowl officers, the three men stared in amazement at the huge tornado of ducks swirling into the fields like large blackflies around something warm-blooded. They had seen similar sights many times before, but each time they had to shake their heads in wonder at the amount of living bodies in the air.

Darkness slowly crept in on the men and ducks until only the lights from the city of Willows to the north provided faint illumination of the rice fields. Pulling the collars of their government-issued, ex-military, sheepskin-lined bomber jackets up around their necks to keep the damp out, the men patiently waited. Far to the north, east, and south, they could hear the occasional sound of gunfire from market gunners, hammering away at their dirty business of slaughter in the Sacramento Valley. With collective grimaces, the men held their positions in the hope that the next shoot, if there was to be one, would be targeted at their flocks so they could extract a measure of revenge for having been in the wrong place at the wrong time until that moment.

By one o'clock in the morning, nothing had happened except that more and more ducks continued pouring into the rice fields. *The new ducks are probably those disturbed by market gunners elsewhere and, hearing the feeding going on in this neck of the woods, dropped in to load up on the fattening rice grains as well,* Kerhr grimly thought.

At one-seventeen A.M., the stillness was suddenly broken by the riveting sound of twenty shots being rapidly fired! The roar from the wings of many thousands of fleeing waterfowl announced that the shooting was directed at the flocks the officers had been patiently watching. Jim, almost asleep, flew off the rice check he had been sitting on and began looking in the direction from which the shots had come. Nothing could be seen, but he and Paul continued scanning. The shooters had been so close that the two men could now smell the faint odor of freshly burned gunpowder drifting in the cold, damp air!

Then Kerhr spotted a darkened human figure running along the base of their rice check. Kerhr, who had been a first-string tackle in earlier days on his high school football team, put a tackle on the fleeing man, and Jim heard the impact even from some distance away!

"Yeoow!" yelled the man as he and Kerhr sailed into the rice field mud at a high rate of speed.

At the same time, another man ran right by Hiller and got a necktie tackle from the warden. After getting smacked in the throat by Hiller's strongly muscled forearm, all the runner could do when he hit the ground was gurgle for air....

Fairchild, Savage, and Gerow ran across the rice field toward where the shooting had occurred. Savage corralled a man trying to run toward Willows carrying a shotgun and, grabbing him by the neck, threw him to earth and disarmed him. Gerow discovered another man hiding under the rice straw, dragged him from his hiding place, and disarmed him as well after a short scuffle. Both of those men were later discovered to be carrying Remington Model 11 shotguns with their plugs removed so each could fire five shots. The men Hiller and Kerhr had stopped were found to be carrying Winchester Model 97 pump-action shotguns with no plugs as well.

All of the captured men denied doing any shooting and pleaded that the shots the officers had heard had come from somewhere else. However, the smell of the barrels of each runner's shotgun showed that the guns had recently been fired. The officers herded their prisoners back to the place where the "drag" had occurred and, with the light from their flashlights, found the ground littered with dead and dying ducks. They also discovered where the four men had crawled to a nearby rice check, stood, and fired their shotguns into the massed feeding ducks. The ground around their footprints was littered with freshly fired shotgun shells that just happened to match the gauges of the four seized shotguns and the extra shells carried in the suspects' pockets.

The prisoners were seated in the muddy damp of the rice field in a forlorn clump, and with three officers watching over them to prevent escape, Hiller and Savage commenced picking up the dead and wringing the necks of the dying ducks left over from the drag. Two hundred and nine ducks later, the carnage was cleaned up except for the 20 to 30 percent of that number that had crippled off into the night, only to later to die a violent death in the jaws of some predator.

Three of the four men, identified as Thom Paladina, Brock Ambrose, and Terry Jussila, were from San Francisco. The remaining shooter was Albert Coates from Willows.

The nine men (including prisoners) carried the broken bodies of the ducks to the nearest officer's car. Savage and Hiller retrieved their hidden patrol cars, loaded all the ducks and four prisoners into the two vehicles, and drove to the Sacramento National Wildlife Refuge headquarters. There the officers gutted and stored their evidence in the refuge's military-surplus walk-in freezer. Then they drove their four shooters to the federal lockup in Sacramento. Turning east onto the Maxwell-Colusa highway just at daylight, Hiller, driving the last sedan in the federal officers' convoy, passed Charlie Dennis coming into his hometown of Maxwell from the east. Charlie was driving his Model A and gave a friendly wave as the two carloads of officers and prisoners passed.

"I need to keep an eye on that Dennis fellow," thought Hiller as he waved back with a phony grin. "His reputation from our files indicates that he will take a duck or two over the limit every now and then."

However, he had a carload of prisoners and needed to pay attention to the road until they were safely in the federal lockup in Sacramento. So he continued toward Colusa, keeping his eyes glued on the road ahead.

As Charlie Dennis turned the corner off the Maxwell highway to his house, the floorboards in his Model A gave way, and 117 ducks fell out onto the highway behind the convoy of federal officers. Charlie later told me that he never went back and picked them up but fled to the safety of his home. However, ninety-nine ducks fell to his gun on a rice field between Two and Four Mile Roads the very next evening to make up for his recent loss. In the meantime, passing neighbors happily loaded up the dropped ducks until none of the evidence from Charlie's previous evening's drag remained.

The four prisoners were booked in Sacramento for using unplugged shotguns, taking overlimits of ducks, and early shooting of waterfowl.

The next evening found the tired but happy flying squad (a group of officers gathered from all points of the compass to concentrate on a problem area) from the evening before staked out on the east side of Colusa County. The men watched swarms of ducks coming out of the Butte Sink and spiraling down in their typical tornado fashion onto the Sartain and Boggs families' rice farms. Since they didn't have enough men to stake out both good-looking bunches of ducks, they flipped a coin.

"Heads," said Savage as he picked up his silver dollar from the dirt. "We will sit on the Boggs properties tonight and hope for the best."

Once again the routine began of hiding their vehicle and sneaking back into the area where the huge flocks of ducks from the Butte Sink were feeding to set up a stakeout without spooking the birds or being seen by the illegal gunners. Tonight the officers wouldn't have to wait long. About nine-thirty, an extensive rattle of shots blew up the evening quiet on Terrill Sartain's land in a large harvested rice field just below the Colusa-Gridley highway!

Damn, thought Hiller with a grimace, *that is too far away to try and catch the culprits in the field.* However, something inside him said to head that way anyway.

"To hell with it," shouted Hiller. "Let's roll!"

The three men ran to where their car was hidden. As the engine roared to life, Hiller slowly backed it out of the shed in which it was hidden and started without lights down a farm road toward where the shooting had occurred. Leaving the ditch-bank road after a few minutes, they dropped down onto Putnam Road, a main graveled byway, and headed north. As they sneaked along below the White Mallard Duck Club, with only the sound of gravel under his tires telling him that he was still on the road, Hiller's instincts told him to stop, but he kept going anyway.

Bam! went the crashing sound an automobile makes when it runs into another of its kind.

After sitting stunned for a moment, Fairchild and Gerow quickly bailed out of the vehicle while Hiller turned on his one remaining headlight to see what the hell he had run into in the dark of the night. Before them was an old rattletrap of a Dodge four-door sedan with four startled faces in the front and back seats peering back at him. Racing to open the doors, Gerow and Fairchild quickly emptied that vehicle of its occupants. However, it took a few moments because the surprised men had to climb across piles of freshly killed ducks! Keeping the marauders under control under the barrels of their pistols, the officers stared in disbelief at the scene. Both vehicles had been moving down the same road without lights to avoid detection—Hiller's car north toward the Colusa-Gridley highway and the shooters' car south toward the White Mallard Duck Club, where the men planned to hide their recently killed ducks in an abandoned storage shed. The outlaw car's driver turned out to be Angelo Conti from Gridley. The passengers turned out to be Angelo's oldest son, Marco; David Pingree; and Stewart Allison. Based on reports from several paid informants, Hiller knew the last two were duck buyers from the Sacramento area. The Contis were dyed-in-the-wool market gunners, as had been their kin clear back to the late 1800s.

The number of ducks in the back seat and on the floorboards showed that the men were in possession of huge overlimits. The officers handcuffed them in pairs and made them sit on the road while they sorted out the situation. Ninety-eight ducks came from the backseat and an additional sixty-three from the trunk. The bulk were pintail, with a smattering of mallard and wigeon rounding out the numbers. The trunk also produced four very muddy Winchester Model 97 12-gauge pump-action shotguns that had been freshly fired.

Soon the sound of tires running on the gravel were heard, and Officers Savage and Kerhr arrived on the scene. The grins on their faces as they eyed the huge pile of freshly killed ducks on the roadside showed that they realized the flying-squad concept was paying big dividends.

After drawing all the ducks along the roadside so they would not spoil, the officers and their prisoners were soon on the road through Colusa en route to the federal lockup in Sacramento. But first they stopped for some coffee and gasoline, just to let a few early-stirring locals see the handcuffed men and trunkloads of ducks.

There is more than one way to skin a cat, thought Hiller with a grin as the locals gathered around the catch of the day in abject silence. However, two days later a local informant told him that at that very moment, just a block away in Weber's Market, another four hundred recently killed ducks awaited buyers from Yuba City to pick them up and move them into the markets in San Francisco.

The four culprits were booked and charged with destroying federal property (the patrol car Hiller had been driving) and possessing overlimits of waterfowl. Since they hadn't been observed shooting or in the field, Hiller figured that was the best they could do in the way of charges.

Two weeks later, both of the recently apprehended groups of shooters appeared before Federal Judge Tyrell. Hiller, who was also a deputy U.S. game management agent, had spent some time with the judge before opening the flying squad's activities in the field in the hope of convincing him that the slaughtering of ducks had to stop. He wasn't sure whether those talks had had any positive effects, but his answer wasn't long in coming.

The first four men captured in the Willows area pled guilty to possessing unplugged shotguns while hunting migratory game birds, early shooting of waterfowl and possessing overlimits of ducks. Silence reigned in the courtroom as the judge figured out what penalties he was going to issue.

"That will be ten dollars for using unplugged shotguns to take migratory waterfowl, ten dollars for the early shooting, and fifty dollars for the overlimits for each of you," he finally said. Hiller had hoped for bigger fines, but this was a start, and he would continue to work on the judge to see if he could convince him that bigger fines were necessary in order to bring down the out-of-control illegal killing of waterfowl. However, for the four men, the sum of $70 apiece was no laughing matter. That amount was about two months' wages for a farmhand in 1948, according to Hiller. But he knew they could raise the money in an evening or two of blowing up more ducks to sell.

In that same courtroom also stood the four men who had rammed the government vehicle Hiller had been driving. They also pled guilty, and Judge Tyrell fined them $50 each for their overlimits and made them responsible for paying for the damage to the federal vehicle.

The feds, like the state Fish and Game, had little money, and Hiller grinned at the thought of having the bad guys fix the government vehicle so it could be used once again to pursue those illegally shooting the duck. He knew the local violators would understand the irony as well as he and his fellow officers did.

The next afternoon found Hiller's flying squad west of the small farming town of Gridley on the Colusa-Gridley highway. On the way, they had spotted three vehicles stopping along the Colusa-Gridley highway to watch several huge flocks of ducks and geese just north of the road swarming into several adjacent rice fields to feed. Soon ten men armed with shotguns got out of those vehicles and started rapidly across the fields toward the flocks of birds. Sensing this might turn into a real shoot-fest, the flying squad forgot the Boggs Ranch detail they'd had in mind and instead split up to take "the bird in the hand." Hiller and Kerhr moved farther down the road toward Butte Creek, parked, and walked toward the birds to provide coverage on the west side of the flock in case the shooters ran in their direction. Fairchild, Boomhower (who had replaced Savage this night, and Gerow were to park their car among the shooters' vehicles, give the ten hunters a few moments, then work their way behind the bunch from the south and east. If the ten got carried away, the federal agents and state game wardens would have them trapped on two sides—or so it seemed.

Soon Hiller and Kerhr had walked into the edge of the flock of ducks and geese now numbering about thirty thousand and secreted themselves at the western side of the field. The din was unbelievable as the many happy ducks and geese greedily cleaned up the rice grains left in the fields after the harvest. It was nature at her best, thought Hiller with a smile of appreciation.

The beauty of the peaceful scene, however, was not to last. The ten hunters had not-so-nice plans for the birds' afternoon. The birds continued to swirl into the fields with much carefree noise and aerial grace. Birds from adjoining areas, hearing the mass of feeding waterfowl, soon began arriving in large numbers as well, and in a short period of time, the number had swelled to about forty thousand birds. Birds flying a thousand feet overhead, observing the feeding spectacle in the rice fields below, made noisy vertical drops, many times flying upside down as they sailed into the feast on the ground. That rapid descent by hundreds of birds created a stir and racket such as many hunters of waterfowl have seldom experienced. The tornado of living energy in the forms of thousands of ducks and geese spiraling into the field was nothing short of wondrous to the officers observing it. As was typical of such feeding masses, more ducks and geese were on the way from all points of the compass in the Sacramento Valley.

The ten men had long since disappeared as they sneaked toward the flocks of feeding birds. For a long time the happy din continued—until, as if a switch had been thrown, the birds got instantly quiet and then roared to life and wing in one massive white living sheet! Their flight was accompanied by a string of shots numbering no less than fifty! The air under the center of the flock rained broken white forms no longer free to fly as they pleased. As the ducks and geese noisily fled the scene, the rice field under the flock of falling bodies was nothing but a moving carpet of white forms struggling as they died or fleeing as cripples on foot. The ten men erupted from behind a rice check where they had been hidden and ran and walked across the rice field, shooting crippled geese on the ground and wringing the necks of those unfortunate enough to be helplessly within reach.

Hiller and Kerhr, enraged at what they saw, sprang into action. Running in a crouch, trying to use the rice checks as cover, they headed for the ten men. On the other side of the field, Fairchild, Gerow, and Boomhower, also surprised at the ferocity of the shooting, raced across the rice field from behind the shooters, hoping to get within arm's length before the culprits spooked like a flock of quail to the four winds of the compass.

The five officers appeared upon the scene almost simultaneously, to the surprise of the shooters. At once the ten gunmen realized the five oncoming men were not of their ilk, and they took to their heels, racing across the rice fields toward their cars. The foot races were on! Hiller and Kerhr had it easy, as four men came tearing right by them, not realizing the officers were as fleet as they were. Soon they had run down and handcuffed two of the four. The other two scuttled off into the vegetative cover of Butte Creek and then headed south for the escape their cars offered.

On the opposite side of the field, Gerow caught his man first. A fat man in his late fifties was no match for the athletic officer and was soon huffing and puffing in a set of handcuffs. Fairchild also caught his man after a short chase, but Boomhower had his hands full. A stocky man ran by him and dodged being captured by swinging his shotgun barrel at the onrushing officer. When Boomhower ducked, the man turned north and ran across the rice field like the wind. Boomhower was up to the challenge and, after about a half-mile muddy chase, caught his man with the aid of a flying tackle.

Soon the five apprehended men were gathered in the center of the killing field among the broken bodies of the birds. The officers gathered everyone's identification, and then the work began in earnest. Leaving one officer to guard the seated prisoners, the other four began picking up dead and dying geese and ducks. They picked up 144 assorted geese and 69 ducks. When confronted with such a pile of bodies, those sitting on the ground in handcuffs had nothing to say in answer to the officers' questions. Even with the prisoners helping to carry armloads of birds, it took all ten of them three trips back and forth to recover all the dead and crippled birds.

When they returned to the place where the shooters had parked their cars, they found three sad-faced men who had escaped the officers in the field only to discover that their cars would not start so they could finish their getaway. Gerow had earlier removed the distributor caps from the shooters' vehicles! Realizing they had no chance of escape because their license plates would identify them as the owners, the culprits had chosen to take a seat on one of the running boards and await their fate. The remaining two men had gone to ground and remained unidentified because those captured refused to identify their equally guilty friends.

Hiller, the flying-squad leader, made a decision that is still practiced today when necessary. He seized the three vehicles the culprits had used to get to the killing fields and held them as "fruits of the crime." The reason was that the vehicles had been used as instruments of the crime in bringing the shooters to the scene; as a legal result, they could be seized as evidence under the provisos of the Migratory Bird Treaty Act. The thirteen men set about drawing all the geese and ducks so they wouldn't spoil, and once that was done, the birds were loaded into the trunks of all the cars along with the prisoners' shotguns. With the distributor caps all back in place, each officer took control of a car. Hiller took the lead with three prisoners, and Kerhr followed with another three. Gerow and Fairchild each took one prisoner, and Boomhower brought up the rear with a car fully loaded inside and out with evidence birds.

The eight men were booked for taking migratory waterfowl with the use and aid of unplugged shotguns and taking overlimits of Canada and lesser snow geese. The numbers of ducks killed during this daylight "drag" did not exceed the legal limit of the day, so the shooters were not charged with taking overlimits of ducks. However, the birds were seized as evidence just the same because they had been taken by shotguns without the state- and federal-required plugs in their shotguns.

The following Wednesday, the eight shooters from the Gridley duck and goose shoot appeared in federal court in Sacramento. They did not seem as happy-go-lucky as they had been in the rice fields a week earlier, and a look of worry was on every face. When asked by Judge Tyrell how they pled, David

Wright, Bart Youngfield, Adam Spinney, and Peter Steele, all from Gridley, pled guilty to the charges as they stood in front of the judge with long faces. Meanwhile, in the back of the courtroom, the remaining four shooters, Billie Ray Sartain, John Petes, Darrell Long, and Gary Steubens, all from the Sacramento area, were locked in an argument as to how they should plead. Every one of them had been before Judge Tyrell earlier as a result of being captured by a bunch of hardworking California State Fish and Game wardens in the Suisun Marshes. They had killed a bunch of sleeping pintail on a grassy spit of land in a marsh, coming away with over a hundred ducks.

Judge Tyrell could see that this illegal killing was becoming a problem in his court. Cases of this type would continue to clutter his docket if the hardworking officers had their way. That thought brought a frown to his face and furrowed his brow.

Then, leaning over his desk as if to emphasize a point, he pronounced sentence on the first four unfortunates from the Gridley snow goose shoot: "That will be twenty-five dollars each for use of the illegal shotguns and another one hundred dollars for killing an overlimit of geese. Can any of you gentlemen pay the fine I have just imposed?"

For a stunned instant, the four men stood frozen.

Then there was a collective, "No, sir, Your Honor."

Bart stammered out, "Your Honor, most of us work on farms. We only make about fifty dollars a month if we are lucky!"

"You should have thought of that before you blew up the geese and ended up in my courtroom. Bailiff, call the U.S. marshals and have them incarcerate these men until they can arrange to pay their fines," barked Judge Tyrell.

Hiller and the rest of the flying squad stood there in disbelief. Never had a federal judge done such a thing! The pronouncement of the sentences brought the quiet argument in the back of the room to an abrupt halt. The arrival of several U.S. marshals put an even deeper gloom on the Sacramento men, especially when the Gridley four were led away in chains. Moments later it was the turn of the remaining Gridley goose-shooting four to stand trial before the federal judge, whose face showed that he was not in a good mood.

"And how do the four of you gentlemen plead?" asked Judge Tyrell.

"Not guilty," said Billie Ray Sartain. "We four demand a trial," he continued as the others remembering the fine imposed on their friends and all nodded in unison.

"You certainly are entitled to a jury or court trial, and that date will be two weeks hence in this courtroom at ten o'clock in the morning, unless you prefer to be heard in the district court."

"No, sir, Your Honor; trial in this court will be just fine," squeaked Billie Ray.

Seeing no more people waiting to be heard, Judge Tyrell said, "This court is adjourned.

"Jim Hiller, I want to see you in my chambers, *now!*" added the judge as he left the bench in a swirl of black robes.

Hiller, not sure what to expect, stood quietly in front of Judge Tyrell as he signed the incarceration papers for the four unfortunates from Gridley. Looking up from his paperwork at Hiller, Judge Tyrell said, "How was that? Any better than the time before, Jim?"

Hiller's heart gave a flip. Instead of getting his ass chewed, he apparently had an ally in the old judge!

"Yes, sir! I think you sent a loud and clear message. Especially once word gets out that killing an illegal mess of migratory birds will end you up in federal court."

"That is clearly my intention, Jim. I don't have the time to clutter up my docket with your bird cases in the future. So let this be a lesson to you. Stay the hell out of my court! This court is meant for major federal crimes, not your dinky damn bird cases. If you can't keep clear of me, I will have to take my concerns to the chief federal judge for Northern California."

Jim's heart sank once more. Now it appeared that he did not have a friend in the court but rather an antagonist. Unwilling to give in easily and realizing what was at stake, Hiller took a gamble.

"Your Honor, no disrespect, sir, but you are the *only* place I have to go with my cases. Without you and your court, I am nothing and have no enforcement program. Without you, I would have to take my cases to state courts, and most of them are as crooked as a dog's hind leg. And Your Honor, the responsibility for protecting the migratory bird resource *does* clearly rest with the federal government. So you see, sir, I have nowhere else to turn. You are the migratory birds' and my only hope!"

Judge Tyrell sat for a while and gave Jim long, hard look. Then he said, "All right, I guess you have a point. Just don't clutter up my court with a bunch of crummy little cases. Bring me the good ones, and I will take care of you. Bring me crummy ones and you will have a limp in your giddy-up from me taking a bite out of your ass so big that it will make the hole in the ground a strip mine leaves look like a dent. Do we have an understanding, Officer Hiller?"

"Yes, sir," said a cautious Hiller, "we do. Just understand, sir, that with a few exceptions, I am dealing with misdemeanors under the Migratory Bird Treaty Act. I don't have much choice because I am obligated under law to treat everyone the same. My men and I will make every effort to bring you only the best cases, but sometimes, as is necessary, you will be dealing with simple misdemeanor cases."

Judge Tyrell threw up his hands in resignation and said, "All right, have it your way. Now, get out of here. I have better things to do than to sit here and argue the law with you."

Not wanting to piss off the ornery judge any further, Hiller let the door hit him in the last part over the fence as he hurriedly left the office.

The four shooters from Sacramento were found guilty two weeks later and fined $200 each, basically for troubling the court with an unnecessary trial. Those four convicted shooters had eyes as big as dinner plates when they were led away in chains by the U.S. marshals to be incarcerated because they too lacked the necessary funds to pay their fines.

Hiller and other officers, both state and federal, were making a difference. But at a huge cost to their families and their health. The effects of burnout, such as alcoholism and divorce, were rampant among such men, and such problems eventually struck at least four members of this flying squad.

CHAPTER 12

Canvasbacks in San Pablo Bay and a Miscarriage of Justice

In 1970, I resigned my commission as a state Fish and Game warden and accepted a federal commission as a U.S. game management agent. Two weeks later, I was transferred from Colusa to Martinez, California, in the San Francisco Bay area. My new district, instead of being just half of Colusa County, took in the whole northwestern half of California, from Monterey to the Oregon line. It was way more than one man could handle as a law enforcement officer, but what the hell—I was young, in fairly good shape, had two guardian angels, and had a wife who would let me run like the wind on my vision quest when it came to chasing poachers. What more could I want?

One dawn found me at a local marina preparing my patrol boat for a detail near Mandeville Island in the San Joaquin Delta. That area was some distance from my previous valley home, to say the least. Even though I was no longer in the Sacramento Valley, I was still being governed by instincts based on what I had learned while working in that arena. In essence, since I was still close to the Sacramento Valley and many of the valley's ducks were illegally moving in commerce into the cities in my new district, it was almost as if I had never left home. Plus, as I was later to discover, the individuals I was soon to cross swords with had been feasting on Mother Nature's cupboard in the Sacramento Valley like a load of maggots for years!

After pumping the bilges on my patrol boat, I checked my engine gauges and made sure I had all the equipment I would need for the day. I planned on working the large waterways just off Mandeville Island because of reports I had received about folks running power boats up to the huge rafts of resting waterfowl and shooting into them. That was not only a common violation but one with state and federal implications, and I thought it would be a good day to ruin someone's Christmas if they did so in my presence. Little did I realize I would end up saving a man's life and in the process make one of the biggest illegal canvasback cases of my career!

Moving out through the many waterways and around the islands toward my destination, I took the time to enjoy the numerous flocks of ducks in the air. I also listened to the volume of shooting on each of the islands because almost all of them held high-class private duck clubs. Especially since those clubs had a history of having a hard time counting the number of ducks taken by their members on any given day, if you get my drift.

Rounding the southern tip of Mandeville Island, I reduced my speed and gently ran the bow of my patrol boat into a dense stand of tall reeds. From that partially concealed position, I could relax and use my binoculars to scan a huge watered area loaded with rafts of loafing waterfowl to the south and west. Then to complete my cover I ran a fishing pole over the stern as if I were nothing but a simple fishermen.

For the next hour or so, everything went according to Hoyle. Then I noticed a small ten- or twelve-foot V-hulled boat coming across some large open water. The boat was way too heavily loaded in the stern, and its bow was riding dangerously high out of the water.

What a dummy. That damn guy doesn't have a clue about boat safety, pushing a boat loaded in such an unsafe manner. One good swell and over he will go, I thought, shaking my head in disbelief.

That thought had no more than flashed across my mind when I saw my unsafe boater hit an unseen swell from the earlier passing of a larger boat—and upside down he went in a heartbeat!

Jesus! I thought as I leaped to my feet to get a better look with my binoculars.

By then the boat was already slipping beneath the waves, and I could just barely see the operator. Jumping back into my seat, I swiveled around to my controls, started the engine, and gunned my boat out of the reeds and into the open water. Slamming the controls into forward, I firewalled the throttle and soon was up on step. By now the flipped boat no longer showed; it had slid beneath the waves! All I could see was a small black dot in the water representing the head of its operator. By now I was fairly flying across the bay. My small dot was getting harder and harder to see, and I remembered that when I had looked him over earlier, the man had not been wearing a life preserver. I pushed my throttle ever more forward and continued watching closely for fear of losing his location. When I had drawn within thirty yards of him, I saw the man weakly struggling and then disappear beneath the water. A second later, I got to where I had last seen his head, leaned way over the side of my boat, reached down, and grabbed at the still swirling spot. Feeling my fingers hit a mass of hair, I grabbed and hung on with all my might! With my other hand, I grabbed the throttle and shut the motor down. The boat nose-dived and then careened in a tight circle, propelled by a huge following wave that lifted the heavy patrol boat three feet up on its crest. Still I hung onto my handful of hair for all I was worth. The man's head was still about a foot under water, and if I hadn't been as big and long-armed as I was, I probably would have missed my grab at his head! Lifting him with my left hand, I reached over with my right and grabbed the man by his pants. With a heave fueled by adrenaline, I jerked the gasping man over the side of my boat and safely onto the deck. I rolled him over so he could gasp for air, and he puked up water and his breakfast. After a few more moments of coughing and puking, he rolled back over and slowly sat up. His eyes were still showing an enormous amount of white, and he was gulping air like a carp. Between bouts of gasping and now crying, the man began to thank me over and over again. All I could do was sit there and thank God for letting me be there for this chap and being large and strong enough to get the job done when it was looking so black.

Finally the man began to calm down and said his name was Donald Cappio, and he was from San Francisco. He was an owner and chef at a fancy restaurant, was married, and had three kids. With those words about his family, he broke down once again and began sobbing. Getting a hold of his emotions, he told me he had been fishing for black bass before he had sunk and then, with a shiver, said he had left his life preserver home but had decided to go fishing anyway. He whispered, "I can't swim!" as if trying to not let God know of his recent indiscretion.

Then, making the sign of the cross on his chest twice, he rose and gave me a bear hug that darn near lifted my almost 340-pound carcass clear out of its seat.

I told him who I was as I dug a coat out from the extra set of clothing I always carried in case I fell in and lent it to the now shivering man. I thought I saw him pause a bit when I mentioned I was a federal game warden but let the moment pass in light of the need to get him back to his car and the warmth his heater would bring.

Back at the marina, he paused before getting into his car and said, "I can't let you go until we have a talk. I owe you my life, and so does my family. I will never forget you for what you did and am forever grateful. If there is anything I can do, you just name it. You and your family will always be welcome at my restaurant and will forever eat for free for what you did for me here today. Please let me honor you with such a favor for what you did; it is the very least I can do."

I just nodded as if I understood and would take him up on his offer sometime in the future. What the hell else could I do? He was making so much of the event that I was starting to get embarrassed. I had done what I had to do, and anyone else would have responded the same way. He was a human being in trouble, so I helped as best I could. Nothing more, nothing less. Then a thought hit me, and I let it roll off my lips without even thinking. Damn guardian angels again.

"You know, Mr. Cappio, there is something you could maybe do for me. As I said earlier, I am a federal game warden, and I know there still are ducks coming into the cities in the Bay Area from the market hunters in the Sacramento Valley that are being illegally sold in the restaurants for duck dinners. If you ever run across such a situation, I would be very pleased to receive information. If I can't prove a case based on such information received with further intelligence I develop personally, I won't bring it before the court. I believe in always protecting my sources of information and would sacrifice a case rather than divulge any source. So rest assured, any help you give me will go to my grave if necessary unless I can prove the case independently."

For a moment he looked long and hard at me and then said, "Give me your name and phone number and I will see what I can do."

Happy to oblige, I gave him my card, and after another monstrous bear hug on his part, we parted company, I to go back to the marshes to catch bad guys and Donald Cappio to go back to his family and give all of them big hugs of joy at still being alive.

The incoming winter storm from the west and the accompanying winds had made San Pablo Bay a violent cauldron of choppy whitecaps. The water was so rough that many species of diving ducks were making for quieter waters along the marshy shores of the bay until the storm had passed. Harper Slough was a large, sheltered, marshy waterway into which canvasbacks and other divers would flood for relief during bad weather. Into that slough settled the small flock of canvasbacks I had been watching through my binoculars just at dusk as they looked for the quiet such waters offered. Also quietly resting or sleeping there, as yet unknown to me because I was still new to the area and unable to see into the slough from where I stood, were about five thousand more of their kind!

The canvasback was considered by many to be the best eating duck because of its selective, high-quality vegetative food habits and large body mass. Its feeding habits made the meat very moist and delicious compared to that of other ducks. That made it a highly prized and valued duck in the eyes of the market hunters of the day and the restaurant markets in which they plied their trade.

Riding on the sheltered waters away from the winter winds, many of the canvasbacks and other diving ducks had their heads tucked under their wings and were sound asleep as night fell. Unfortunately, this resting area was known to others than those in the bird world. I didn't know it at the time but learned later that four sets of eyes harboring evil thoughts also observed the ducks quietly riding the smaller swells of Harper Slough. Unaware of the men concealed along the water's edge at a dangerously close range, the slough's diving ducks, happy to be out of the weather, continued their sleep. Across the bay, the lights of the city blinked softly as the four men made ready in the now gently falling rain and dark of the night. *Boom-boom-boom-boom* thundered the shotguns in unison as the lead from their shells tore into the rafted ducks. Many canvasbacks never knew what hit them, dying as they slept, while others, attempting to take wing, were struck down by the deadly hail of shot from the massed guns just yards away. Within moments, except for the dying, it was all over. The four men sank back down into the covering shoreline vegetation and nervously examined their surroundings for any sign of activity that bespoke the law in hot pursuit. However, they were rewarded with the stillness that comes from a deserted point of land in a marsh setting at eight o'clock in the evening on a cold, stormy night when most folks were enjoying the warmth of their homes.

However, a mile away and downwind from the carnage stood a large man recently transferred from the town of Colusa in the Sacramento Valley to the city of Martinez in the San Francisco Bay area. Some of the lessons learned working the night shooters in the rice fields in the Sacramento Valley were now being put to use in the many back bays and estuaries of San Pablo Bay.

The mass shooting had not gone unnoticed, and I understood that a great killing of ducks sheltering out of the wind in some small estuary had just transpired. Carefully looking in the direction where the shots had occurred, I stood on top of my Rambler American patrol car, squinting into my binoculars for any sign of light or movement. Seeing none, I mentally marked the area and, getting back into my patrol car, began slowly moving toward the area on muddy back roads without the use of lights. Soon I was forced to abandon my search for the shooters because it seemed there were dirt roads leading every which way, and to just wander around might spoil any chances of apprehension by spooking my prey. Working under the old maxim that if a violator gets away with an illegal act, he will return later under the same circumstances and commit the same violation again, I relaxed. I parked in a central area so I could observe any unusual comings or goings at that time of the evening and quietly waited for my gunners to show their hands.

I was told later that, after waiting for about twenty minutes in the thick vegetation, the four shooters rose from their hiding place and continued to watch for any signs of unwanted human activity. Seeing none, Frank Firugi slipped into his hip boots, walked down to the edge of the estuary, and began quietly picking up dead canvasbacks collected along the windward shoreline and throwing them up to his accomplices on the bank. Since the wind was blowing into the estuary and the tide was coming in, the men had an easy job picking up the dead birds as they floated to shore. Those wounded in the shooting either swam off to be eaten by harbor seals or gulls or hid in the protective vegetation to be eaten later by land predators. Diving ducks other than canvasbacks that had been killed in the shoot were just tossed into the shoreline vegetation by the shooters to be eaten by predators or rot.

Soon Frank had thrown 137 dead canvasbacks up to his brother Victor; their boss, Frank Spencer; and another man, A.C. Bertoni, who worked at their San Francisco restaurant. Bagging the birds, they walked out to their concealed car and tossed the gunnysacks into the trunk of their Oldsmobile, along with their shotguns and hip boots. They looked around again for any signs of discovery, lighting up some Toscanni cigars and just standing by their car to watch for any other vehicle's lights on the back roads in their neck of the marsh. Seeing none, they got into their car and slowly drove for about a quarter mile on the muddy road without using their headlights. Turning on their lights once they felt safe, they sped down the muddy road onto an adjacent state highway and out of the area at a high rate of speed.

From half a mile away, I saw the headlights suddenly come on and speed away on an unseen dirt road. Jumping back into my car, I attempted to locate the road the other car had just taken, only to be thwarted once again in my pursuit when my chosen road ended at the edge of a canal. Gritting my teeth in frustration, I backtracked, turned on my lights, and eventually was able to move into the area vacated by the shooters, who were now long gone. Finally locating the right road, I got out of my patrol car and examined the muddy road for fresh tracks. There they were, and it was obvious from all the slipping and sliding that the occupants had been in a hurry to get the hell out of Dodge. Slowly following their tracks, I discovered where they had parked the car out of sight in a patch of willows. Then I followed the tracks made by four men with the light of my flashlight toward the edge of the estuary some sixty yards distant. Crushed grasses and muddy footprints, some still filling up with water from the marshy ground, led me to the place where my suspects had lain in ambush at the edge of the estuary. Looking out over the water with my flashlight, I saw that the water was covered with duck feathers from a recent shoot, and after a little effort working along the shoreline, I picked up twenty-three crippled and freshly shot canvasbacks and greater scaup. Wringing the necks of the cripples, I stacked them in a pile for later retrieval. Then I found the spot from which the men had shot into the resting ducks. I collected twenty 12-gauge shot hulls whose smell told me they were freshly fired. Then I realized my estuary was filling up with more canvasbacks winging in as they sought shelter from the madly howling winds and rough water of the storm on the adjacent bay. It became evident to me that in times of rough weather, canvasbacks would seek shelter in the estuaries, including the one where I now stood. I lodged this knowledge in the back of my mind for future reference.

Gathering up my twenty-three evidence birds, I silently walked back to my patrol car. There I gutted the birds so they wouldn't spoil and tossed them into the trunk. Once in the car, out of the wind and rain, I thought, *I need to spend some more time in these marshes. Especially since these guys got clean away, and with another weather event like we have howling here tonight, they more than likely will return. When they do, let's hope I will be here to greet them with open arms.* With many of the markets in the vicinity still selling wild duck dinners, I wondered if this might have been a commercial hit as the rain pelted my vehicle like there was no tomorrow. From the look of all the feathers in the lagoon, I knew they must have killed several hundred ducks, and the only outlet for that quantity would be commercial. With that thought spinning around in my head, I headed for home and some much-needed sleep.

Frank Spencer backed his Oldsmobile up to the back of his restaurant on Thomas Street in San Francisco, sprang from his seat, and hurriedly unlocked the door. Tony, Victor, and A. C. quickly grabbed gunnysacks of ducks from the trunk and hurled them onto the floor in the back room, where they would be out of sight of anyone but trusted employees. After closing the back door, the four men began cleaning the birds in the kitchen sinks, drawing them so they would not spoil. Then they tossed the bodies into the restaurant's cooler so they would quickly cool out and be ready for preparation the following evening in the form of a delicious wild-duck dinner. The four men then went to the bar by the dining room and poured themselves a double shot of Jack Daniels each to celebrate their successful hunt. Little did they realize that the hunt was now on from a direction they never expected.

Arriving the following morning at my office in the post office building in Martinez, I noticed my answering-machine light was flashing. After going through my stack of mail, I turned on the machine and made ready a notepad and pencil. Man, did I get a surprise! The first message was from none other than Donald Cappio, the man I had saved from drowning earlier in the season. Donald made it very clear that he would hold me to my promise of nonexposure if I couldn't make the case on my own with the information he was about to give me. As he went on, I almost fell out of my chair.

He detailed the illegal canvasback hunt from the evening before, listed the names of the shooters, told me how they had pulled off their shoot, explained how the birds had been transported, and gave me directions on where they were being kept and how they would be sold to selected and trusted patrons in De Nobli's Restaurant in South San Francisco. He said his brother Ricardo, a chief cook at DeNobli's, had discussed the hunt with his friend Anthony Firugi over several drinks. Firugi had laid out the entire operation and had even taken Ricardo into the locker where the birds were kept to show him what they had killed. Then Donald put the icing on the cake. Ricardo had told him that Firugi had said the four shooters would be doing the same thing in the same location once the next winter storm blew the ducks off the bay and into their favorite estuary and killing field. They had been doing this for years, killing thousands of canvasbacks, and had never once been caught!

There was a long pause, and finally Donald said, "I know this doesn't even come close to paying you back for what you did for me, but it is a start. Take care, my friend, and may the Blessed Virgin Mother always cover you with her grace."

The message ended, and my brain hit high gear. Leaning back in my chair in the quiet of my office, I began to run bits and pieces of information through my mind. I thought over what I was going to do over the next two weeks in the San Pablo Bay area to help the canvasback, including getting long-term weather reports. I realized I needed to get out in the area during daylight hours so I could learn all the roads and how best to catch multiple shooters once a shoot had occurred. It also occurred to me that this was the time of year when the canvasbacks and other diving ducks would storm into the calmer waters once the chop got too great to comfortably ride it out in the big waters. I smiled with satisfaction at the confirmation of my notion that the canvasback shoot had been related to a commercial venture. Now I had to do a little preliminary groundwork and then wait for Mother Nature and my guardian angels to do what they did best.

A week later, I was rewarded with another big blow. But this time, when Mother Nature huffed and puffed, my patrol car was hidden under an old surplus camouflage parachute a short distance from the suspect estuary. I also had an ace in the hole. Earlier in the week I had called my old friend Glenn Ragon, who was a deputy sheriff currently on vacation in Colusa County for a month of duck hunting. I had met Glenn when I was a rookie game warden in Humboldt County and he was a cattle deputy in the backcountry. We became instant friends and still are today after over forty years. Glenn was a unique individual—a war veteran, ex–navy diver, built like a brick outhouse, and horseshoe-nail tough. He feared nothing, and the greater the challenge, the more he rose to the occasion and loved it. He was only too eager to come down and give me a hand, and I set it up with a large grin. No matter how tough the four canvasback shooters were, and no matter what they tried once we closed the trap, they were now doomed to capture.

Lying back in the brush a short distance from where the canvasback shooters had hidden their car the first time, we patiently watched and waited. For the next four hours the two of us lay shivering in the bushes as a steady cold winter rain pelted off our inert forms. Figuring my shooters were not coming, I stood up to get the blood flowing to my many numbed and wet parts. Glenn did the same, and we stood there in the rain like two soaked rats. I figured I would follow my personal Rule Number 2 before we left the area, which was to wait just ten minutes more after deciding to leave. That rule had been a good law enforcement tool over the years, and I am glad I used it that evening. On minute eight, we saw a vehicle turn off the nearby state highway and began to snake toward the estuary behind us. When it was about a hundred yards away, the lights went out, but we could still hear the engine running as it continued its approach. Earlier in the evening, Glenn and I had sneaked over to the quiet backwater we were staking out and through the lime-green light of the Starlight Scope had seen several thousand ducks resting on those calm waters. "At least the ducks are doing their part," I had said with a grin.

Soon the vehicle splashed its way to where my suspects had parked in the willows for the shoot I had witnessed during the last storm, and on came the dome light as the men quickly stepped out of the car. We could hear quiet conversation over the sound of the rain pelting off their vehicle's roof as another light, this time the trunk light, came on. In the soft light through the heavy rains, Glenn and I could see four men grabbing raingear, hip boots, and shotguns from the trunk. Then the light disappeared as the trunk lid closed. The four lads quickly dressed in their gear, then turned and started for the estuary and the unsuspecting sleeping ducks.

I had made several sets of nail boards, which were nothing more than small boards with long nails driven clean through. As my shooters sneaked over to the estuary, I walked over and placed the nail boards beneath each tire of their hidden car. If the shooters somehow got away from us, they wouldn't be able to drive far.

Glenn and I had decided we would wait in an area between the shooters' car and the killing field. We could witness the shoot, and when the men came back toting dozens of heavy dead bodies and tired from their recent exertions, we would put the grab on them. I would be the one to rise up out of the swamp in the dead of night and confront our culprits, while Glenn would quietly close in on them from the rear. I would use my Starlight Scope until they were in our pincher trap, and we would close the trap once my flashlight went on.

Around midnight, the estuary was full of canvasbacks quietly bobbing in the waters softly illuminated by the lights from the surrounding cities. For the longest time nothing happened. Then the night was lit up by the flames from the ends of four shotgun barrels erupting death into the sleeping and resting rafts of ducks. That sound was immediately followed by the roar of thousands of ducks taking wing to escape the danger. Then we heard only the hissing sound of rain hitting the water, along with the rustling of shoreline vegetation in the winter winds and the faraway sounds of city traffic. The suddenness of the harsh staccato of the shotguns rending the night air had quickened my heart, but I still held my Starlight Scope steady. For a quick second, the brightness of the muzzle flashes had blanked out the scope, but it soon came back on. For the next twenty minutes, nothing moved along the bank of the estuary. Then four lime-green figures could be seen in the scope, although the outlines were fuzzy because of the rain. They were hastily picking up limp forms and tossing them onto the bank. This activity went on for about thirty minutes before all four men gathered at their pile of ducks and began loading the carcasses onto duck straps. Loaded down with their booty, they began the escape from their killing field back to their vehicle.

Quietly walking ahead of the four shooters to their car, I stood off to one side and waited as they came toward me. When they passed the spot where Glenn was hiding, I saw him stand up in the soft light of the scope and start trailing the men, as we had planned. The shooters stopped short of their car and for the longest time just stood and watched for any sign of discovery. Finally one man walked away from the group and ambled over to the car as if he had every legal reason to be out and about in such weather and at such a time and place. Finding no one by the car, he whistled, and the other three men came hastily in.

Without a word, the men opened the trunk and began tossing their ducks and shotguns inside. After closing the trunk, they all went back for a second load of ducks. When they passed Glenn's position again, I saw him move even closer to the vehicle and find another hiding place. Soon our shooters returned, loaded to the gills with dead ducks. Once again the trunk was opened, and they dumped those ducks inside posthaste.

When they closed the trunk for the second time, essentially barring access to their shotguns, I laid down my scope, stepped forward, and turned on my flashlight.

"Holy shit; who the hell are you?" shrieked the man closest to me.

"Federal game warden, gentlemen. And who might all of you be?" I asked.

The lads just stood there, and no one responded to my question. I think it was mainly from surprise at being intercepted and caught red-handed with no plausible story to explain their being in such an oddball place in the crappy weather and at that time of night.

Still wanting to strike while the iron was hot, I said, holding out my badge and credentials, "Here is my identification, gentlemen, and if you would be so kind as to produce your driver's licenses, I would be obliged."

"Why the hell do you want to see our driver's licenses?" asked a strident voice. "We aren't driving."

I knew the man was Frank Firugi because I had pinched him on Butte Creek Farms in 1969 with an overlimit of pheasants; possession of two hen pheasants, which were closed-season; and no hunting license in possession. When I asked at that time if he was the Frank Firugi in Hugh Worcester's book *Hunting the Lawless,* he responded that he was and added, "Just write the ticket, asshole." I grinned as I recognized the voice of this man. Now it was my turn once again to turn the screws.

"I identified myself to all you gentlemen, and I asked for some form of identification from you. The reason is that my partner and I watched the four of you ground-sluice a mess of ducks sleeping in that estuary behind you just moments ago, in violation of state and federal laws. You will either be ticketed if you comply with my request or booked in jail if you do not. Is that clear enough as to why I requested your driver's licenses?"

I could see my words cut clear through the men standing before me in the rain. Then Firugi took me on once again.

"Well, asshole, if you think we just blew up a bunch of ducks, where is your evidence? We ain't got no guns or ducks, so how about that?" he asked with a sneer.

"As I said earlier, my partner and I saw the whole thing, including the part where all of you stashed your shotguns and ducks in the trunk of this car after your first trip out of the marsh. Now, if you would like, I can take a crowbar from my vehicle and pop open this trunk to prove my point, but I am not sure that is what the owner of this fine car would like," I replied, enjoying the little game we were playing.

The man who turned out to own the car, Frank Spencer, said, "That won't be necessary. The ducks and our shotguns are in the trunk. Give him your licenses, boys," he continued. That seemed to defuse the situation and validated the information I had received from Donald Cappio on my telephone answering machine about Spencer being the boss of this little group.

Seeing that the group would comply and not raise hell, Glenn turned on his flashlight. Boy, did that create a stir of surprise—I think the four men had believed I was alone, even though I had mentioned the presence of my partner.

With driver's licenses in hand, Glenn and I marched our shooters back to the kill site. I left the four men standing on the bank with Glenn as I began walking the shore picking up left-behind cripples. One hour later I had picked up thirteen more canvasbacks, sixteen greater scaup, and four redheads. With those birds in hand, we walked back to Spencer's car and opened the trunk. To my thirty-three ducks just retrieved, I added 153 canvasbacks from the trunk of Spencer's car along with four unplugged shotguns. Glenn soon brought my patrol car onto the scene and began gutting all the birds to avoid spoilage while I took information from the men for later issuance of citations.

In the end, all four men were cited for taking an overlimit of ducks, late shooting migratory waterfowl, not having federal duck stamps in their possession, use of unplugged shotguns, and possession of an overlimit. Each man later pled guilty in magistrate's court in San Francisco and was individually fined $500. In those days, the maximum these men could have received under the Migratory Bird Treaty Act was $500 per offense and/or six months in jail. In my opinion, owing to the deliberate nature and seriousness of the crime, they should each have been fined $2,500! However, the Ninth Circuit court where these cases ended up was not known for having any guts when it comes to meting out proper punishment to outlaws and lawbreakers.

This travesty was especially galling in light of the fact that all four men had been apprehended and convicted years earlier by federal agents working for Hugh Worcester for selling sport-shot waterfowl in contravention of the Migratory Bird Treaty Act—a felony! Most other courts would have taken those earlier convictions into consideration when meting out punishment for subsequent similar violations. But the San Francisco courts ignored the obvious when it came to this serious matter. If these outlaws had been apprehended in the Sacramento Valley area under the jurisdiction of federal Chief Judge McBride, they probably would still be in jail. As it was, Judge McBride received all our seizures once the cases had cleared the docket and used them as food to help several charitable organizations, as he was wont to do.

My law enforcement sense tells me that as long as those four men lived, they walked on the dark side of the world of wildlife, skirting the laws that protected the critters and taking more than their share at every opportunity.

Donald and Ricardo Cappio have long since passed to their rewards. Now that both are gone, I have resurrected this story because, as I said earlier, I would not divulge a source of information if it would harm that person. Now that everyone in this case is dead except Glenn and yours truly, I feel I have kept my promise.

CHAPTER 13

They Were There

In June 2007, my wife, Donna (acting as my cameraperson), and I traveled to Colusa, California, in the northern Sacramento Valley. My mission was to try to interview old-time commercial-market hunters of waterfowl on film to preserve a segment of history for the Smithsonian Museum in Washington, D.C., before it was lost forever. Commercial-market hunting of North American waterfowl was, in my mind, a historical practice every bit as important as the history of the mountain men, the buffalo hunters, the wolfers, the sea-otter and fur-seal hunters, and the whalers. I knew I was racing against the march of time. In fact, I was probably twenty-five years too late because many of the old-time market gunners had long since stepped over the Great Divide. Still, I was determined to talk to as many of those old gunners still living as would share their tales before they were all gone. Little did I realize the uphill fight I would have, as the closed society of market gunners had strict unwritten rules against disclosing such information—especially to a conservation officer.

Commercial-market gunning of the Sacramento Valley's great hordes of waterfowl began in full force when hundreds of thousands of Argonauts adventured to the gold fields of California to stake their claims and strike it rich. Within months of their arrival, endemic species of game animals such as the tule elk, bighorn sheep, mule deer, black and grizzly bears, and pronghorn had been shot almost out of existence and plopped into the stew pots of thousands of starving miners. It was only natural that many of those unused to the toils of mining soon turned to market hunting and began harvesting the remaining populations of shorebirds, ducks, geese, and swans for the hungry maws of the miners and rapidly expanding populations of city folks. In so doing, they created an industry whose magnitude, in my opinion, was almost unique to California. True, market gunning of shorebirds and waterfowl was part of the history of the Texas marshes, many of the marshes in the southeastern United States, and the Chesapeake Bay region of the Northeast for many years. However, I suspect many more water birds were harvested by illegal commercial-market gunning, and for longer (from before 1918 when the Migratory Bird Treaty Act was passed until the early 1970s), in California than in any other region of the United States.

By 1910, some people became alarmed at what they saw of the killing fields of the Sacramento Valley and the inevitable waste that followed, especially without the benefits of modern-day refrigeration. Soon their clamoring for conservation of waterfowl and related shorebirds could be heard clear to Washington, D.C. As a result, in 1918 a treaty was signed between the United States and Great Britain (signing for Canada) that in theory legally curbed many of the excesses associated with the market gunning of waterfowl. Gunning of most species of shorebirds was outlawed altogether (except for snipe, rail, woodcock, and coot), as was the commercialization of sport-shot waterfowl.

However, by that time commercial gunning had come to be considered almost a birthright by many of the gunners, and the new state and federal conservation laws were mostly ignored. The illegal market hunting problem was exacerbated and intensified by the lack of conservation officers, lax court systems not considering the slaughtered birds as proper victims, poor support from the

Limits of the day on a duck club in Sacramento Valley around the turn of the twentieth century. (Courtesy Glenn Wellborn).

Canada and Lesser snow goose shoot around the turn of the twentieth century in Sacramento Valley. Note the horse-drawn "gut wagon," with the cages in the back to transport live decoys. Also note the pile of formed wire hangers in the lower right of the photo. They were used to prop up the heads of geese once killed, acting as additional decoys. (Courtesy Glenn Wellborn)

government's legal counsels, and a general attitude of public acceptance of the market hunting industry. The illegal practice was further supported by markets with insatiable appetites for duck and goose dinners in the nearby metropolitan areas and in rural communities where people were struggling to make a living.

As a result of those historical factors and the ready supply of money from the sale of ducks and sometimes geese, the market gunning of such species continued unabated until the start of World War II, when many of the market gunners went off to fight in the European and Pacific theaters. In addition, because of the magnitude of those conflicts and the demand for military supplies, there was an acute shortage of gasoline, rubber tires, automobiles, and shotgun shells. Thus, anyone wishing to carry on the market hunting tradition found it difficult. However, a few years after the war ended and U.S. industries had turned from producing tanks and guns to making tires, gasoline, and shotgun shells for the civilian population, the killing and selling of migratory waterfowl resumed with a vengeance. Soon hundreds of thousands of ducks and geese were flowing into the ever-hungry markets and the silver dollars were flowing into the hands and pockets of the market gunners once again. This killing of waterfowl for the markets and home freezers continued until the early 1970s. By then, state game wardens and federal agents were getting more numerous and aggressive. People's attitudes were slowly changing toward more conservation with less support for uncontrolled killing and marketing, and the adaptive thinking of the courts and prosecuting attorneys was not far behind. Large fines and prison sentences were meted out to those apprehended breaking the conservation laws, and for the first time, many consumers in the big cities began turning away from greasy rice-fed duck dinners to more heart-friendly meats such as turkey. Lastly, the great clouds of waterfowl blackening the skies began diminishing, and the increasingly smaller numbers further alarmed the Fish and Game agencies and conservationists as well as many of those, believe it or not, directly involved in the business of extinction.

That was where I came into play. I was a California state Fish and Game warden in the Sacramento Valley from 1967 until 1970. Then I accepted a commission with the U.S. Fish and Wildlife Service as a U.S. game management agent and later a special agent, continuing my duties in that enhanced capacity in the Sacramento Valley. I was promoted and sent to Bismarck, North

Typical Sacramento Valley plains goose shoot around the turn of the twentieth century. Note the wire rods in the lower center of the picture that are holding up the heads of the dead geese, thereby increasing the spread of decoys. All the "decoys" in this picture are dead Canada and Lesser snow geese, numbering over 100. (Courtesy Glenn Wellborn)

Dakota, as a senior resident agent in the fall of 1974, and from there, my career took me across the country. However, those years from 1967 until 1974 chasing wildlife outlaws in the Sacramento Valley for their gross killing and sometimes selling of the ducks and geese only whetted my appetite for control over such activities throughout the rest of my career. My profession as a conservation officer became more than just a job. The need to control such senseless and gross outrages against the natural world became quite simply a vision quest. With the cooperation and understanding of my wife, I routinely worked seven days a week and as much as sixteen hours a day in the field in order to put those in the business of extinction out of business. As a result of such efforts, many thousands of individuals, duck clubs, market hunters, politicians, duck draggers, and poachers came to know me personally and professionally.

The Sacramento Valley and its bloody yet unique history, along with its many great people, never left my heart. Once retired from federal service in 1998, I began writing books about my conservation law enforcement experiences, becoming an eight-time published author, and a two-hour Discovery Channel film was based in part on some of the stories from my books. But I always hungered to return to my beloved Sacramento Valley and preserve what history I could from the stories of those old-timers who had lived during the halcyon days of the market gunner.

This chapter contains narratives from some of the few remaining gunners from yesteryear who would speak to me about those times. Most had passed over the Great Divide prior to my arrival in 2007, and a fair number of others whom I contacted refused to discuss their gunning legacy because of embarrassment, guilt, dislike of what I used to stand for, or all of the above.

Those who chose to be interviewed shared some of their adventures and tales so that others could enjoy at least a quick peek into the pages of a unique time in history and experience to a small degree the excitement of the chase, the roar of thousands of frantically beating wings, and the smell of gunpowder before it was wafted away forever by the winds of time.

Peter Grevie

Probate Referee Peter Grevie is a bear of a man, standing over six feet tall and tipping the scales in excess of three hundred pounds. Aside from his grizzly-like mass, one is impressed by a meaningful twinkle in his eyes and a genuine smile of welcome. His story, like that of many others of the same ilk, is unique in the historical annals of the Sacramento Valley duck dragger and sometime commercial-market gunner.

Peter's great-grandfather arrived in the Sacramento Valley in 1861, having traveled there from Missouri. Moving into the Johns area of Colusa County, he began dry-land farming in order to support himself and his family. Money was scarce and times were difficult for those working the land. Like others in the farming community, Peter's great-grandfather found himself not only working the land but actively involved in the killing and marketing of waterfowl as a sideline in order to survive. Wild game, especially the plentiful migrating ducks and geese, graced his table more often than not because of their abundance. In those early days, Colusa County did not raise rice, and the farmers concentrated on other seed grains almost exclusively. The lands, unlike today, were not leveled but rolling and during the rainy winter season filled with many watered potholes, thereby creating a haven for the ducks, geese, and gunners.

Peter Grevie, former "duck dragger" and commercial-market hunter and his wife, Bernie, in 2007. (Courtesy Donna Grosz)

Grevie's great-grandfather's method of operation was to use a trained horse (a method followed by many other early-day gunners) and ride out toward the huge gatherings of ducks and geese as they fed in the grain fields until the birds became nervous. Then he would dismount and continue walking beside the horse, still closing in on the feeding birds. The ducks and geese, no longer able to distinguish the rider from the horse, would relax at the sight of a familiar animal and let it approach to within shooting range. Then, taking his double-barreled Damascus 10-gauge shotgun with hammers, the man would slip the gun over the back of his horse and discharge both barrels into the masses of now close-at-hand feeding waterfowl, killing them by the score. He would gut the birds in the field to lighten the load, then load them on the horse and bring them back to the farmstead. Those not stored in the basement or hung in the barn and eaten later by the family would be shipped from the Southern Pacific railroad station in Arbuckle to cities such as San Francisco or Marysville. The profits from such sales were used to operate the farm and help pay some of the family's living expenses.

Years later, his grandson, Peter Grevie III, continued in his father's footsteps, hunting waterfowl in order to feed his family during the perennial hard times experienced as a farmer—but he, unlike his father, never shot for the commercial market. In fact, times were such that Grevie III made a point of never wasting a duck or goose, except maybe some foul-tasting shovelers killed by mistake during a wing-shooting or drag-shooting episode. Like other fathers of the time, he passed his hunting skills down to any of his children who cared to heft a gun and harvest the land's bounty. In those days, kids started doing everything earlier, from learning to drive to killing the ducks. The Peter Grevie IV whom I interviewed was just ten when he sneaked out into a flock of lesser snow geese and ground-sluiced the first of several thousand he killed throughout his life. He noted that the current crop of kids living on the land does not show the same enthusiasm youngsters from earlier times did, especially when it comes to sneaking and shooting feeding waterfowl. He remembered even being taken from school by his dad when the great flocks of ducks were in the valley in order to help with the killing, cleaning, and hauling of the hundreds of birds from the fields to their basement for storage (the birds were hung for up to two weeks in the winter's chill air before being eaten). In fact, such removal of kids from school when the birds were in the valley was commonplace, and the teachers did not object, realizing it was a way of life for children raised on the farms.

Peter Grevie III, not unlike Peter Grevie IV, was known to harbor a little bit of the devil during his many hard times on the land as a young man. After a stint in the Pacific theater of World War II, he and a friend hopped a freight train to Red Bluff in northern California. While there, Grevie III purchased a used Model T Ford for $7 and drove it back to Colusa County. Once home, he installed a war trophy he'd picked up in Japan while on occupation duty: a used air-raid siren. Driving south of the town of Colusa after a bout of drinking with his buddies one day, he chanced to pass a barn known by local outlaws as a stopping-off place to pick and clean the hundreds of ducks and geese illegally slaughtered in the fields. The piles of feathers from picked ducks and geese sometimes topped fifteen feet in height in many such barns by the end of the hunting season. Then, when the winter winds came, doors at each end of the barn were opened, and the feathers were blown across the country and out of sight.

Grevie III cranked up the air-raid siren as he approached the barn so that he sounded like the approaching law, and every door and window of the building instantly sprouted illegal duck shooters fleeing for their lives to avoid the shame of being captured by the hated game wardens. The urgency of their escape was increased by the presence of about five hundred illegal ducks currently being picked and cleaned in the barn. It took many nips from a bottle of quickly proffered whiskey before the fleeing illegal shooters' feathers were smoothed down! Peter Grevie III kept up his active life until 1963, when he suffered a stroke after living a hard life as a farmer. Thereafter, his activity on the lands slowed, but he still managed to hunt and eat his beloved ducks at every opportunity.

As a young man, Peter Grevie IV spent many an hour stalking the valley's ducks and geese when the migration was in full swing and the weather conditions were right. He and several of his still living friends (whom he declined to name for this story) would dress lightly because sneaking up on the feeding birds was hard work. They would soon be sweating, especially after the shoot, when the dead and dying birds were hastily gathered from the rice field.

In those days, he explained, one could shoot ducks almost anywhere because most landowners didn't mind the shooters hunting on their lands. Pulling the plugs on their shotguns and careful to only bring older, less valuable guns that could be discarded or seized in case they were apprehended by the law, off they went. The best operations involved sneaking up on flocks of ducks or geese that were feeding deep in the fields up to half a mile away from well-traveled roads. Once close enough to the birds to shoot, the men would rise up, and for a split second the ducks would raise their heads as they became aware of the danger. The first shots would be fired across the raised heads, killing as many as possible. In some cases, so many raised heads were mowed down by the shot streams that it looked as if someone had gone across the ducks with a mower! As the remaining ducks rose en masse, the shooters would swing their shotguns from side to side as they fired in order to kill as many birds as possible. The entire shoot would last no more than twenty seconds. Any longer and the law, if any officers were in the fields close by, could echo-locate on Grevie and his group of shooters, and the chase would be on.

If the group shot geese, they would be breasted on the spot in order to reduce the weight carried from the field. If they planned on wing-shooting the field later, they would take the breasted goose carcasses, push welding rods under their chins, and then stick the rods into the ground, thereby creating goose "decoys." These disposable decoys were handy because they did not need to be carried to or from the fields.

If ducks were shot, they would be gutted in the field in order to reduce their weight. Then they would be placed in the leather loops of a special home-made duck strap (a carrying device) that could carry twenty-five ducks per side, or about one hundred pounds each trip. Those ducks not eaten by the Grevie family would be distributed to the landowner on whose property the shoot had occurred, or to needy families in the area. According to Peter Grevie, nothing was wasted, except perhaps the foul-tasting shovelers (a type of puddle duck known for eating a lot of vegetative matter and having a strong flavor) that were accidentally killed in the shoot. During the cold winter months, the shooters might draw the ducks and leave them in the field for pickup the next day, thereby further reducing the chances of being apprehended by the wardens while leaving the field after a noisy drag had occurred.

Another trick of the trade utilized by Peter Grevie was unique. Immediately after the shoot, Grevie would take his shotgun, which had a hook installed on the back of the stock, and loop it inside his jacket sleeve. The device allowed him to carry the shotgun hidden under his coat while freeing both hands to gather up the dead or dying ducks.

Peter Grevie recalled an incident that occurred when he was still in high school. The weather was raining and blowing, and the ducks and geese were flying everywhere. He borrowed his dad's Chevy Impala sedan, and off he went into the fields. Soon he had killed so many ducks that he had filled the trunk of his dad's car! About then, here came his dad looking for him in another family car, a 1964 Ford Galaxy. Pete's dad was happy to see his son was all right because he had been reported as missing from school. Instead of giving his son a butt-chewing, his dad was also happy to see his Chevy's trunk full of ducks. They switched cars, and Pete's dad took the trunkload of ducks home to pick and clean while Pete continued hunting. Pete finally quit shooting when he had filled half the Galaxy's trunk with ducks as well! Pete's dad later wrote the school a note saying his son had been sick that day and requesting an excused absence.

Throughout the interview, Peter Grevie relived incident after incident in which anywhere from 70 to 180 ducks had been killed in an outing and hauled from the fields. In one incident Grevie and several friends got into a huge flock of lesser snow geese and killed so many that they filled the bed of a three-quarter-ton truck; when those birds were later piled up on a garage floor for picking and cleaning, the stack was four to five feet high! Grevie also told a story that involved his wife, Bernie, another old friend of mine. It seemed that Bernie loved eating ducks and geese so much that she told Pete she would clean and pick every one he brought home for the table. Pete and his buddies, with the three-quarter-ton truckload of dead lesser snow geese dumped out on the floor of the garage, told Bernie she was expected to pick and clean every one of them! The men left, only to return later to find Bernie sitting in the garage crying over all the geese she had to pick. God and my wife have yet to forgive Pete for that little joke.

When asked how many birds he had killed in his lifetime, Pete was unable to give me any kind of estimate other than saddened words indicating "at least several thousand." When asked about his commercial-market hunting experiences, he mentioned that he had sold ducks to a friend, whom Pete declined to name because he is still living, who in turn moved the ducks into the Bay area of San Francisco for resale. He did mention that he killed and sold enough ducks one year in the late 1960s to buy a new Ford three-quarter-ton, four-by-four pickup! His methods of killing ducks for the markets were similar to those he used when dragging ducks for the family's table.

Toward the end of the interview, I just let Peter reminisce. He spoke of the ducks and geese being so numerous in the days of old that they would keep one awake at night with their calling back and forth as they flew overhead. He remembered that he could hunt just about anywhere, but if he and his friends were going to violate the laws, they generally stayed on familiar ground, namely, near their communities and known farmsteads. The state game wardens were never really a problem, but everyone looked out for and feared the federal agents. To get caught by the feds and sent to federal court in Sacramento was a frightening and expensive experience. He also told me that after he became friends with me—I was a local game warden at the time—he gave up killing ducks as he had in the past. He felt that the supportive attitudes of people in the Sacramento Valley regarding slaughtering the feeding birds were on the wane by the late 1960s and early 1970s. He also felt that his earlier illegal drag shooting and market hunting activities were part of the reason why his kids would never see the flocks of birds he had seen as a young man, or even be able to hunt ducks in this day and age.

Pete slowly said, "I know myself and others like me are not totally responsible for the loss of waterfowl in the Sacramento Valley today, but I would bet we had a lot to do with it." He grew quiet for a moment, then said, "God will have to create another earth like this one before we see such wonders like the great clouds of ducks and geese I saw of old. I will never ever kill another duck again as long as I live."

JESS D. TURNER

Jess Turner is not a large man, but one cannot help but be impressed by his genuine smile and steely dark eyes. He is a veteran of the Korean War era. Within him, plain to see, is that battle-tested hardness showing he is still a paratrooper at heart. To back that up is a stand of rifles and shotguns on the wall of his den, with a centerpiece .30-06 Garand as a reminder of the character of the man sitting before me. Jess had an easy and relaxed style even when being interviewed by a law enforcement officer who would have thrown him in the bucket for some of his earlier illegal adventures if he'd had the chance. But that difference of backgrounds and philosophies hardly fazed Jess as he easily swung into some of his duck-dragging and market hunting adventures from days long gone and never to be recaptured.

His father was a man of the soil with just enough means to scratch out a bare living for his family. Like many other men of the time, his dad was a big hunter of deer, pheasants, and ducks to help feed his family. According to Jess, his father did not hunt game for the markets but only for the dinner table of his family and maybe some close friends in need.

Jess, like his father, was also a big hunter, especially for ducks. During his younger days and during high school, Jess never hunted for the market but shot exclusively for the family dinner table. After a stint in the army as a paratrooper in Korea, he returned home in 1951 and, finding work scarce and living hard, went to work for Al Lawrence, a well-known local market hunter.

Jess Turner with a large overlimit of mallards and pintail, circa 1950s. (Courtesy Jess Turner)

He assisted other hunters shooting on Al's duck club, and, according to Jess, "in the process, I killed a lot of ducks, which I gave to Lawrence." Where those birds went, based on Al's market hunting reputation, is anyone's guess, but more than likely they went into the commercial markets of San Francisco. After being apprehended for purchasing sport-shot migratory waterfowl, Al Lawrence was sentenced to a stint in federal prison. While there, in a reflective moment, he told one of his guards that he had killed and sold at least fifty thousand ducks in his day! Shortly after Al was released from prison, he became ill and passed away in just a few days. With Al's death, Jess moved on with his life.

But hunting was in his blood, and Jess continued his duck shooting at every opportunity around his work schedule. One morning early, he was called from his home by a man named Tony Stefano, who said he was a jewelry salesman. He asked Jess if he would sell him some ducks because he knew he was

Jess Turner sitting in his den being interviewed by the author in 2007. Fay Turner, recovering from recent knee surgery, sometimes acted as a "drop off" driver for her husband when he was illegally "dragging" ducks at night for the commercial market. (Courtesy Donna Grosz)

a big-time duck hunter. Jess luckily put him off with a nonanswer. The next day the chief of police in Williams asked Jess if he had sold any ducks to Stefano. Jess replied that he had not, and the chief said he had better not because Stefano was a federal undercover officer for the U.S. Fish and Wildlife Service. After those words of warning, Jess never sold Tony Stefano any ducks. But when he called a friend of his, who was a bartender in Maxwell, the next day to warn him about Stefano, his friend said his words of advice were too late—he had just sold Stefano sixteen ducks that morning! That bartender was later prosecuted in federal court for his illegal sale of sport-shot ducks to the undercover agent.

Jess started commercially market hunting ducks in 1953, never selling any to the commercial markets in the Bay area but just to local people who didn't hunt or wanted ducks for their dinner tables. He bought a Belgium Browning shotgun in Willows for $155 and with that gun began his illegal duck dragging and commercial-market hunting business. According to Jess, he could only find part-time work and needed the extra money the sale of ducks brought into the family coffers in order to make ends meet. He said he never used a Long Tom extender (which added extra shells to the magazine) but preferred to just pull the plug on his Browning for the five shots it offered when killing ducks for the market. He always shot his ducks in and around the Williams area because he knew the land like the back of his hand. There was comfort and safety in that knowledge. He preferred using number 7-1/2 shot fired from high-base shells and when shooting at night needed no more than a quarter moon. The birds were spooky at night, and with less light, Jess and his partners could more easily sneak up on the birds. Plus, with that amount of light after the shoot, they could more easily locate their kills and cripples, thereby avoiding waste.

The author standing behind Jess Turner, former duck "dragger" and commercial-market hunter in 2007. (Courtesy Donna Grosz)

Jess and his close-knit group of gunners dressed lightly for their activities and crawled straight at the ducks. When ready to shoot, one of the men would shoot high into the air, alerting the ducks. Then all the men fired directly into the mass of the ducks' raised heads and then at the flock erupting off the ground for the maximum kill.

Jess sometimes had his wife, Fay, drive him, Parker Wallace, and Doug Thayer (a Fish and Game employee in later years) to the area where they planned to shoot. After the shoot, Fay would pick them up at a prearranged time and a different place than where she had dropped them off. The men would gut the ducks in the field and bring them out when they came, or they would leave them in the field overnight if the weather was cold and pick them up the next day. The ducks were tied in bunches with binder's twine and hauled from the field if it was safe. They

Jess Turner (left), commercial-market hunter and "dragger" and one of his shooting partners, Parker Wallace, with a large overlimit of mallard and pintail ducks, circa 1957. (Courtesy Jess Turner)

generally killed less than two hundred birds per shoot and would take them to a barn on Jess's property to be tied in bunches of ten and hung to further cool out. They preferred to shoot pintail and mallard (pintail were considered the best), and after the shoot, the word would be let out to the local people who wanted to buy ducks to help themselves to the bounty hanging in the barn. The buyers would go to the barn and pick up the ducks they wanted. The best price Jess ever got for his ducks was $1.25 each, but generally they sold for $1 a duck. If the men had killed any wigeon (medium-sized duck), which were considered not top of the line for eating, they generally gave them away to anyone who wanted them. Jess said they killed a lot of geese in his day, but they were not for the market but for the dinner table. He was not aware of any commercial markets for the geese during the 1950s.

Jess told one story about Al Lawrence and Red Murphy (market hunters) having 2,700 ducks stashed between Princeton and Maxwell. Those outlaws heard the wardens were in town and, fearing discovery of their large cache of illegal ducks, enlisted help from a local mortuary. With two hearses filled to the brim with dead ducks instead of the usual stiffs, off they went to peddle their ill-gotten gains in San Francisco and made a clean getaway, not to mention a tidy profit for their ingenious efforts.

He also told of a time when he had sixty pintail in his folks' freezer, well over any legal limit. Hearing that the wardens were in town and maybe on his trail, Jess, Doug Thayer, and Parker Wallace loaded all the birds into a military duffel bag for hiding. Only afterward did they realize that printed on the outside of the bag were Jess's name, rank, and serial number from his military days, a dead giveaway as to ownership!

Jess Turner, Sr. (left) and Jess Turner with an overlimit of mallard and pintail ducks, circa 1956. (Courtesy Jess Turner)

Jess found duck dragging and market hunting competition to be fierce in the 1950s. Many times different shooters would converge on the same flocks, and then care had to be taken not to mistakenly shoot in each other's direction or get into a hell-raising in the field over whose ducks were whose. With one of his trademark grins, Jess said it was a standard joke in the valley that there were so many market hunters selling ducks, they had trouble not screwing up and trying to sell to one another!

The market hunters' favorite shotguns were the Remington Model 11 (semiautomatic and forerunner to the Browning semiauto) and the Browning auto. Many market gunners such as Al Lawrence, Red Murphy, and some of the Fonseca clan preferred using Long Toms because such a fixture (magazine

Jess Turner (left) and friend Jim Bower kneeling under a large overlimit of mallards, pintail, and wigeon, circa 1950s. (Courtesy Jess Turner)

Jess Turner with an overlimit of White-fronted geese, circa 1950s. (Courtesy Jess Turner)

extender) gave a shooter six more shots to pour into the ducks. Jess said he was aware that some of the Long Tom gunners would file the sear on their shotguns, allowing them to shoot full automatic! With a chuckle, he wondered why some of those gunners hadn't blown their own heads off.

The hordes of ducks successfully gunned for the markets in the early days would either be driven to the Bay area for sale in the shooters' vehicles, shipped out by Greyhound bus, or sent by train in sacks, milk cans, or just tied in bunches with shipping tags attached.

Jess also told of a group from the Bay area that came to the Sacramento Valley in an attempt to start up a commercial venison market, offering $125 per deer. The local populace met that commercial-market hunting approach

Doug Thayer (left) and Jess Turner holding a large overlimit of mallard and pintail ducks, circa 1950s. (Courtesy Jess Turner)

with little or no support. Apparently some code of honor among the valley's shooters found the marketing of deer carcasses offensive. Ducks were all right to sell, but not deer. However, Herb Murphy, butcher and part owner of the Williams Meat Market, had a flourishing illegal deer market where he killed and sold deer for $125 each.

Good years, according to Jess, for the market hunters were the 1950s and '60s. There were birds everywhere, and the appetite of the Bay area and local markets for rice-fed ducks was insatiable. However, change was in the wind.

Fines for killing too many ducks were becoming a major concern for the shooters. Some judges were sending folks with heavy trigger fingers off to prison, and with fines of $25 per duck over the limit, many shooters began backing off. Another problem for the market gunners was when they found themselves going to court when apprehended for violation of the conservation laws. State judges had a habit of letting many shooters from their voting jurisdictions off with a slap on the wrist for killing too many ducks. However, as the barely punished shooters left the state court in glee, federal officers waiting just outside the courtroom would slap handcuffs on the just-freed men and whisk them off to federal court in Sacramento (it wasn't double jeopardy, as you might think, because a state *and* federal crime had been committed, allowing prosecution for the same offense in both court systems). There, more often than not because of state and federal prosecution for the same violation, a hammer was dropped upon their dragging operations.

As the interview wound down, I let Jess reminisce about the old days. In so doing, I got a surprise. Fay, Jess's wife, had a story for me as well. When she was pregnant and big as a horse (well, maybe a small horse, to hear her tell it), she had an opportunity to go into a rice field near Salt Creek in the moonlight and see for herself what a horde of feeding ducks looked like. Since she was late in her pregnancy and in no condition to run if surprised by the law, she would not let Jess take a shotgun along. Out into the field went the market hunter sans shotgun as ordered, along with his loving bride.

They crawled up to the roaring, feeding ducks (with some difficulty on Fay's part), and she got a firsthand look at what the drag shooting fuss was all about. However, she said Jess had a hard time keeping from slobbering all over himself or having a heart attack with so many ducks close at hand just waiting to be shot and he with no gun to do so. Little did Fay realize what a rare opportunity it was for her to see Mother Nature at her very best.

With a grin of remembrance, Jess told another tale about him and Doug Thayer one afternoon getting into a huge flock of feeding lesser snow geese next to state Highway 20. After they shot the flock, they picked up forty-five dead birds for their efforts. Taking them over to a place near the Davis Road, they commenced cleaning the birds because they knew a lot of people would take them if they were gutted. In a weak moment, the two men began throwing all the guts and gizzards high up into a bunch of nearby willows for all the world to see. Finished with their gutting and tree displaying chores, they headed home. The next morning, Jess was accosted by the local constable, who told him a women had seen the two men throwing the guts into the willows and claimed it had made her sick. He told Jess that he and his partner had until ten that morning to clean up the mess, or else! Since neither man had a chainsaw, they had to use axes to chop down the trees adorned with all the snow goose guts and then drop the offending displays into a ditch out of sight. That was the last time they decorated the trees with the essence of lesser snow goose.

Jess remembered his birthday in 1957 or 1958, on the 23rd of January. He was home celebrating with family when a bunch of his local buddies—Trent King, Vernie Engrahm, Pete Engrahm, Joe Kemp, and a man named Perry who used to own Garrison's Military Surplus Store in Williams—came roaring up all in a lather. They asked if they could pull their shotgun plugs in Jess's garage for a shoot because there were "thousands" of ducks out on Nissen's property nearby. Leaving his birthday party and guests with his trusty shotgun in hand, Jess went along with the others. They crawled up on the unsuspecting ducks, but, due to a small mishap, only four of the six men unloaded their guns into the feeding horde. When the smell of gunpowder dissipated, 232 ducks and one hapless hen pheasant who just happened to be in the way lay on the ground in front of God and everybody. Gathering up all the birds, they took them to a friend's barn out on King Road that had a two-place duck picker. There they picked and cleaned the ducks and then went home with their ill-gotten game. Jess brought home sixty pintail for the table and only then rejoined his hastily abandoned birthday party.

It was only fitting that this duck drag occurred during the closed season and was Jess's last drag, closing his own season for such illegal activities forever.

DOUG TURNER

Doug Turner, son of Jess Turner, is a chip off the old block of granite. During my interview with him, it was apparent that he had his dad's strap-steel-tough character and his mom's quickness of step and wit. He also has the bearing of a respected senior law enforcement official, a position he currently holds in the community as a lieutenant with the Colusa County sheriff's office.

I knew from personal experience as a conservation officer that Doug, like about 90 percent of all the other male juniors and seniors in the high schools (when he was attending) throughout the Sacramento Valley, illegally wing-shot at night, or dragged ducks during the winter months when the migratory waterfowl migration was in full swing. For the most part, their fathers and grandfathers had done the same, with some even market hunting, and as youngsters in the 1960s and '70s, they followed suit. To them, it was not only a way of life and almost a God-given right but a unique blood sport providing the thrill of the chase to a degree not readily found elsewhere.

Doug's family had a history of dragging and selling ducks, and to the extent of dragging, he followed suit. Like many others his age, he realized that as a juvenile, he was subject to only a slap on the wrist if he were caught breaking the conservation laws. Blowing up ducks allowed one some bragging rights at school and also put some food on the table at home. In a young man's mind, what else was there? They had the resources just waiting to be blown up, it was the historical thing to do, everyone else was doing it, the people in the valley didn't seem to mind that type of lawlessness, and the thrill of the chase topped it all off.

Doug's dad didn't condone his son dragging ducks, telling him that he, Jess, had had to do so to support his family. In Doug's case, it was just for the sport because his folks were good providers, and Jess didn't support that kind of illegality. But being strong-willed and falling in with the rest of the young men of his community at the time, Doug went forth into the rice fields of Colusa County to do battle with the duck.

He and his mates would spend time watching the ducks during the day to see where they were feeding. Many times that pursuit carried over to some of their dating activity. Doug said that many times while on a date, he would stop out in the country at night and listen for the sounds feeding ducks make (like the sound of a harvester running). He had to laugh, saying that some of his dates thought he was stopping just to make out.

He looked for mallard and pintail as his species of choice to shoot, and selected a flock or group of flocks as they fed in the fields. He knew the birds would return to where they had fed last or the approximate location, so those were the areas he and his buddies chose once they decided to pull a shoot. Doug usually shot with only two companions, later reduced to one as he grew more concerned about being apprehended. He preferred stalking the feeding birds on moonlit nights so they could navigate the areas chosen to shoot and after the shoot be more able to easily pick up their killed and crippled birds. Partial moonlight was also beneficial if they were jumped by the law and needed to see to escape. He confessed that they never went out on rainy nights to drag ducks. It was too miserable, so they would wait until the weather cleared before venturing forth once again. Anyway, the birds were so numerous that they didn't have to punish themselves by shooting in bad weather. When asked about night shooting in the fog, Doug indicated it was somewhat problematic. For just wing-shooting during the day, he said hunting in the fog was great, but not so much for shooting during the night. He and his buddies had done so, but it was difficult to locate the center of the flock to shoot in such weather, and the drags they pulled on such occasions were not all that successful. Doug, like other duck draggers of the day, would hunt on those where they were familiar with the terrain. Knowing the lay of the land made it easier to sneak up on the ducks and also to flee if the law was at hand and took up the chase after they had pulled their drag.

After locating the ducks, Doug and company would usually let the birds work up to their position of ambush. If that failed because the feeding ducks changed direction, they would crawl up on the birds. Doug reported that oftentimes they were surrounded by hundreds of feeding ducks extremely close at hand. He mentioned one instance when one of his shooting buddies was able to grab the close-at-hand ducks and kill them as they fed alongside the soon-to-be shooters lying in ambush on a rice check.

Doug's weapon of choice was a Winchester Model 12 20-gauge, shooting high-base shells. Doug would only allow one volley of shots to be fired from his and his buddies' unplugged shotguns. There was no reloading because a local game warden had warned Doug that was how they caught many of the valley's draggers, by echo-locating on follow-up volleys. He once had a fellow shooter who shot numerous times at the clouds of flying ducks circling overhead after the first shots were fired on the ground. Doug said he never hunted with that chap again.

Doug and his fellow shooters would dress lightly and wear work boots because soon they would be sweating as they crawled or picked up the dead and dying ducks. As a matter of course after the shoot, Doug would sit on a rice check and his buddies would bring him all the cripples. Since neck wringing was problematic because heads would sometimes come off, making it tougher to carry the birds from the field, he would bite the still-living ducks through the eyes, crushing their skulls and killing them instantly (an old market hunters' trick). Sometimes he would kill so many ducks using that technique that he would be smeared with blood. He mentioned with a laugh that sometimes he'd come home after a night shooting session covered with so much duck blood that it would freak out Fay, his mom! He also said that biting through the heads of geese in order to quickly kill them did not work. Their skulls were thick enough that if you tried to bite through their heads as you did with ducks, you could lose some teeth!

Doug said that sometimes the ducks were so hungry, they would flood into a field night after night until the leftover rice or milo was all gone. When that happened, Doug and his partners would shoot those flocks sometimes five times a week. And if they didn't, someone else would take advantage of such easy numbers and blow up the same ducks!

After a successful shoot on his future father-in-law's land, they would gather up their ducks and sneak to a nearby barn, where they would stash the birds under the hay. Then, leaving their shotguns concealed in the barn, they would wash up in a nearby water trough and walk to the farmhouse to make sure there were no game wardens in the area. If all was quiet, they would return to the barn, and each shooter would bring out one legal limit of ducks. That way, if they were intercepted by the law, they would not be in violation by having an overlimit in their possession. They would take the birds home to their respective houses, clean them, and place them in their family freezers. Doug was not one to waste game and usually the next morning would go back to the field they had shot the evening before and pick up the ducks they previously overlooked.

Sometimes they would take their ducks to a motel in Williams that had a picker and use it to pick and clean their ducks. Then they would store the birds in a nearby freezer with the numbers and ownership written on a tally sheet on the picking-house wall. Doug had to laugh at this indiscretion because if a game warden had come in and looked on the marker board, he would have had proof of a mess of illegal shooters with overlimits.

Many times when his family freezer was full of ducks, he would go around Williams in his future brother-in-law's beat-up truck and give the birds away to anyone who wanted them. He chuckled as he compared himself and his future brother-in-law, who would be the one driving the clunker truck, to modern-day Robin Hoods. …

Doug confessed that the last drag he'd ever done was the one I heard, after which I had chased him and his future brother-in-law for hours (see Chapter

4). He said that episode scared him straight, and he never again illegally shot any ducks. He has told that story over and over to his son, who today is an excellent sportsman and an ethical hunter as a result of learning from his dad's transgressions.

At the end of the interview, as I had done in the others, I just let Doug reminisce. One story he told was of his only venture into an illegal commercial deer market. He and four of his buddies decided they would slaughter a bunch of deer, turn them into jerky, sell it around high school, and make a killing off their classmates. Well, they killed the animals on a local ranch that had been suffering deer depredations, then trimmed them out, brined, and jerked the meat. Their venture into this commercial market, however, ended in disaster. They took the meat to school, where it was eagerly purchased by their schoolmates. That was when the wheels came off the wagon. Doug and his "venison company" had not cured the meat long enough, and many of his purchasers got sick. As if that wasn't bad enough, their smokehouse got too hot, caught fire, and burned the smoker and the building housing the illegal enterprise to the ground. Thus ended the great venison-jerky caper.

After that tale, Doug grew introspective. He recalled that the number of ducks in his day had been unreal. Many times when they blew up the ducks at night, the flocks of fleeing birds would blot out the moon! He shook his head as this picture from days long past slipped across his memory. He said that in his dragging days, the country had been full of illegal duck and goose shooters, and almost everyone did it. As he put it, "Illegal duck killing wasn't a big thing. Most everybody did it, but it was almost an unwritten code that one stuck to shooting within the season but broke every other law in between.

"I am not really proud of what I and the rest of my generation in the valley did during those times. But we truly didn't think it was all that bad, the illegal killing, that is. None of us ever thought it was damaging since there was always a never-ending flow of birds. But we soon discovered it didn't take many more years of such abuses, and now we can't do that anymore. I know the birds are gone for many reasons, but our illegal killing of such numbers couldn't have helped. That is why I spent so much time working with my son on his hunting ethics because I was part of that destruction, and I wasn't going to let him follow in my footsteps. If nothing else, I have made him into an ethical hunter, and that has to count for something."

Wallace "Ed" Dowell and Raymond "Pudge" Dowell

When I first met the Dowell brothers, I was amazed. Ed was eighty, and Ray was seventy-nine, yet both looked and acted as if they weren't a day over fifty! Here were two men who were ramrod-straight, possessed the reflexes of cats, and had the memories of men in their twenties and a superb clarity of recollection. I soon discovered that both had a quick wit and a sense of the history from which they had come. They also possessed a unique understanding as to why they were there for the interview and a willingness to share Sacramento Valley duck dragging and commercial-market hunting history of waterfowl as they had lived or observed it some sixty-five years earlier. Both were highly educated, and of note was the fact that Ray had surveyed over 280,000 acres of the Sacramento Valley during his active years as a surveyor. Not only that, he was considered one of the best wing-shots in the valley, or, as many called him, a "shootist." Ed was the family historian, and what a memory he had, even as to exact dates of events from many years before. In addition, Ed had been and to this day still is honored as one of the valley's superb track men in high school. His athletic prowess continued right through college, where at Saint Mary's College in Oakland, California, he held the 440-yard school record. In his later years, Ed won a gold medal at the Senior Olympics in the Los Angeles Coliseum in the 400 meters in the 40–49 age division and set a record that lasted eight years!

Ray Dowell (left) holding one of his hand-carved decoys, and Ed Dowell. Both men were "duck draggers" in their day, and Ed was one of the fastest runners in the Williams area—able to run down a crippled pheasant! (Courtesy Donna Grosz, 2007)

If I had run across these two breaking the law when I was still a young conservation officer working in the Sacramento Valley, I would have been hard-pressed to round them up because of that athletic prowess and their understanding of the valley's terrain. Those skills and abilities are surpassed only by their understanding of the life histories of the wildlife and the history of the people living in the Sacramento Valley.

The family and natural history rolled off Ed's tongue as if it were only yesterday instead of yesteryear. Ed told me that eight generations of Wallaces had lived in Colusa and Yolo counties in the Sacramento Valley. Prior to that, Great-Great-Grandfather William Ward Wallace and his brother had been successful farmers in Missouri, owning numerous hogs and cattle. However, upon hearing that California had lots of rich soil and cheap land, William headed west by wagon train in 1852. He served as an assistant wagon master and was accompanied by his wife and daughter. Because William and company got a late start and didn't want to chance the Sierra Nevada Mountains in the winter, remembering what had happened to the Donner Party, the wagon train turned south on the Santa Fe Trail. Upon their arrival in Los Angeles, William and his family boarded a boat and headed north. Once in Monterey, they traveled inland to the Sonoma, California, area. There Wallace formed a stock-raising partnership with Captain Salvador Vallejo (brother of General Mariano Vallejo) for several years. Wanting to have a bigger outfit and hearing about the wonders of Bear Valley in western Colusa County, William left the Sonoma area with his family, traveled northeast, and established a large cattle ranch. William Wallace raised eight children and passed on in 1902 at the age of eighty-three.

His brother Ben stayed in Independence, Missouri, in the livestock business and raised his family as well. One of his granddaughters, a young lady named Bess Wallace, wanted to marry a Missouri dirt farmer. Her family, being in the livestock business, believed that a dirt farmer would not amount to anything and at first refused to let Bess marry her man. Finally, after holding out for four years, they relented, and Bess married one Harry S. Truman, the love of her life. The rest is American history.

Ed and Ray's grandfather, Frank Wallace, was born in Williams, California, in 1882 and as a young man worked at Brim's Hardware in the same town. Their mother, Elvera, was born in Williams in 1911 from the marriage of Frank Wallace and Tena Ochs. In 1925, their future dad came down from Montana

Doug Keith (left) and Ray "Pudge" Dowell with a few too many ducks, which were taken in the Willows area in 1948. (Courtesy Ed and Ray Dowell)

and went to work for the California Highway Department, remaining in that capacity for the next forty years. Ed and Ray were born in Williams to this union and grew up in the heart of the greatest duck, goose, and pheasant hunting area in the state.

Ed and Ray talked about the tremendous numbers of waterfowl and pheasants when they were growing up as nothing short of unbelievable! No matter where they went during the winter months, the air was always filled with skeins of waterfowl and the roadsides were lined with thousands of pheasants. With that kind of environment, it was only natural that Ed and Ray would turn their expansive energies toward hunting. This was during World War II, and Ray's first shotgun was a Winchester Model 12 16-gauge. This was when he was in the eighth grade, and when he went pheasant hunting, he would take Ed along because his brother was such a fast runner that he could run down a wounded and running rooster pheasant. Since they didn't own a dog, Ray made do with his lightning-fast brother. Ray maintained it was nothing to kill fifteen to twenty pheasants every outing, and all of them went onto their family's table. He maintained that he had never shot for the commercial market (neither had Ed) but only for the table or to help other, poorer shooters kill birds (Ray to this day is known as a "shootist," or crack wing-shot on game birds). Both men did their fair share of ground-sluicing, or drag shooting, of feeding waterfowl during daylight hours, but again, the birds went onto the table and not into the commercial markets as many others of their day did.

Ray talked about riding on the running board of a slowly moving Model A on the Marengo Ranch one day, and as the pheasants ran alongside the road or exploded into the air from the ditches, he would wing-shoot them with his shotgun. He had learned to back-lead the birds as they attempted to flee and to compensate for the vehicle's speed, aiming behind the flying or running birds. He said it was common for him to kill twenty to twenty-five pheasants in such a manner.

Both Ed and Ray recalled the valley being full of lesser snow geese, and those were the type of geese most frequently killed. Many people just breasted them out and then breaded and pan-fried the meat. White-fronted geese were the best eating, according to the brothers, and the most sought after but were in the valley in lower numbers than all the other goose species. Many times their flocks numbered only twenty-five to fifty birds, whereas the lesser snow geese would number in the thousands. Since the white-fronted geese were so wary, a lot of folks would carry a .22-caliber rifle in their vehicles and shoot them in the rice fields from a distance. Canada geese were also in the valley in fairly large numbers during the 1940s but were considered the wariest of all the geese.

Ray remembered a time when he was working in the Williams Meat Market (a haven for stored, illegally shot waterfowl for the commercial markets), and Fred Hill brought in two Canada geese he had killed. One weighed twenty-two pounds and the other weighed twenty-four pounds, according to the butcher's scale—extreme weights even by today's standards! He remembered another Canada goose killed in Willows, a city just to the north of Williams, that weighed in at thirty-six pounds (probably a world's record)! That bird was stuffed and placed in a local hotel in Willows for the patrons to view.

Ray recalled another time when several thousand pintail ducks were feeding off Lurline Road just north of Williams. He had his friend Doug Keith slowly drove by on the road alongside the feeding ducks. Ray stood up in the moving automobile with Doug at the wheel and shot into the horde of ducks several times. Then they realized there were several parked cars sitting along state Highway 99 just yards away, full of folks who were watching Mother Nature and her ducks in grand review. Flooring the gas pedal, the two illegal shooters fled the scene. Later, after the other vehicles had left, the two boys went back and picked up about forty to fifty dead ducks before fleeing the scene once again. That was in 1944, and people didn't report the illegal duck shooters then, as they didn't in like situations some thirty years later in the same area when I was the local Fish and Game warden. ...

One day in 1943, Ed and Doug Keith, still in high school, were beckoned by Mr. Davidson, their principal. He asked if they wanted to go on a duck shoot (this was in March, long after the close of duck season), and the boys eagerly agreed. Driving north on what they called the Old Muddy Road just north of Williams, they came upon many feeding ducks in the rice field on both sides of the road. Mr. Davidson shot twice into the feeding ducks, and then it became apparent why he had invited the two boys along. They were to be his dogs and retrieve the illegally spring-shot ducks. Taking off their shoes and socks, the two boys waded a small canal, went into the rice field, and picked up a slug of ducks just killed by Davidson. There was a small bridge over the Old Muddy Road under which they hid the illegal ducks. Then they heard frantic calls from their principal to hurry and get back into their vehicle. Davidson had spotted the local game warden, Taylor London, fast approaching in his patrol car. Stopping the principal with his red light, the game warden got out and approached the three scared culprits in their car.

"Having any luck?" asked Taylor

Davidson replied in the negative, and, having seen what had gone on just moments before, Taylor asked if he might look in their car. Given the green light, he opened the trunk and, finding a shotgun, broke open the breech on the double barrel, extracting two still-smoking shot-shell empties! The barrel was still warm from the recent firing. Finding no ducks, and having seen the boys emerging from beneath the bridge down the road, the game warden took them back, figuring that was where he would find the just-shot birds. Much to everyone's surprise, when Taylor looked under the bridge, the ducks were gone! About then Ed spied what looked like a hog moving across the rice field to the east. He stared in disbelief at what turned out not to be a hog but a man crawling along and dragging a sack full of ducks! Luckily, the game warden did not see what Ed was looking at. As it turned out, the man, who had been stalking the same field of feeding ducks, had seen the turn of events with the game warden. He had taken his chance to sneak in, grab the principal's ducks, and flee the scene. Ed thought that was all right because the man had several hungry children to feed, and his actions helped the three real culprits get clean away.

Another time on the east side of the Sutter Basin, Ed, Paul Nix, and Carl White from Knights Landing went looking for a large concentration of feeding ducks one evening. Not finding any right away, they continued looking until they located a likely-looking bunch that they could approach unseen. As they crawled up on the bunch of ducks, Carl and Paul would get their heads close to the ground and listen intently. If they didn't hear a grinding sound, they would readjust their position until they heard what was locally called the "grind" (the sound thousands of duck gizzards make when grinding up the rough-hulled rice grains prior to digestion). All three men finally got into the position they liked from the sound of the grind, rose up, and each fired only three shots. Then they rose up from their hiding place and began bagging their kill. They put twenty ducks to a bag and then left the bags and the rest of the ducks not picked up (cripples) in the field. Walking back to their vehicle, the three men drove off without using any lights until they were far away from where they had made their drag. Paul Nix said they would pick the ducks up the next day about noon, which they did. Ed said he would never shoot or drag ducks at night again after that episode. When I asked why, he replied, "It was illegal and offered no challenge. But Ray and I did make some good sneaks on the birds during the daylight hours throughout our times in the valley."

Ray remembered a time when he was a sophomore in high school and was working at the Williams Meat Market (which burned down in the 1960s). Herb Murphy (a known market hunter), butcher at the meat market and part owner with Johnny Coleman (another poacher), asked Ray to accompany him on a drag. That afternoon, Herb, Ray, and another man whose name Ray could not remember drove out of Williams north toward Maxwell. They turned off onto Lurline Road and drove several miles east looking for duck concentrations and suspicious vehicles that might belong to game wardens. They finally located a large feeding flock of ducks, and the drop-off man let Herb and Ray (who was not carrying a shotgun) out of the truck. Herb had his Model 11 Remington semiautomatic shotgun with a Long Tom extension and six or seven gunnysacks. It was just at dusk when they crawled up on the ducks until they could hear the grind. Herb whistled, and when the ducks' heads rose up to see where the danger was, he let fly with two shots into their exposed heads and necks. Then, letting the birds get up about fifty feet in the air, he let go with the rest of his shells, killing and wounding a large number. Running among the dead and dying, Herb picked up the cripples and bit them across the eyes, killing them instantly. When they had gathered up a mess of birds, but not all that were killed or wounded, Herb took out a knife with a hook at the end of the blade. In one swift movement, he opened up a bird at the vent and with a swipe with the hook on the end of the blade quickly eviscerated the duck. This went on until Herb and Ray had collected and sacked ninety-five ducks. Then Herb said they had better leave, and the two of them dragged the sacks full of ducks back to the road where they were to be picked up by their driver. The driver, hearing the shooting, had waited about thirty minutes and then came slowly driving back down Lurline Road by the pickup spot (most skilled commercial-market gunners could shoot, gut, and sack the ducks and be out of an area in an hour or less). The two men waved from the cover at the side of the road, letting him know they were there as the driver slowly passed by. Driving to the end of that road, the drop-off man made sure no one was in the vicinity who might be the law. Then, coming back down the road when the coast was all clear, he stopped, and Herb and Ray heaved the

Herb Murphy was butcher and part owner of Williams Meat Market, as well as a commercial-market hunter, "dragger," and deer poacher. (Courtesy Ed and Ray Dowell)

Williams Meat Market in Williams, photo taken before it burned to the ground. This meat market was one of the largest collecting and shipping points of illegal ducks on the western side of Sacramento Valley (Courtesy Ed and Ray Dowell)

sacks of ducks into the back of the truck and piled in. The pickup, now being driven without lights, continued west across state Highway 99 and even farther down a back road. Stopping out in the middle of nowhere, the three men just sat and watched the area they had just left to see if they had a tail. Seeing no one in their wake, they went back the way they had come and, turning south on state Highway 99 toward Williams, stopped at a numbered culvert. There Ray and Herb hid the ducks in the culvert out of sight. Then they turned on their lights and proceeded into Williams like any normal vehicle. Once at the meat market, Herb called his contact in San Francisco to inform him of the kill and the stash location under the numbered culvert. Early the next morning, that contact drove up from San Francisco and picked up the ducks still hidden in the culvert. Then, driving back to Williams, the man paid Herb in cash for the ducks and left.

According to Ray, one to two thousand ducks a week moved through the Williams Meat Market during the height of the waterfowl migration. Not only would Herb ship his birds out from the meat market, but other gunners would sometimes bring in their ducks for Herb to purchase and ship to his San Francisco contacts as well. Herb would take the illegal ducks, tie them off in legal bunches (whatever the limit of the day was), then tag the bunches with tags under other people's names, real or imagined. Ray would see as many as twenty bunches of ten ducks each hanging in the cool room one day, and the next day they would be gone. Even Al Lawrence, a notorious local market hunter, reportedly sold ducks at the Williams Meat Market to his friend Herb Murphy.

The only person Ray could remember purchasing ducks from Herb Murphy and moving them to San Francisco (normally such transactions, being illegal and a felony, were kept under wraps and not discussed even with other shooters by most market hunters) was by a man named Shirley Corlette. He had alleged mafia ties in San Francisco, and Ray saw him many times purchasing ducks from Herb. In fact, he was such a good friend of Herb's that he often stored his cash in the meat market's large iron safe in the back room. Ray told of once being beckoned over by Corlette and handed a roll of cash to hold for a moment, which Corlette told him amounted to $35,000! Corlette was also involved in the trafficking from the black markets in the Bay area to Williams of sugar and coffee, which in turn were sold to the locals. According to Ray, no one went without sugar and coffee in Williams during the war when Corlette was around.

Ray and Ed remembered that during the war and shortly thereafter, prices for dressed pintail and mallard ran from $1.25 to $1.50 per duck. For wigeon, a smaller and less desirable duck, the price was $.75 each. Ray's only recollection of goose prices was $2 per dressed bird paid by a man named Bob Bowen, who allegedly took them to the Bay area for resale. He also remembered that a wild-duck dinner in San Francisco and other markets sold for twice the price of a tame-duck dinner. Once a wild-duck dinner was purchased at a restaurant, the diner was told to enjoy his meal and keep his mouth shut!

My personal experiences with the people in the valley, historical information from law enforcement files, discussions with many still-living old-time game wardens when I was assigned to the valley, and personal interviews with other folks who had known Herb Murphy (no kin to Bill Murphy, another old-time market hunter) indicated that the Williams Meat Market, before it burned, had probably been one of the largest collection and shipping points for illegal ducks en route to the Bay area's commercial markets from the west side of the Sacramento Valley. Estimates ran as high as ten thousand to twenty thousand ducks per winter season (birds were shot out of season as well until they began feeding on grass, thereby reducing their marketing and eating qualities) moving through its doors, and who knows how many during the lifetime of the market! The market was centrally located in relation to some of the greatest killing fields in the Sacramento Valley, so market hunters funneled some of their birds through the facility throughout its existence. Herb was a very effective market hunter himself, and his being a part owner and butcher at the facility facilitated such illegal operations. The building was located on a direct major highway system leading into the Bay area, where many of the markets were located, and for several years the market had a mafia tie from that location to some of the main marketplaces in San Francisco.

Herb also marketed deer during those times. He would go out to the King Ranch west of Williams and kill black-tailed deer, then dress and hang them in his meat market or slaughterhouse west of Williams. Buyers would come from San Francisco and pay him $125 per deer. He would also sell deer to big-city hunters who came up to drink and chase women under the guise of a deer-hunting trip. When ready to leave, they would approach Herb, purchase a deer, and take it home, I am sure with collateral hair-raising wild tales of the chase and their excellent shooting abilities.

When asked about prices that may have been offered for pheasants, Ray and Ed couldn't remember any. Ed indicated that most pheasants were shot for the dinner tables. However, Ray remembered one incident when he went out on the Marengo Ranch, where his girlfriend lived, to accompany big-city hunters on their pheasant hunts. If they missed, it was his job to see that they had pheasants to take home. One time Ray stopped with a group of city-slicker pheasant hunters by a big ditch full of tules and crossed over by a wooden bridge. Six pheasants got up at once upon hearing the truck stopping, and Ray with his unplugged Winchester pump Model 12 shotgun killed six birds with just six shots. Reloading and crossing the bridge, he threw some rocks into the tules from that side, and five more pheasants rose into the air, only to fall from five well-placed shots from Ray's trusty shotgun. It was occasions like that that lent credence to Ray's Sacramento Valley reputation as an excellent wing-shot! Ed, who was also a good shooter in his day, claims that his brother is without equal as a wing-shooter.

When I asked how many pheasants he had killed in his lifetime, Ray thought for a minute and said, "From eight hundred to a thousand, easy!" When

I asked how many waterfowl he had killed, he struggled with his answer. Then he said, "Well, probably five to six hundred geese, probably more. … As for ducks, probably two or three thousand, an easy three thousand … maybe more now that I think about it."

According to Ed and Ray, towns such as Willows, Maxwell, Delevan, Artois, Williams, Arbuckle, Princeton, Gridley, Woodland, Colusa, and Yuba City were the main market gunning centers. But they added that almost anywhere there were ducks and hungry people, the ducks fell to the gun. Ed said, "The Sacramento Valley was full of hungry people and lots of birds, so it was a way of life."

Ray and Ed also said that one could make as much in one night of successful gunning and the subsequent sale of the ducks as they could as a farm worker during the entire winter during the 1930s and '40s. So it was easy to understand why so many folks went into the market gunning of ducks in order to survive.

Ray and Ed's Great-Uncle Ward Wallace had found the going hard as a farm worker in the valley in the winter. So he went out commercial market hunting and then, taking a pickup load of ducks (after dropping some off to Ed and Ray's house and the homes of other family members), went to San Francisco. The next day he would be back with $200 to $300 in his pocket, which was more than he could make all winter as a farmhand.

In my short time in the valley, I ran across at least a dozen farmers, including some who were community leaders, who flat-out told me the reason they commercially shot ducks was to save their farms. In every case, if farm profits were lower than expected when the bank note came due and the ducks were in the valley, out they went to kill and sell ducks in order to make their payments. Rice farmer Terrill Sartain told me he had done so in the 1950s more than once in order to save his farm—and would do so again if the need arose.

At the end of my interview with Ed and Ray Dowell, I asked if they had anything to add. There was a long, thoughtful pause; then both men had almost the same thought: "We were lucky to be born and have lived in that era. Then it all started going downhill real quick."

HAROLD "COCKY" MYERS

One morning Peter Grevie; my wife, Donna; and I drove to the small town of Arbuckle, located just south of Williams in the Sacramento Valley. Arbuckle was home to many old-time market hunters and duck draggers from times long past. That morning we were en route to the home of Harold "Cocky" Myers, whose family has a long, rich history of farming; duck dragging; commercial-market hunting; and loyal, honorable service in the military, particularly during World War II.

Entering a beautiful and well-kept home, we soon met Harold Myers and his wife, Joan. Harold, never a large man, is showing the inevitable signs of the passage of time. A strong handshake and steady gaze into our eyes was his greeting, accompanied by a genuine welcome into his home. However, he was a bit reserved, which was to be expected when meeting strangers for the first time—especially a former conservation law enforcement officer coming to talk with him about the lawless pursuits of his early days.

As my wife prepared her video camera, the film of which will ultimately go to the Smithsonian Institute in Washington, D.C., I found Harold quickly laying down ground rules for the interview. He informed me that he would frankly discuss many friends and family members engaging in activities that were illegal during their day. However, he did not want any of their names used in my proposed story because many were still alive, as were their kin, and he didn't want to embarrass anyone. I knew it was more than just that: There is also a code of silence that still rules among the brotherhood of illegal duck gunners. I have attempted to provide the historical context of what Harold told me during the interview without using the names of most of those involved, as he requested. However, I did include some names from the past only because their activities were publicly known or known through the legal system. Honoring Harold's request for silence detracts from what could have been written about some of Arbuckle's history, but I agreed to his terms nonetheless.

The Myers family traveled from Wisconsin to the Arbuckle area in the 1850s. They were of hardy farm stock and, once on the land, continued their age-old farming traditions. However, in those days, and later even more so with the advent of rice as a major crop in the valley, the farmers' lands were swarmed with hordes of first hungry geese and then ducks. Many fields of barley and other crops were stripped bare in a matter of hours when they were discovered by the ravenous flocks. Fields of clover or alfalfa suffered the same fate once the flocks of waterfowl arrived, hungry after a long migration, much to the chagrin of those trying to make a living off the land. Harold spoke of times when he was a little boy when the airways in the winter months were constantly filled with flocks of birds looking for a place to land, rest, and feed. And that density of waterfowl didn't end during the day but continued into the night, with so many geese calling that oftentimes the noise kept people awake.

According to Harold, the duck hunter, the drag shooter (so named in his opinion because of the sacks or bunches of ducks dragged from the fields after the shoot), and the commercial-market hunter of waterfowl soon became welcome friends to the desperate farmer. Even movie stars were among the hunters who swarmed into the Arbuckle area, following the news of the arrival of millions of waterfowl, to be guided on duck and goose hunts by local farmers and other area residents.

It wasn't long before stories of mass killings of ducks and geese became part of the common knowledge. Over four hundred ducks killed in one nighttime drag, at least one thousand ducks killed in a day by several commercial-market

Unknown movie stars after a morning's shoot in Sacramento Valley around the Arbuckle area, circa 1920s. (Courtesy Charlie Geyer)

hunters—so many birds were killed that their gizzards and livers filled a fifty-gallon barrel, and some men shot until they couldn't shoot anymore—such tales were typical of the day.

When the hunting season closed and the crops were planted, depredations by geese on the spring wheat began, and so did the illegal gunning all over again in order to save the crops. In late summer, when the rice headed out and the ducks returned to resume their depredations, the illegal killing under the guise of "herding" reared its ugly head once again.

Harold said his dad did not extensively shoot ducks or kill for the market as other family members did. He was kept busy with the usual demands of farming and raising a family, leaving the killing to others around him. However, other members of the far-flung Myers family not only sport-hunted heavily but were involved in duck dragging and in some cases in commercial-market hunting for the markets in the San Francisco Bay area.

When dragging ducks, Harold and his companions would sneak out into the fields being used by feeding waterfowl, sometimes getting so close that when they decided to shoot, they had to first scare the ducks and let them get some distance away in order to make effective use of their shot patterns. Then, with their shotgun of choice, usually a Browning AL-5 with the plug pulled to make it capable of firing five shots and using number 6 shot, they would shoot into the fleeing ducks at close range. They would kill from 100 to 150 ducks per drag. They would gut the birds and either leave them in the field for retrieval the next day once the "heat" was off or bring them in that night if the coast was clear. The most Harold and his friends ever killed in one evening was about four hundred in several shoots, and Harold said he didn't know why they killed so many because they had trouble giving them all away. He added that there were so many ducks in the valley and on the farms that for the most part, the shooters could go out each morning and kill whatever they wanted without having to go through all the work of dragging them illegally at night.

Harold told a story of a time in the late 1950s when he and several close friends went out and killed a large number of ducks. Having so many and needing assistance to pick and clean them, they went to Gerald Hawn to borrow his duck picker. Then they got the loan of another local farmer's cool box in which to store the picked and cleaned ducks, and the work began. The plan was to take thirty picked and cleaned ducks at a time to the cool box, located some distance away from the picker, which meant they had to pass the Villa Bar. Harold laughingly recalled that he got to drinking too much each time he passed the bar, so on one of his later runs he forgot that he had ninety picked and cleaned ducks in the back of his pickup as he stopped for another drink. Once inside, he realized there were two game wardens sitting there in the bar! He lost all desire to stop in the bar, but he still had to take the time to have a drink to avoid suspicion. If he instantly headed for the door, he felt the game wardens would be on to him, and they had only to follow him outside to catch him with the goods! Ultimately, Harold got clean away, but he and his group of buddies were not allowed to use that duck picker again once Hawn found out about their near discovery. (Most valley game wardens and federal agents figured that a person wouldn't have a duck picker on his premises unless he planned on picking *a whole lot of ducks.*)

Harold told me that when the birds were numerous in the valley, he and his cohorts would often illegally drag ducks many nights in succession. Knowing the game wardens were onto their illegal activities, the draggers would do all kinds of things to throw the law off their track and make the job of catching the illegal shooters a lot more difficult. One tactic was to frequently change the locks on the gates to their farm properties because the game wardens had keys to those locks. Or they would take a bulldozer out to a dirt road frequently utilized by the game wardens to reach the shooting areas and plow a hole in the center of the roadway. They knew the wardens would be running without lights in order to get closer to the shooters, and the plan was to cause the officers to wreck their vehicles by driving into the hole! This would allow Harold and his cronies to make a clean getaway and have a good laugh at the expense of the game wardens.

Another story he told involved an episode with U.S. Game Management Agent Jim Savage. Savage had a reputation for being a good, hardworking federal agent, and the word got out that he was making a serious effort to shut down the illegal slaughtering and night shooting of ducks in the valley. Savage owned a big Labrador retriever that he used to help him at night, especially when working the rice fields alone chasing the duck draggers and commercial-market hunters. Knowing he was after them, a group of draggers one night *shot his dog!* That took a lot out of Savage because for a conservation officer, losing his faithful dog is like losing a child. Harold said the local people, upon hearing about the dog-shooting episode, thought it was too much; it turned people's stomachs.

Harold told me about Joe Shaw, owner of a local restaurant and gas station years ago in Arbuckle. Joe also had a duck-buying and commercial duck-selling business on the side. He would purchase ducks from local shooters, store the birds until he got a large bunch in hand, and then transport them to San Francisco for sale to the Chinese restaurants and poultry-processing facilities. Joe was later rewarded with a stint in McNeil Island Federal Penitentiary for this commercialization of sport-shot ducks after being apprehended by U.S. Game Management Agent Hugh Worcester's special flying squads and covert operatives (I have divulged Joe's name because his violations are a matter of public record).

Toward the end of the interview, I let Harold just speak his thoughts about the old days. He talked about how the local state wardens were not really feared, but just about everyone was leery of being caught by the federal officers and, once apprehended, having to go to federal court in Sacramento. He repeated that unless you had been there, you could not imagine just how many ducks and geese there had been in the valley during its heyday. Today they seemed to have considerably lessened in number, he added. He talked of how people in those days made so little money as farmers or farm workers that many were driven to the easy money associated with the illegal commercial markets. The birds always seemed so numerous that people seemingly didn't care if you violated the law—the money was quick and good, there would always be more birds over the next horizon or during the next migration, and the commercial appetite for duck dinners was unbelievable. There were always more buyers and markets than could be supplied with birds, and that was reflected in the prices of more than $1 per duck on average, which was big money in those days. Harold figured with those prices and one good shoot, a man could make more off the ducks in one night than he could make in one month as a farmhand. He felt that the commercial duck killing and selling in the Arbuckle area declined right after World War II. He believed it was because a lot of the commercial shooters didn't come back from the war, and those who did had had enough of killing. The fines had gotten too high if one were caught for night shooting or having too many ducks in possession, and it seemed that folks just shot for their dinner tables and were no longer interested in shooting for the commercial markets.

When Harold seemed to run out of what he generally had to say, I asked him how many ducks he thought he had killed in his day. He thought for a moment and then said, "I am not really sure since so many times I was collectively shooting with my friends and we all were killing them. So individually I don't have any idea how many I killed in a lifetime." Then he paused again and after a long moment said, "I killed a lot of ducks."

Vance Boyes

Walking into the office of Vance Boyes, an investment broker in Colusa, I was pleasantly surprised. Vance is a large physical specimen, middle-aged and in tremendous shape, and kept that way through a busy schedule and involvement in athletic activities. He is a big-game hunter and deeply committed to his community and family. He is obviously not only a skilled businessman but a successful one as well. Once into his interview, it became obvious that he is also well-educated and highly motivated, possesses an excellent work ethic, and comes from a long-established Sacramento Valley family.

At first Vance was so full of energy and had so much to say that it was hard to keep him on topic. But soon he settled into the interview, and the stories he had to tell about the Boyes family, from Revolutionary War times through early California history and the days of the market hunter, poacher, and duck dragger in the Sacramento Valley to the present, staggered the imagination.

Vance Boyes's family goes back to the Revolutionary War and the role it played in the formation of the United States. One family thread is represented by Great-Grandfather John Kentucky Boyes, born in 1845, who settled in the small California town of Shasta in the 1860s.

In September 1864, two Yana Indians entered the home of the William Allen family on Old Cow Creek, Shasta County, and confronted Mrs. Catherine Allen, née Boyes, and her four children. Before this episode was over, Mrs. Allen had been killed and her four children severely beaten and left for dead. The next day, Mrs. John Jones was killed in Bear Valley, a scant fifteen miles from the previous day's killing. This attack was presumably carried out by the same two Yana Indians who had killed Mrs. Allen. Those two events so enraged the area's settlers that two large parties of men were formed, and within a two-month period, five hundred Yana Indians were wiped out! This killing field included men, women, and children along with one Mexican who was mistaken for a Yana Indian. These attacks effectively wiped out the entire Yana Indian population in California. In that party of enraged settlers doing the killing was John Kentucky Boyes, an eighteen-year-old single man at the time.

In 1878, John Boyes married Ada Beck and moved to Princeton, California, in the Sacramento Valley, had four or five children, and became that town's sheriff for a time. He was known as a no-nonsense sheriff who wouldn't hesitate to shoot a man if he believed him to be guilty of a crime. John Kentucky Boyes died in 1926 at the age of eighty-one.

Grandfather William Boyes Sr. was born in 1890 in Fort Collins, Colorado, and moved to the Princeton area in the Sacramento Valley around 1893, Bill as he liked to be called, went into farming. Like many other men of the land at that time, he also went into the commercial-market hunting of ducks as a secondary means of support. Vance told me that his grandfather killed more ducks and geese than just about anyone else in the Sacramento Valley during his heyday. Historically speaking, Bill Boyes Sr. rivaled Sam Gridley as one of the greatest market hunters of all time. Bill was one of the last great commercial-market hunters living before he died in 1971, and a reference to his being "the last great market hunter" is even inscribed on his headstone.

Vance Boyes, once a duck "dragger" and poacher, holding a four-barrel 10-gauge shotgun used to shoot into masses of feeding waterfowl. (Courtesy Donna Grosz, 2007)

Bill was a mere lad of seventeen around the turn of the century, when he drove and operated a "gut wagon" (used to carry the thousands of ducks and geese shot by market hunters) for his commercial-market hunting stepfather. Vance said his grandfather got the notion of going into the market hunting business for himself because of the readily available markets, abundance of waterfowl, good money, and no limits on what the shooters killed. He teamed up with his brother Harry, and the two formed one of the most efficient duck-killing machines the Sacramento Valley has probably ever witnessed. Killing ducks by the thousands in the Norman area, the brothers sold their kill to a merchant in San Francisco, who was the stepfather to A. P. Giannini, the Bank of America financier.

According to Vance, canvasbacks and mallards during that time, because of their size and eating quality, were the premier products. In those days those species sold for $.75 a brace (pair). Pintail, the next most sought-after duck by the market hunters around 1900, sold for $.50 each, and the lesser species of ducks sold for $1 to $1.25 per dozen. Although geese had less market value, they were sold as well, with white-fronted geese (the best eating) bringing $5 per dozen, lesser snow geese bringing $1.75 per dozen, large Canada geese $2.50 per dozen, and lesser Canada geese (smaller and usually not in as good shape) $1.25 per dozen.

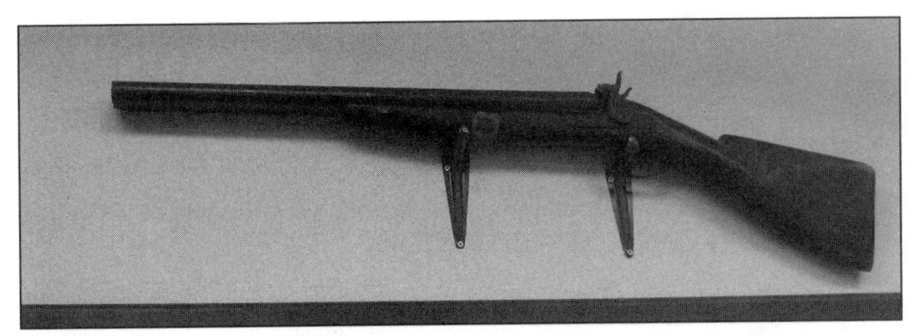

Six-gauge, double-barrel shotgun used by early members of the Boyes family in the Sacramento Valley to shoot ducks for the commercial market. Photo taken in 2007; shotgun is the possession of Vance Boyes. (Courtesy Donna Grosz)

Using the first live goose decoys in the Sacramento Valley, the brothers coupled those "Judas" geese with a 6-gauge shotgun (still in Vance's possession) as their first shotgun of choice (this was before the advent of multishell-capacity autoloading or pump shotguns). Soon the brothers graduated to four-barreled shotguns manufactured by gunsmiths in Sacramento. One of these killing machines was a four-barreled 6-gauge shotgun with outside hammers. The other was a four-barreled 4- and 5-gauge hand cannon (currently on exhibit in Sutter's Fort in Sacramento)! These monster guns were loaded with black powder and a handful of shot and would have possessed the kick of an army mule if it weren't for their extreme weight. The brothers would take these handheld cannons, walk a well-trained horse alongside thousands of feeding ducks or geese (hiding behind the horse so as not to spook the birds), and when the moment was right lay the barrels over the back of the horse and let fly. After gutting the kill to reduce its weight, they would loaded the dead birds on the horse for the trip back to the farmhouse or a nearby barn. After hanging for a while to cool out, the birds would be transported to the train station in Norman or Artois; loaded on the train tied up in barley sacks; and shipped to their buyer, a Mr. Scatena in San Francisco, for resale in the city's many eateries.

Vance told a story about his grandfather and Great-Uncle Harry really getting into the birds during a blustery winter storm early in the century. It seemed the north winds were howling, and the birds poured into the shallow, watered pans that were everywhere in those days (most are gone today because of current land-leveling practices) to rest and get out of the strength-sapping winds. Those were just the conditions for which the brothers had wished, and for the next ten days, they shot over those crowded pans of water full of resting waterfowl, killing at least ten thousand ducks! According to Vance, that was one of their better shoots, but he remembered Great-Uncle Harry killing 185 lesser snow geese with one blast from one of his four-barreled killing machines and 305 ducks another time in one day!

With a proud chuckle, Vance told me more about Great-Uncle Harry. It seemed that he was one of the most powerful men of his day, and not a man to tangle with if he was mad. Harry was also a renowned wing-shooter who many times killed fifty birds in fifty shots! Like his brother Bill, Harry quit market hunting in 1909. According to Vance, both men found that times were getting too tough, especially with the law on their tails all the time (although commercial-market hunting was not federally outlawed until 1918 with the passage of the Migratory Bird Treaty Act). However, both Harry and Bill continued to drag ducks illegally for the table for many years afterward. Before all was said and done, Harry had been apprehended eleven times for wildlife violations but never once prosecuted because as history shows, the courts looked at wildlife violations a little differently in those days—if at all!

Bill, after leaving the commercial-market hunting trade and going broke as a farmer, moved his family from Princeton to the west Sacramento Valley town of Williams. Here, along state Highway 99, the volume of business was better, and the family once again set up their commercial enterprises. Bill became the town barber in 1910 and remained so until his retirement some years later. Vance recalled that his grandfather was a gentleman to everyone he met, and after losing almost everything to farming spent the next thirty years paying back everyone to whom he owed money.

Bill Boyes Jr., Vance's father, was known for his strap-steel-tough guidance and family ethics. According to Vance, his dad never killed and sold ducks for the market but shot only for the table and a few close friends. He was a big-game poacher and duck dragger par excellence, but one with certain ethics and scruples. Game was never wasted, always well-cared-for, shot only when it was in its best body condition, and used exclusively for the table.

Then came World War II, and off to war went Bill. He became an outstanding heavyweight boxer in the military and a rifle shot beyond compare. While in North Africa, Bill had to help supply his company with fresh meat. He would load up into a half-track, head out into the desert, and kill what ever fresh meat was available with his .30-06 Garand rifle. Many times it was three shots resulting in three dead-for-the-table warthogs!

Home from the military, Bill Jr. raised four boys. Like his father before him, Bill raised his sons with certain ideas of what it meant to be a man. "Tough" was a family byword, and he constantly instructed his sons to be as good and professional as they could be. He also gave them a heritage of hunting, which became a tradition and passion. With that passion many times came closed-season shooting of wildlife, overlimits, and the like.

As a town barber like his father, Bill Jr. would cut hair during the day and when the opportunity or need arose pursue his shooting in the world of wildlife during the rest of the day or night. Vance remembered one occasion when Bill Jr. and Johnny Coleman, a butcher in the Williams Meat Market, were coming down state Highway 16 in Colusa County when they spied a large tule elk bull in great body condition. The season was closed on the rare elk species, but that didn't stop the two men. *Bang* went their rifle, and the animal was gutted out and loaded into the back of their pickup. Pulling back onto state Highway 16 with the partially covered elk, which was too large for the bed of their pickup, Johnny spied one of the local game wardens driving ahead of them toward the town of Williams. Turning to Bill, he said, "Think we ought to pass him?" As near as Vance could figure, his dad illegally shot a tule elk from the Cache Creek herd in Colusa County every other year for a period of about ten years.

Vance also remembered his dad killing a large black-tailed deer buck with a single shot in the ear on the Three Sisters Ranch on July 4 one year. The buck was in good condition, and they had a need for some fresh venison, so the deer was gutted, thrown into the truck, and brought home once again to the family's table.

Then there was a time when Bill had killed sixty to seventy ducks just off the north end of San Jose Road while hunting with a friend. They threw limits of drake mallards into the first car and the overlimit into Bill's station wagon. Driving down San Jose Road to Lurline Road in a rare Sacramento Valley snowstorm, they met the local game warden. He checked the birds in the first car and, finding everything legal, began to get concerned about the heavy snowfall and the prospect of getting stuck on the muddy roads. The warden told the two hunters to head out Lurline Road toward state Highway 99 before they all got stuck in the snow, and once there, he would check Bill's station wagon. As it turned out, with all the slipping and sliding, the game warden never caught up with Bill, and as a result, he escaped with a large overlimit.

As is the case many times for folks violating the law, Bill was finally apprehended and prosecuted for a wildlife violation. Vance said that slowed his dad down some because he was a family man and didn't want to be putting out good money to pay the hefty fines associated with such violations.

As I had done with the others I interviewed, I finished by letting Vance reminisce about his family, the old days, and some of his personal experiences with wildlife and the laws of the land. Sitting back in his chair, Vance thought for a moment and said, "I have been an outlaw in the past and knew a lot of other outlaws. However, these stories need to be told so others can have a sense of what it was really like in the days of old when we had lots of game and didn't think much about what we were doing to it.

"I remember talking with Dad about the old days when my grandfather and Uncle Harry used to hunt ducks and geese with a horse. So one day, my dad, brother, and I got a horse and tried that method of hunting. Once in the field with all the feeding birds, we sort of walked at an angle toward the flock but not directly at them. Then, as we got closer, we kept working in on them as they fed until we were within shooting range of the birds. We let go of the horse and started shooting, and it was amazing how well this ruse worked! 'Course the horse took off, and we had to walk back with more than fifty birds, but it was really neat to do something like what my grandfather had done. To the best of my recollection, that was about thirty years ago.

"Then there was another time when my brothers Brock and Reese and I, along with Bobbie Romero, pulled a sneak on the ducks about 1972 or 1973. Getting as close as we dared, we spooked them and then began shooting, swinging our shotguns from side to side as we shot. Before it was all over, we had killed about 250 ducks if I remember correctly.

"You mentioned Louis Cario earlier and asked if he ever bought any ducks. I can't remember anyone selling ducks to him, but I know a number of ducks would be stored in his restaurant in years past at various times. I think he had some connections in San Francisco and maybe those birds went there. I can remember as a kid that if Louis Cairo, who was a family friend, needed some birds for his friends or whatever, I would shoot and take him twenty picked ducks at a time. What he did with those birds I don't know.

"However, I can remember many times taking ducks to the Traveler's Motel in Williams because they had a duck picker and freezer there. They also had customers who would come up to hunt, and if they were not successful, us kids would sell them a few ducks and geese for spending money. Yes, I killed hundreds of ducks and geese when I was a kid of eighteen or nineteen. In fact, I started hunting when I was about eight years old.

"I remember another time when I was with Dad and we were coming down state Highway 20 and I was just a kid of fifteen. It was in the Cache Creek area and just about dusk. Dad and I spotted a large bull tule elk in beautiful shape. Dad told me to take the .243 Winchester and shoot him in the head. Jumping out of our pickup, I crawled to within seventy-five yards of him and tried to put the scope dot on his head but just couldn't make it work. So I crawled closer, to about twenty-five yards away, and tried to put the dot on his head. It was getting darker now and really hard to put the scope dot on his head. So I would put the dot on his shoulder and then move it to his head in an effort to be able to see the dot. I tried this several times, and it was just getting too dark. Finally putting the dot on his shoulder one more time to find it and then moving it up to where I thought his head was, I shot. Down went the elk, and I found out later that I had shot him right in the ear! Dad and I dressed out the animal, loaded it into his 1959 GMC pickup, and brought him home. That was in 1969, I think."

Then Vance said out of the blue, "I really like hunting deer; it is one of my favorite sports." Sensing a real love for that big-game sport in the man, I asked Vance just how many deer he thought he had killed in his lifetime. He thought for a moment and then surprised me with his answer. "In my day, I probably have killed 220 deer or more." When asked how many deer he thought he killed annually, he said, "Both in state and out, probably four to five deer a year."

Then Vance began to wind down, saying, "I probably shouldn't be telling you all of this, but the stories need to be told. Almost everyone in the valley in times past shot and lived on the game that was provided. Some sold the game, and others just shot for their tables because times were tough. In our family, we lived on deer, elk, ducks, geese, salmon, and striped bass. We not only liked eating game, but it helped us survive the tough times as well. Plus, there is no denying it, we lived for the sport and the thrills it brought. Today we are paying the price. The clouds of ducks and geese are no more, and because of that, our children will not be able to experience such wonders. Regardless of the outcome, I hope you can get your book published so those who were not here to see what we saw can at least experience to some degree what it was truly like. An experience that for whatever reason is no more."

After thirty-two years of putting those in the business of extinction out of business, I felt a strong connection with the man I had just interviewed. It was obvious that he came from a special family and possessed some unique genes and talents. He also had a history that I felt was still coursing in his veins. I couldn't help thinking that if a thirty-five inch, five-point black-tailed or mule deer buck; a seven-point Rocky Mountain elk; a large, fat tule elk bull on his out-of-the-way ranch on the west side of the valley; or twenty-five thousand close-at-hand feeding pintail presented themselves, Vance would find himself once again licking his chops and maybe pulling the trigger one too many times.

CHAPTER 14

They Made a Difference

In every walk of life there are those who made a difference, but instant name recognition is rare for those who excelled in protecting the world of wildlife for those yet to come. Wildlife officers, or others who dedicated themselves to protecting the natural world, are rarely known because they are involved in fighting a deadly and never-ending quiet war. Few on the outside notice, understand, or even show any interest in this conflict. Yet it is always being fought by the men and women of the "thin green line," with the same spirit, sacrifice, and intensity others who are more famous put into their labors.

For thirty-two hard-fought years, I had the opportunity across this country to enforce state and federal wildlife conservation laws. I also had the opportunity to meet many people dedicated to and involved in protecting the voiceless in the world of wildlife. Some of those folks remain in my mind as true champions for the critters, and ultimately the American people. Others whom I met on the same fields of battle—well, let's just say they went the way of the wind and had about as much effect.

Today some of these folks have crossed over the Great Divide or retired. Many of them barely left a whisper or ripple in the wind because of their self-effacing ways. Others who are still living are limping about today with bad backs, failing eyesight, and unsteady legs from the many plane, boat, and horse crashes they underwent while on duty, or because of injuries suffered during chases into unseen fences in the dark, or falls into deep ditches, or tumbles into muskrat or beaver holes underwater. Or just lying for hours on the damp, cold ground waiting for those shredding the fabric of this nation's natural heritage to make their appearance. It is to those few I have known and worked with that I dedicate the following lines, which hardly capture the essence, soul, and history of their time. I thank you for the patient hours spent teaching and helping me and others to understand so we could do a better job. Thank you for the dangers endured and long hours away from your families. Thank you for the heart and soul of the commitment called for by our profession and personal calling, which you so freely gave. Thank you for never failing the animals and the natural world, even though your agency, the American people, the politicians, and many others failed you time and time again.

HANK MARAK

Hank Marak, a California Fish and Game warden, was stationed in Willow Creek, California, and his patrol district was one of the most challenging in the state. It had a lot of steeply vertical territory; was loaded with rattlesnakes, poison oak, desert heat, and dangerous rock slides; and was frequented by deer poachers, illegal gill netters, salmon and sturgeon snaggers, and numerous mean-tempered loggers and lumbermen who seemed to break the conservation laws every time they were out of work. It would have taken a dozen good officers to effectively patrol such an area! Yet the state of California had placed one man in the center of all that mess. Hank was a medium-sized man, with sandy hair and a constant wisp of a grin. But that was where the average ended. His courage matched that of men many times his size and number. He also had a sense for rooting out violators and physical abilities that allowed him to chase those outlaws up and down his mountain ranges with the seeming ease of a mountain goat. Those traits were assisted by a sharp mind that could outthink most poachers. He was tenacious in pursuit and, like the best of his kind, almost seemed to be talking directly to the critters about who was doing what to whom, where and when.

He was not only resolute but fair and honorable. It was a given that when the wildlife resources were in his area, like salmon, band-tailed pigeons, or sturgeon during their annual migrations, so were the outlaws. But they knew Hank was there as well. And if it took a twenty-hour day to get the job done, he would be there to carry out the duties at hand!

When I worked covertly in his district, I would often hear the outlaws who didn't have a clue as to my identity say in a respectful tone, "I will kill that son of a bitch if I ever get him in my rifle sights!" But none ever pulled the trigger, for they knew Hank was right in protecting the harried creatures of the land and water. That tone of voice is always a good sign that you are doing your job and the outlaws respect you.

Glenn Ragon

Glenn Ragon, Humboldt County deputy sheriff, is not a tall man but is solidly built and close to the ground, like a fireplug. He has a jutting jaw that speaks to an innate toughness and single-mindedness when it comes to law enforcement that is legendary in Humboldt County to this day. He was an officer who always used his head in tough situations, but if it came to a physical confrontation, you had better bring a lunch because he would soon be taking you to the bucket and your lunch home to eat. It made no difference to him what type of law you violated—if you were wrong, you were taken before the mast. Glenn had an intelligence system like no other I have ever known. Bottom line: Break the law in his district, and it was just a short time before you were caught, thanks to his work ethic and that deadly intelligence system. His patrol area was historically utilized by poachers because of its vast resources and remoteness. It was also staffed by at least three game wardens, and yet Glenn would write more Fish and Game citations in a year than the three wardens combined! He was always there to assist the wardens in any way, and one could hope for no better backup. Glenn was so effective that many outlaws moved their operations out of his area into other, less aggressive officers' districts to continue their illegal pursuits.

When I transferred from Humboldt to Colusa County in the Sacramento Valley as a state Fish and Game warden, I forgot Glenn under a blizzard of work in my new district until he showed up at my front door one day. It seemed that he took several weeks off each year and moved to Colusa County to hunt ducks. He loved to hunt and eat waterfowl. From that moment at my front door sprang a renewal of our friendship that was a plus for the wildlife and a negative for the poachers in the Sacramento Valley. Glenn would hunt when he found time and then go to work with me. Since he was a state peace officer, he could legally enforce any state laws statewide. By damn, Glenn and I had such a chemistry that when we worked together, the bad guys fell by the droves. For several years, the two of us spent time during his vacations running the back roads and rice fields of Colusa County in pursuit of the outlaws and all those involved with the slaughter of waterfowl in the Sacramento Valley.

It wasn't until I was promoted and reassigned to Bismarck, North Dakota, as a senior resident agent for the U.S. Fish and Wildlife Service that this outlaw-catching duo was broken up for the last time and the bandits in the Sacramento Valley got a breather. That was too bad because when we ran together, the sky was the limit. There were many instances that could have gotten ugly if I had been by myself. But with my capable and determined partner at my side, no situation ever got out of hand. One look told anyone with an ounce of sense that laying a hand on either of us would not be in anyone's best interest.

Today Glenn, like me, is pretty broken up physically, but he still has that look of fierce determination and the heart of a lion. When God comes for Glenn, he'd better bring a lunch. Here is one man who made a difference not only in keeping me alive but in saving a hatful of God's critters in the Sacramento Valley in the process.

Joe Galipeau

My brother-in-law Joe, a former chief master sergeant in the U.S. Air Force, is a sprite of a man, hardly bigger than a green-winged teal! Originally from Maine, he is as tough as the granite found throughout that state. We have always gotten along famously, and when he and his family moved to an air base near Sacramento (fifty miles from where I was stationed), it was a partnership made in heaven for the two of us and hell on wheels for the bad guys in the Sacramento Valley. Joe is a big sportsman, especially when it comes to bird hunting. Guess who else loved hunting game birds? It was only natural that the two of us got along. Joe is easygoing, very bright, mechanically gifted, knowledgeable in the ways of the wild, and has a great way with people. Many times he would put in a sixteen-hour shift with the air force and then drive to my home in Colusa. After grabbing a quick bite to eat, he would put in another sixteen hours with me chasing bad guys, especially those slaughtering the ducks and geese. I always had a mountain to climb in order to maintain law and order in my district. The area was rich beyond compare in resources and near several major population centers. It historically was home to commercial-market hunters, duck draggers, and other illegal shooters. Twenty-hour days were the norm, and for anyone who had the misfortune to work with me, that became their norm as well.

Joe was not a law enforcement officer, nor was he trained in that profession. However, he would have made a great one! He is one of those people who has a natural instinct for the work. That penchant came out many times when the two of us tangled with deadly serious outlaws, especially night shooters of waterfowl. Joe has a natural survival instinct, and when things got dicey, I would find him doing exactly what I would have expected from an experienced officer! Uneven odds are daily occurrences for conservation officers, and many do not have the luxury of a second or a backup. When Joe was around, I always had a wise second working the fringes of the "hurrah," keeping my back clear and the bad guys off their feed. It made no difference what dangers we faced: Joe was prepared to dish out as much as he got.

Here is to a man who made a difference in the rice fields of Colusa County catching those slaughtering the waterfowl, even though he *didn't have to.* ... His love for the land, the critters, and his brother-in-law transcended all.

Jack Downs

The first time I met Jack Downs, agent in charge for the U.S. Fish and Wildlife Service, I was chasing those illegally shooting ducks in the early-morning hours in the rice fields of the Sacramento Valley of California. I had decided to call it a day at three in the morning, and after quietly extricating myself from a field that contained about twenty-five thousand feeding ducks, I headed for my hidden patrol vehicle. On my way home, I called the Colusa County sheriff's office and let them know I was coming off my stakeout. They acknowledged the message, and once again, silence filled the airways except for the occasional grinding noise from feeding waterfowl or rattle of shots fired by those dragging the ducks.

Then I heard the faint click of a radio mike, and a voice came over the air on the Fish and Game frequency, saying, "Hey, Tiny, what's your 20 [location]?"

Not knowing whom the voice belonged to but knowing he was another officer, I replied, "Corner of the Maxwell Road and Four Mile. Who is this?"

"This is 207. Wait right there; I would like to meet you. 207 clear."

Pulling off to the side of the road, I waited in the moonless winter dark. I had heard a lot about Jack Downs and his legendary abilities in catching the worst of the outlaws but had never met him. I had always wanted to be a game management agent like Jack, but to date, I had been unsuccessful in joining that small, elite bunch of federal wildlife law enforcement officers. It seemed that there never was an opening in those hallowed ranks. Those fortunate enough to become game agents seemingly lived long lives and died in place with their hip boots on.

Soon I heard the sound tires make running slowly on a graveled road. Looking north on Four Mile Road from whence the sounds came, I saw nothing.

Jack was running without lights so as not to give away his position (a common practice in those days by officers working the night shooters and duck draggers). Soon his sedan pulled alongside my truck.

"'Morning, Tiny. Where the hell are all your compatriots? The valley is full of birds and draggers. Critters could use a little help I would think from the rest of your boys wearing the green."

"Home in bed, I guess," I replied.

"Why aren't you home in bed?" he asked with an impish grin as he stepped out of his vehicle.

"I guess I'm as dumb as you," I said with an answering grin. He just chuckled, and there began a lifetime of friendship that continued until he retired years later.

That was 1967, and between then and 1970, I had many opportunities to work with Jack chasing the Sacramento Valley duck draggers and those on the duck clubs who couldn't count. In the process, I found myself constantly learning from his dedicated and intelligent ways. "Bright" was an understatement. I can't say I ever ran across anyone who possessed that man's skills in dealing with the courts, sportsmen, club owners, outlaws, laws of the land, and ever-present crooked politicians. He was truly the "agent's agent" in every aspect of the profession. Be it as a quiet teacher, supervisor, "catch dog," or friend and ally when we state officers got in over our heads politically and needed his strong federal backing for protection from our own agency, he was there.

In the spring of 1970, I received a career-altering call from Jack. He asked if I wanted to work for him as a game management agent. I did, and the rest is history. I learned by leaps and bounds from Jack as he exposed me to every kind of learning opportunity: duck banding in Canada, attending the national academy in Washington, D.C., as a member of our agency's first training class, fieldwork across California and Nevada, courtroom operations, grand juries, teaching state officers, working in covert capacities, teaching at the national academy, major covert operations, takedowns, and everything in between that had a positive impact on a federal officer. When I left California and Jack's command, I was a young officer who had grown older in the traces in a positive manner unknown to most officers of my time and grade. Jack had seen to it that I came away from our relationship a much better officer and man. That training would serve me well throughout the following years in the profession.

I only had four and a half years' service as an agent when Jack supported my promotion to senior resident agent in Bismarck, North Dakota. Such a move was not usual in those days in the western region unless an officer had between seven and eight years' field experience.

Jack continued to move and shake the very timbers the Service leaned on by creating the concept of the wildlife inspector program as we know it today. He was the special agent in charge in the New York district, which included the ports of entry in New York and New Jersey, at one time the busiest international ports in the world. Literally thousands of tons of wildlife imports arrived daily from around the world, and a pile of those imports were patently illegal as a result of smuggling or false documentation. Any wildlife shipments had to be inspected and approved for importation by the Service. That meant using scarce numbers of special agents from the field to conduct business at the ports of entry. Desperate for more help than his limited number of agents could provide and finding none forthcoming from the Service, Jack created the concept of the wildlife inspector program and pushed it through his regional office. Today approximately one hundred wildlife inspectors are making history across numerous designated and nondesignated ports of entry because of Jack and his insight.

I think one measure of a man's greatness is what he passes on to others. I learned a lot from Jack and tried to emulate him as a supervisor in later years. Because of him, we made a difference, especially regarding those who chose to slaughter the ducks in the Sacramento Valley.

Dennis "Buck" Del Nero

Buck Del Nero, a California Fish and Game warden, and I first met in the summer of 1966 at the Riverside Sheriff's Academy in Riverside, California. Game wardens were sent in those days to this police academy in southern California to satisfy the Peace Officer's Standards of Training requirements for entry-level officers. Buck was a big man in those days, standing six foot four inches tall and carrying a lean 250 pounds on his frame. He was smart as a whip and had that faraway yet knowing look when it came to talking about wildlife law enforcement. At the time, I did not possess the feeling behind that look, or understand it. It wasn't a crazy look, mind you, but seemed to transcend reality. I never really understood it until years later when we worked together as a law enforcement team. Only then did I understand the genius of the man and his innate ability to look into the beyond that led to hundreds of arrests or citations over the years.

In May 1970, I resigned my commission as a state game warden and became a game management agent with the U.S. Fish and Wildlife Service. As an agent, I found myself working the conservation outlaws in many areas throughout the state. That included working the delta area near Stockton due to the heavy concentrations of dove, ducks, geese and shooters who seemed to have a great degree of difficulty in counting what they shot and the time of day or season.

As luck would have it, I received a phone call from Buck, the local state Fish and Game warden, before I wasted a lot of time mucking around trying to learn the Stockton area. Buck had a world of wildlife in his district (mostly game birds and fish) and a lot of mean-spirited, violating sons of guns that any "catch dog" would be proud to have as targets. Many times he needed my federal "skirts" to ride on or hide behind in order to reach into the worst dens of outlaws. Working out a simple battle plan for catching every son of a gun in the valley, off we went into a series of adventures I still remember and relish to this day.

"That's Dante Crudelli," he said as an inconspicuous pickup passed us going the other way on a dirt farm road one day. "He will go into the safflower field behind his barn and shoot dove before the season opener this afternoon."

Looking over at Buck, I thought, *Yeah, right. Nothing like looking into the future ...*

Sure as shooting (no pun intended), we caught Dante killing dove during the closed season that afternoon in his safflower field behind the barn.

"That's 'Baby Fat' Bushalacci. He's heading out to Nomellinis' to shoot pheasants or early-shoot some ducks on the duck club," Buck said as we passed another pickup a day later. This time we hid in an adjacent walnut grove until Baby Fat started shooting and then made a clean apprehension, which included four preseason ducks and an unplugged shotgun.

"We need to go down Road D. There will be a wad of guys shooting dove off the power lines and taking them out of the mullein patches [plants producing hard, black seeds that the dove loved] before season begins," Buck told me. Four hours of hard work on Road D, and we had six shooters for violating federal law with their illegal taking of dove during the closed season from their vehicles.

Many of the rich and poor fell to our "guns" that summer and fall. We discovered thirty-nine baited fields just before the first day of dove season, four baited deepwater duck clubs, gross overlimits of waterfowl taken on the Venice Island Duck Club, overlimits of waterfowl and use of bait on Mandeville Island, early-shooting and overlimits of ducks taken over bait on Jones Tract—and on it went with stunning regularity! It was like being a kid in a candy store. Everything Buck touched turned into hundreds of citations and truckloads of evidence birds. In that first seven-month period working with Buck in the delta, I wrote more citations than any ten officers would normally write in a year! We averaged seventeen major citations a day while working together.

"If we can get on this island without discovery, we will catch the duck club and its shooters with gross overlimits of ducks and geese," said Buck, nodding toward a small island. In response, I placed a magnetic sign on the doors of the truck from my box of tricks, and the two of us boarded the public ferry going to that private duck club. The operator came over to check us out and see what our reason was for being on the ferry. If he suspected we were the law, he would have called the clubhouse and duck blinds (before the existence of cell phones, many wealthy clubs had land-line phones in the blinds just for this reason) before we arrived. I told the operator I was a natural gas technician going to check for a reported leak (the island was over a large natural gas dome storage area). The seal on my front door read, "Pacific Gas and Electric Company." Satisfied, the ferry operator docked without making any calls. Letting Buck off on the bottom side of the duck club's hunting area, I headed for the top end. As we walked toward each other, checking the hunters in their blinds, we found every so-called sportsman in violation! Six hours later, I had cited twenty-three individuals for overlimits of geese and ducks, no federal duck stamps, no state hunting license, unplugged guns, wanton waste, and taking closed-season species (canvasbacks). On that occasion, we just loaded the duck club's sixteen-cubic-foot freezer full of overlimits of ducks into the back of my truck as evidence. We found that it contained over four hundred picked and cleaned mallards and pintails!

By the time we boarded the ferry to leave the island, the word was out. The ferry operator briskly walked over to my truck with an obvious bit between his teeth.

"You bastards! Why didn't you tell me who you were?" he sneered.

"Why?" I asked. "So you could tip off the shooters and the club?"

He just looked at me for a hard minute and returned to his ferry duties. The next time Buck and I hit that club, that ferry operator had been replaced. …

I was now a true believer in that look Buck got in his eyes whenever he saw a mess of ducks working a marsh, a row of dove on a power line, a certain individual driving down the road, and everything wildlife- or human-related in between. Buck was the most uncanny officer I ever ran across who seemingly had total knowledge of the happenings in his district. Not to mention the fact that he knew everybody, and seemingly knew where and when they would violate even before they did! We met a lot of honest sportsmen during that period as well as lawbreakers. But that first seven-month period we worked together (not all the time either, because I had other duties in my Sacramento district), Buck and I seized over 3,500 illegal ducks and about 1,000 geese! I lost count of how many hundreds of dove we seized and the number of baited fields we discovered. In one day, Buck and I seized over 650 ducks and geese on just two duck clubs! Our best bag for the day on illegal dove was just 377. Tell me we didn't have some great chemistry to go along with our "help" from upstairs!

We also shared a strong desire, almost a vision quest, to catch every violating, trigger-pulling son of a gun within reach. I think we damn near did, and a lot of them twice before our tour of duty was over! When Buck was on patrol, no one was safe. When the two of us were together, a lot of fat cats paid the price. In fact, it got so bad for the bad guys that many Mondays, the director for the California Department of Fish and Game, one G. Ray Arnett, and his chief of law enforcement, Charlie Fullerton, would have a get-together with my boss, Jack Downs, and Buck's boss, Jim Wichtum. The purpose of this political form of "piling on" was to iron out the "unfair" treatment and harassment issues of those mashed fat cats who had gotten caught with their greasy hands deep in Mother Nature's cookie jar. However, the complaints were all to no avail. Buck and I would descend into the pits of the delta the following week and extract another bucket of knotheads with heavy trigger fingers and empty heads. I wrote over five hundred citations that seven-month period in the Stockton area and never lost one case in federal court! That figure does not include the citations Buck issued for his local state courts. Not bad for a couple of country boys.

I won't identify the city, but Buck and I got invited to a Ducks Unlimited chapter-founding dinner one evening. As we sat down, we happened to get a list of names of that chapter's founders and major donors. Between Buck and yours truly, we had cited 208 of the 211 for major migratory bird violations!

In September 1974, I was promoted and sent to Bismarck, North Dakota. That transfer broke up the "dirty duo," as Buck and I were called locally. Over the years I have lost track of the big lug since his retirement. Buck is one in a million, and I was blessed to have had an opportunity to ride on the coattails of such a man and officer.

Tim Dennis

Tim Dennis, once a rice farmer and deputy U.S. game management agent, was from a long line of Sacramento Valley pioneers. He enjoyed his line of work and was a great hunter and lover of waterfowl. He also lived in a place where and time when game wardens and their profession were not loved by many people.

Colusa County had historically been a commercial-market hunting area because of the great clouds of waterfowl inhabiting the Sacramento Valley during their earlier migrations. Literally hundreds of thousands of migratory waterfowl were shot over the decades and sold in the markets of Sacramento, San Francisco, Los Angeles, Reno, Marysville, Yuba City, and sometimes as far away as Chicago.

It was still somewhat that way when I arrived in Colusa County as a state Fish and Game warden in the fall of 1967 and when I became a game management agent in 1970. Many people would not talk to me once they found out I was a conservation officer, or if they did, it was never more than a few guarded words. But changes were taking place. A lot of the old-time market hunters were dying or retiring from the field, the demand for a duck dinner was waning, and the great clouds of ducks were almost becoming a thing of the past. Because of the decline in waterfowl populations, I made a point of being out and about when the critters were in the valley. I began catching more than my share of outlaws, both young descendants of old-time shooters and casual violators. Soon the general bad feeling about game wardens in some circles increased because of my successes. I lived, ate, and slept with the ducks, and soon those crazy enough to stray across the line were running afoul of the law. That was what I was paid to do, and I earned my keep.

But there was always more work for me to do than possible. For a long time, I just increased my time in the field until my body was requiring only four hours of sleep per night to meet the new demands for my time. I was young, and the catchin' was good, so I kept my face into the wind and worked my way though as many bad guys as possible. I could have used some help, but other than occasional support provided by Glenn Ragon and Joe Gallipeau, none was forthcoming until one fine fall day.

I was mowing my lawn to avoid having my wife remind me for the fourth time to cut the six-inch-tall grass when a three-quarter-ton, blue-and-white Ford pickup drove into my driveway. Out stepped a man who was built like a brick. He wore a cowboy hat and strode purposefully over to me.

"Hello. I'm Tim Dennis from Maxwell. We haven't met, but I already feel I know you from the talk of the local outlaws in my dad's restaurant. I don't know if you know it or not, but you sure as hell are making a dent in their gunning pastime."

Grinning at the news, I said, "Well, I hope so. There seems to be a fair number of them out and about, be it daylight or dark. And most of them seem to be having trouble counting when they are out killing." However, still suspicious of many of the valley folks, I didn't say any more because it always seemed to get back to me, many times in ugly tones.

"That's why I am here," Tim said as he shook my hand with a firm farmer's grip. "I have pretty well got my work done for the year as a rice farmer and decided I would give you a hand at stopping some of the slaughter."

Now, still being fairly new in the valley, I reared back at his unexpected offer. First of all, all I needed was to let an insider see how I was catching so many folks. I could just picture that fellow running off and blabbing my tricks of the trade. Then there was the issue of Tim not being a law enforcement officer. Don't get me wrong—I was happy for the offer of help. But I really didn't know this chap and sure as hell didn't want my "catch dog" secrets to get out.

"Well, thank you for the offer. One of these days I will give you a call, and we can give it a whirl," I said casually.

I didn't really mean it, for all the reasons I just listed. We parted company, and for the next month, Tim would call regularly to ask if I needed any help. I always politely declined. I just didn't have the time or trust, so I kept him at bay. Then one day Tim called and asked if he could ride along with me.

Feeling somewhat trapped and embarrassed at having kept him at bay for so long, I accepted his offer.

"I'll pick you up tomorrow morning about seven, and we will spend a day in the outback," I said.

"I'll be ready and meet you at the Maxwell Cafe," he answered.

With the ending of that simple conversation began a friendship lasting until this day, even though we have been apart for almost forty years. The following morning, I picked Tim up, and we headed west out of Maxwell toward a little mountain town called Stonyford. We hadn't gone more than a couple of miles when I noticed a pickup moving slowly along the country highway ahead of us. Coming up on it from behind, I caught two citizens from Maxwell (Tim's hometown) illegally road-hunting pheasants. Three illegal pheasants and two loaded guns later, I finished up with the lads. Throughout the process, I had seen the two miscreants giving Tim long, hard, dagger-like stares.

Afterward I said to Tim, "You just made a couple of enemies."

"No big deal," he said. "They needed catching for a long time, and I am glad I was there to let them know that from now on if I see them doing something like that, they will get reported."

I couldn't help but marvel at the sand Tim was showing. Especially in light of the sentiment of a lot of the folks in the valley regarding my profession.

As luck would have it that day, we caught two deer poachers, four more chaps with loaded guns, two fellows shooting dove off the power lines from a motor vehicle, and an even dozen on Lake Ladoga with fishing violations! It was just one of those days when everything quietly fell into place and I was at the right place at the right time. Unfortunately or fortunately, as one might look at it, Tim was hooked on this law enforcement thing! When I dropped him off that evening, he made it abundantly clear that he wanted to do more of what we had just accomplished, and to be frank, so did I. Tim turned out to be a great guy and companion. He had no agenda other than stopping those violating the wildlife laws of the land. On top of that, he had a wealth of knowledge of the geography, landownership patterns, and history of the area. Such a resource was a boon to any local conservation law enforcement officer.

For the rest of my time in the Sacramento Valley as an officer, day or night, I now had a companion who was rapidly developing into a close friend. I took Tim everywhere, and soon he developed into one hell of a "catch dog" in his own right. No challenge was too big for the man, and many times, we went right into the lion's den after the lawless. Many of the people we caught were his old friends, family members, fellow dirt farmers, or school buddies. That made no difference to Tim. They all fell to the long arm of the law, and many times after the dust had settled, they chewed his hind end for running with the law. Unfazed, Tim would inform the miscreants that their days of lawlessness and slaughter were over and they and others like them must stop or suffer the consequences. Soon I began to notice that some of the worst local outlaws were beginning to walk away from their lawless pursuits. I don't know if it was because I was making inroads into their subculture, because of having Tim in my camp, or a combination of both. But either way, we made a great team. I will never know the full extent of the crap Tim took from his friends in the valley for throwing in with the hated game warden, but it had to be considerable. But Tim never wavered. He had a real love for the world of wildlife and was bound and determined to see that his kids and everyone else's had an opportunity to enjoy it as well.

When I resigned my state Fish and Game warden's commission in May 1970 in order to take a commission with the U.S. Fish and Wildlife Service as a game management agent, our work continued. Tim had such a love for what we were doing and such a knack for the profession that I often wished he had the academic credentials for the job. However, he didn't have a college degree, and that pretty well cut off any avenue for him to go into the wildlife law enforcement profession. However, in those days, we had deputy U.S. game management agents, though they were for the most part already credentialed officers. With that in mind, I hit up my boss, Jack Downs, to see if it were possible to somehow credential Tim. After all, he showed great promise, was loaded with common sense, quickly grasped the position's duties, and was a natural "catch dog." Jack wasn't sure if credentialing someone other than a full-fledged officer was possible but said he would contact his boss in Portland and see.

Several weeks later, Tim and I were in Humboldt County working sportsmen taking Pacific black brant (a true sea goose, able to manufacture freshwater from saltwater) during the regular hunting season. Jack met us at Glenn Ragon's house in the mountains above Eureka for a Dungeness crab dinner and afterward made a surprise presentation.

"Tim, raise your right hand," said Jack.

All of us were surprised at that odd request, but Tim did as he was told. Jack swore him in and presented him with his own set of U.S. deputy game management agent credentials! Man, talk about stunned. Both Tim and I just stood there looking at that silver badge in Tim's hands. That wasn't all. Tim, because of the abilities he had shown, was to receive a salary, an expense account, and a government vehicle for official use. In fact, I think he was the only person in the United States at that time so honored! Needless to say, it was a memorable day for both of us and a bad one for the outlaws.

For the next four years in the Sacramento Valley, always in the face of a fair amount of local animosity, Tim continued to enforce the federal laws. We worked together on his rice farm (I would take several weeks of annual leave in the spring) to get the crop in. Then come fall, Tim would swing into law enforcement, and the two of us would cut quite a swath.

Never once did Tim let me down, and there were some tough times when we surprised bunches of outlaws doing what they did best. Tim was so steadfast that most miscreants just rolled over and took their punishment. We did canoe work in the Butte Sink, airboat work in the flooded Yolo Bypass, and stakeouts for deer poachers to assist the state wardens. We worked covertly on the abalone tides; staked out large ranches and their particular nests of illegal mule deer shooters in Modoc County; stalked the fat cats killing too many ducks and geese in the San Joaquin Delta; chased deer poachers at night on the private ranches in the Sacramento Valley; and worked the rice fields at night in Colusa, Butte, Glenn, and Yolo Counties chasing the night shooting duck poachers and few remaining commercial-market hunters.

Not once did Tim ever lose a case in state or federal court or do anything unprofessional to embarrass the Service. I have worked with a lot of officers over my career throughout the United States and along the border of Canada. I can say with certainty that Tim Dennis was one of the finest, most professional officers I ever had the honor to work with. He never had to get involved, but he did. He stepped into the mud and blood of the arena, carrying the torch as well as anyone. I thank him for that, and the critters do as well. He made a difference when a difference was really needed in stopping the slaughter in the Sacramento Valley. …

John Cooper

The first time I met Special Agent John Cooper was as his new supervisor in his office in Minot, North Dakota. When I walked in, the first thing he said as he looked up was, "Holy cow, where did all the light go?"

That was my first exposure to a man who always had a lighter side to his soul and heart. John had come to the Service from the Naval Investigative Service. He had a deep. abiding interest in the world of wildlife and was self-taught. John was bright, sharp-eyed as an owl, was totally dedicated to the resources of the land, and accompanied all those virtues with a sense of joy at being alive. I guess two tours of duty in Vietnam will do that for some people.

Being new to the area, I had John introduce me to the many resource problems in North Dakota. I had a Canadian border running the length of the state with all its warts and related ports of entry, rampant drainage of Service-owned or -administered wetlands by a hatful of half-crazy dirt farmers, over 150 national wildlife refuges with their attendant problems, numerous tribes of Native Americans scattered throughout the state with their unique problems, illegal airborne hunting of furred critters up the tailpipe during the winter season, rampant illegal grazing of cattle on Service lands, and a budget that was virtually nonexistent!

Every time we got together, the training would commence, since I had come from a region without any of these problems. I soon realized that John was an exceptional officer. He had a wisdom beyond his years relative to the resources and their complexities. His knowledge of the federal laws was outstanding, and when he applied them, it was with a fairness and seriousness of an officer senior to him in years. He had an easy manner and an intense dedication to the profession at hand. He had won over the hearts and minds of other Service employees in his district, especially some of the hard-headed, anti-law enforcement types.

For the next two years, John and I worked our way through many problems that had been left sitting on the Service's books for years. It seemed that just about every time we enforced the laws, it ended up being a first law situation, or off to the Supreme Court the issue would go. Fortunately, we had two of the country's finest assistant U.S. attorneys in Dave Peterson from Bismarck and Lynn Crooks from Fargo. With their iron-solid support and keen minds, John and I never lost a major battle!

In September 1976, I was promoted again and sent to Washington, D.C. I lost track of John but did not forget him. In June 1981, I was promoted once again and sent to the Denver office as the special agent in charge. I was pleased to discover that John Cooper had been promoted to the senior resident agent position in Pierre, South Dakota (in my new district), and our relationship took up where it had left off.

Once again, I had an exceptional officer in a place where wildlife issues abounded. John seemed to be always amid the swirl of action, calmly and skillfully working through the legal and often dangerous issues. Many national law enforcement issues were generated under John Cooper that ended up in the Supreme Court, and every one of them was settled in favor of the government!

John's skill in pursuing and prosecuting complex legal issues became legendary. I never discovered any sign of loose ends or sloppy work in his investigations. He was exceptional in all he did and said. Soon he became a spokesman for the Service in many arenas, most of which required the very best of an officer. He was also a good friend and valued counselor. It was a once-in-a-lifetime experience for almost any supervisor.

Before I retired in 1998, John had resigned his commission and became in essence the state Fish and Game director for South Dakota. Today John is recognized as a major force in the world of wildlife conservation, and I expect he will remain so until he steps down from his new position working for the governor, or moves across that Great Divide.

Robert Hodgins

In February 1979, I transferred to Minneapolis, Minnesota, to be assistant special agent in charge to Special Agent in Charge Bob Hodgins. For the next two years, I got an education from my boss that has never been, nor ever will be, equaled! Bob came to the Service straight from his position as director of South Dakota Game, Fish, and Parks. His appointment generated one hell of a lot of animosity in the Service's Division of Law Enforcement because it was perceived by many as nothing more than a political appointment to one of the highest positions in law enforcement—a position highly sought-after by many among the rank and file of senior law enforcement. However, within months, agents from across the country began to realize that Hodgins was an exceptional manager, law enforcement officer, leader, and human being.

Bob is now dead. But in the two-year period that I worked for the man, I got a rare and exceptional schooling. Bob was one of the brightest people I ever worked for. His recall of events that had occurred five or more years earlier was legendary. He could remember a person's name, the event, the case disposition, and many other points of value from previous investigations. I remember him going frequently to his secretary, Barbara Anderson, and saying something like,

"Remember that falconer in Illinois that Karen Halpin caught three years ago with the extra birds hidden in his car? Would you pull that file for me, please? His last name was Jones. and he was from the Springfield area."

I had a master's degree and a pile of years of service, and I couldn't even remember where the bathroom was! How Bob did that memory thing was a mystery to me and a marvel to his field officers, whom he called his "gumshoes."

There wasn't a day that went by when he wasn't in my office teaching me a thing or two about being a better manager, supervisor, agent, or human being. His mind was constantly flowing with ideas like a creek during the spring runoff. Those ideas led to numerous investigations, ways to cut corners (we were always broke), ways to beat some extra money out of the Service higher-ups, ways to build a fire under a gutless attorney without pissing him off, how to best settle pissing contests between the officers in the field or the ladies in the office, a new way to get through the budgetary minefield without getting caught, how best to trap the chief of law enforcement (who was no slouch himself when it came to being downright devious)—and on it went. There were days when I was so full of his thoughts and ideas that I would go home and just sit on the back porch for a while to let it all settle into place. He suggested not only fresh ideas, many of them revolutionary, but how to successfully implement them. He was forever saying things like, "Big T, get your butt in here. I got an idea on how to settle the squabbling between the two Illinois senior resident agents."

Bob's love for his staff and field officers was legendary. To him, his folks were almost like his kids (Bob was a World War II veteran). His love for the resources was legendary as well. I don't know if it came from his South Dakota prairie upbringing or something else, but suffice it to say, if you messed with the resources in his district, the wrath of hell would be down around your ears once Bob found out! We always had the youngest agents in the land in his district. We couldn't afford senior officers drawing higher salaries because our annual budget was so low. But I remember that in 1979, we had sixteen covert operations going on at the same time with these badge-carrying youngsters, the most in the nation! Before all was said and done, we rounded up over 470 bad guys as a result of those investigations.

In those days, our region had over sixty-five million people, many of them pounding the resources as hard as they could. Illegal commercial fish houses on the Great Lakes, fish houses taking fish tainted by PCBs from Lake Erie and selling them in the fish markets of New York, overlimits of ducks and geese being taken in Illinois, politically crooked state Fish and Game agencies, illegal movement of spawning and speared walleye off reservations, illegal wildlife flowing across the Canadian border, illegal importations of endangered species into the port at Chicago—it was a virtual law enforcement blizzard. "Hodge" sat calmly at the helm in this whirlwind. He would shift agents from one battlefront to another just as fast as they finished a detail. His selection of the right kind of personality for each job was uncanny. And his care for the natural resources was matched only by the concern he had for his young gumshoes.

Never had I seen a better field general working with limited means, dragging down some of the worst outlaws the country ever experienced. And if we were short-handed, Bob would be right in the middle of the action with his young officers. Even if that meant going into the bowels of Detroit to claw some miscreant out from under the woodwork in the ghetto, Bob was right there with a calm demeanor—and a 12-gauge shotgun in hand in case things got out of control. He was only an average shooter with a handgun, but there wasn't one of us who wouldn't have laid down his life for the man.

I was blessed in being able to share several years of my still formative management life with Bob. He taught me a world of things, much of which I continue to use to this day. He was without a doubt one of the most exceptional and influential leaders I have ever had the honor to serve. When he died, the Service lost one of its very best; grown officers cried and the critters lost a great friend.

Nando Mauldin and Dave Kirkland

Separating the exploits of these two special agents, even though they often worked individually, would be a travesty. Both worked for the branch of Special Operations for years, covertly investigating some of the worst wildlife crimes in America. They were like two peas in a pod: intelligent beyond belief, extremely dedicated to catching everyone breaking the law, possessing mental capacities that boggled the minds of us normal folks standing around looking on, and possessing a dedication to the natural resources of the land and the American people that is unequaled today.

They took on the most dangerous and complex covert operations of the day, bringing almost every one of those targeted souls to the mast without losing a defendant in the legal morass we call our system of justice. They worked investigations routinely involving commercial-market hunting and abject wanton waste of this nation's most precious natural resources. Both were naturals in the darkened world of deception called covert operations. One was an ex–Pennsylvania game warden and the other was a warden out of New Mexico. Yet both brought something from their previous experiences and backgrounds that made them brothers when it came to dedication and vision. Those traits were liberally sprinkled throughout every operation in which they were involved. No mater the complexities, those two would stride through the world of wildlife's battlefields as if it was old home week. At least, that was how it looked to those of us on the outside looking in.

I can remember them doing covert work in my district in the 1980s. Twice they came separately into my office, putting their fingers over their lips to quiet all questions as to how the investigation was going. Then they would sit down with a legal pad and begin writing. When they were done, I would pick up those pads and find dates, times, details of illegal sales or purchases, models of firearms, full names of dozens of outlaws, Social Security numbers of the shooters, calibers of firearms used to illegally kill, how many shots were fired on a given day, serial numbers of numerous weapons, weights of bullets used—and on it went! Incredible, to say the least, and a trait I haven't seen equaled to this day! After pouring out days' worth of their memories on paper, they would look up and casually say with a relieved grin, as if it was no big deal, "*Now* we can go and have a beer!"

I have no idea how many outlaws fell to these two officers over their storied careers. It had to be in the hundreds, if not thousands, over their years of opportunity. Hell, I would bet they can't even tell you. Oh, the stories and close calls they could write about. But knowing the modesty of those officers, their stories, both hell-raising and deadly, will never see the light of day or be added to the pages of the history of this nation.

These two men went after the nation's very worst under the deadliest conditions time and time again, alone, for over fifteen years. They worked by themselves, often without sidearms or backup, all the while extracting a brand of poison that was destroying a major part of our nation. Fully aware of the dangers, they continued their missions with dedication and focus. They and their families paid a high price that most Americans give but little thought. It is in part owing to men like these that there are still natural resources left for the rest of us to enjoy.

Larry Davis

Another exceptional state Fish and Game warden with few equals in the wildlife law enforcement profession was Larry Davis, who worked for the state of Utah. I had the honor of meeting Larry many years ago at a joint briefing between Service and Utah officers before a waterfowl task force operation in the marshes of the Great Salt Lake. He looked just like me—a beat-up old warhorse who had seen lots of "trails plowed under." But that was where all similarities ended. I spent many years working with a variety of state officers nationwide. Most were very good in their trade, some were not worth the powder to blow them to hell, and a few were exceptional. After working off and on for years with Larry, I believe he exceeded that description of "exceptional" when it came to his trade and profession. Larry was always quiet, laid back, extremely professional, and curious. He kept his eyes always searching, possessed a knowledge of the land's history rivaling that of Jim Bridger, was superefficient when it came to catching outlaws, and was also an outstanding human being.

What started out as a joke by task force organizers assigning the two oldest officers together ended up a disaster for the bad guys and for the assigning and competing officers as well. In a group of such multitalented officers, it was always a goal to be first in numbers of citations issued by the end of the assignment. I think they thought we two old guys would fall asleep under the first sage bush we came to and provide no competition to the sixty or so young bucks in the task force. But in the following years of friendly competition, in numbers of citations issued, Larry and I beat the socks off any two of the next-closest teams every year but one!

Sixteen- to eighteen-hour days were the norm for us. We traveled far and wide over the Utah marshes, snagging bad guys. Between Larry's knowledge of the area, his genius, and our noses and gut feelings for the illegal, there were times when the culprits were stacked up in front of Larry by the score waiting for their tickets. One of the things I noticed about Larry was his intense love for the land, its history, the American people, youngsters, and the critters. No matter what it took, he was always there to extract the greatest good for the resource. And it seemed that the harder we worked, the better we got.

Even more important than catching the outlaws was Larry's grasp of the laws and the life histories of the wildlife. Also exceptional was his ability to deal with people. He is absolutely unreal and uncanny in that art form that so many in our line of business have failed to master. But not my partner. He could talk the socks off a horse, and in so doing discover other violations lying hidden just beneath the discussion. More than once, I just stood in awe as I watched him doing one of the hardest things on earth, namely, dealing with his fellow humans!

Larry retired in August 2005. What a loss for those living inside and outside the world of wildlife! And what a loss I hope the state of Utah will someday come to realize and appreciate.

ROBERT PRIEKSAT

Without a doubt, one of the most dedicated and tenacious officers in the land when it comes to stalking, cold tracking, and apprehending the lawless individual is Special Agent Bob Prieksat. I made it my business over my many years in law enforcement to study people. Most are easy to read, and a few are very difficult. Bob wears his intentions clearly on his sleeve. It is very plain to see if he is hot on your trail—all you have to do is look back. His total dedication to the natural resources and the laws of the land is exceptional, if not legendary everywhere he has served. Coming from a long line of pioneer prairie stock, he has learned to see most things in a straightforward manner. It is that ability to focus and his dedication to the moment that make Bob the outstanding officer he is and has been for the last twenty-plus years of his state and federal wildlife law enforcement career. First as a South Dakota game warden and then as a special agent for the Service, Bob has dedicated himself to the world of wildlife. His work intensity is matched only by his outstanding ability in the legal arena. He is an exceptional thinker, strategist, and calculating infighter when dealing with the laws, legal representatives, and our sometimes questionable system of justice. His towering intellect is matched only by his work ethic. I think it is fair to characterize Bob in understandable law enforcement terminology: If he gets on your trail, the only thing you can do to get him off is shoot him!

Many dozens of outlaws over the last fifteen years taking wildlife in one state illegally and transporting it across state lines have come to know him personally. Without a doubt, based on his investigative history, current caseload, and rate of convictions, he is the number-one Lacey Act investigator in the nation. That is no small feat, considering the number of good officers scattered throughout the land offering competition.

Bob is currently in charge of North and South Dakota. Both are rich in natural resources and deep in complex wildlife law enforcement issues, many of which are national in scope. But it is a typical Bob Prieksat–managed operation. If there are problems, address them. If there are more problems, *find* a way to address them. And, if there are a world of problems, *get it done!* He's a tough man for a tough job. Bob knows extinction is forever, and if he has his say, it won't occur on his watch.

Russ Pollard

Another unusual officer I met over the years is Wyoming Fish and Game Warden Russ Pollard, recently retired. Russ is a quiet, unassuming man with a winning smile and flashing dark eyes that can look clear through you. However, below that exterior lies an officer with uncanny investigative abilities. With a set of miss-nothing eyes, an intelligence bordering on the unnatural, and the instincts of a superpredator, Russ was truly a superb hunter of men.

Having worked many times over the years with Russ, I had numerous opportunities to watch him in action as he dealt with the sporting public. During major interstate roadblocks operated in several Western states to check the American sportsman, I often just sat back and watched Russ, the master of such activities, in action. Quickly assessing vehicles laden with game as they entered the inspection area, he almost scented the air for something out of place. With a few questions, Russ might simply be done with one set of hunters except for a routine inspection of their game. However, with the next vehicle, he would again be winding the air with all his senses. Many times something would catch his attention—an unspoken word, a furtive glance, or a nonanswer—and with that, Russ would swing into action. He would gather up hunting licenses and tags, and his careful scrutiny alone seemed to flush many of those hiding something out from under the leaf litter. With just a tiny piece of evidence, he would run a violator to ground.

Watching Russ do what he did best allowed me to get schooled in senior law enforcement techniques by one of the nation's very best. More than once I have seen Russ use a single document or nonanswer to turn an inspection into a full-blown criminal investigation. Those investigations resulted in numerous wildlife seizures and arrested defendants hanging their heads as they trooped off to settle up with the state of Wyoming. His expertise did not end there. During quiet periods, he would move over to other stations' inspections and just scan their operations with the eyes of an eagle. Soon he would sense something that the other officers had missed and would quietly slide into the inspection much to the ultimate chagrin of the violators.

His method of interviewing was another example of excellence. No wasted words, just accuracy in trailing the loose leads and intense eye fixation of the subjects. Within moments he would be off on the trail of illegality, running his interest to ground in one quick swoop … after sensing all the time that it was there! Oftentimes when Russ swung into action, a group of his peers would walk over and look on in incredulous disbelief, trying to gain insight into the man's uncanny supersensory and investigative powers. His intensity in such operations was matched only by his smooth manner and outstanding professionalism when dealing with the American public. But make no mistake, when he was on the trail of the hunted, even those of us standing off to one side could smell the blood.

I tip my hat to a man who never rested his senses when enforcing the law and constantly exceeded the standard set in the profession when it came to "long-shooting" violators. I have always highly respected any officer who could reach out and touch someone needing the long arm of the law for "guidance," especially one showing no outward signs of guilt. Many thousands of critters have been saved as a result of Russ's work on the wildlife fields of battle. Violators who encountered the man more than likely remember how this seemingly quiet individual ran them to ground, usually in a heartbeat. I can only hope those people learned a lesson for the future.

Russ continues to serve our country in foreign lands that have turned deadly. I can only hope that he returns safely—and in the meantime, any enemy who challenges him had better watch out!

Pat Bosco

I have known Special Agent Pat Bosco for many years. I first met the man sitting on a hiring panel for special agents many years ago. Officers from the field whom I considered knowledgeable and trustworthy kept calling me from across the country, saying this guy Bosco needed to be hired. It seemed that the man had made an impression on what I considered solid officers, so I took a deeper look. I discovered that Pat was a wildlife inspector in New York City who did not have a college degree (a requirement by the Chief of the Division of Law Enforcement in those days). That alone portended a hiring fight! I also saw that he had simultaneously worked three jobs (one as a garbage collector) and gone to college in the evenings at the same time trying to earn a degree. As near as I could tell, the man was doing all that on about three hours of sleep per night! I thought anyone who put that much effort into trying to become an agent needed to be selected. After I underwent many arguments with the chief over hiring someone without a degree (the chief wanted us to look like the FBI), Bosco was selected.

I can't ever remember a new agent hitting the road running harder than Pat. He did everything at a speed advertising a skilled, focused, and driven work ethic. Associated with that was a high degree of intelligence, a vision, and an intense desire to serve. The man was a human dynamo! No matter what Pat did or got involved in, it was accomplished in record time and done exceptionally well; his conviction rate was also exceptional. He had worked hard all his life to get into the ranks of the agent corps, and by damn, he was making up for lost time.

As an instructor in state and federal institutions, there was none better. As a teacher to younger officers, he was exceptional. As a criminal investigator in the Service, he approached Special Agents Bob Prieksat and Jim Klett for tenacity and investigative excellence. In covert operations, he charmed the socks right off the bad guys every bit as well as Nando Mauldin and convicted every damn one of them. And as a friend to just about everyone, he is without equal. The Service had made a selection that ranked among its very best. The critters were rewarded by the man's intense and dedicated efforts, the officers surrounding Pat benefited greatly from his leadership talents, and the rest of us picked it up a notch in order just to stay even with Pat's efforts and the energy field surrounding him.

This man worked extremely hard just to show that he could make a difference, and rest assured, he has!

Tom Warren

There was a very unusual bearded giant residing on the military facility at Fort Carson in Colorado as the army's environmental director at the time this was written. He is in charge of seeing that the tanks and other military vehicles don't tear the hell out of the archaeological sites or destroy the resident endangered species and of protecting the landscape from overusage resulting in erosion and the destruction of game and nongame species. This mountain of a job is done very well by a mountain of a man with an iron handshake.

Early on, I discovered that the valuable work by Tom and his law enforcement staff didn't end on Fort Carson. Tom was into wise use and protection of wildlife and plant resources nationwide. After several meetings with this giant of a man, I discovered that his agenda included helping me in my eight-state region. The help was given in such a way that one would never see Tom's hands at the controls. He was a quiet, modest man whose aim was to serve the American people and see that future generations had natural resources to view and enjoy, as their families had over the previous years. Tom stayed in the background while his support efforts and other unique qualities as a conservationist took center stage with a rush like the charge of an African lion.

As the Service's chief law enforcement officer in a region of 750,000 square miles of resource-rich states, I had major problems just about everywhere I looked: a basically nonexistent budget, one-third of the nation's nonresident hunters in the area during hunting season, endangered species everywhere getting whacked, eagles by the thousands being taken illegally, oil field pollution, international borders overflowing with illegal wildlife, transmission lines killing untold hundreds of thousands of migratory birds, poison everywhere thanks in part to many sheepherders on public lands, commercial-market hunting in the national parks ... I think you get the message!

To handle all those issues, I had twenty-four hard-charging officers. Hell, Custer had better odds than that! But those odds were reduced time and time again through the quiet helping hand and leadership of my friend at Fort Carson. He was constantly at my side, offering gifted counsel and support in our mutual problems and endeavors, be it the loan of his officers for details, training, sharing equipment and intelligence, or just a shoulder to cry on. No better team from separate entities existed than we two giants from a world apart.

Over the years, I began to fully understand my bear of a friend. Together we would discuss monster interstate roadblocks, task force operations, covert operation takedowns, or large covert operations requiring his extensive support assistance in order to be successful. Many times Tom had ideas of how I could save money (always essential) or acquire the needed surplus equipment from the army to be used as cover or construction for an undercover project.

More often than not, he came up with the very thing that pushed my deep-cover operations into the success column. In fact, because of Tom's efforts and forward thinking, the Service was able to purchase and operate a half-million-dollar undercover ranch in order to look into illegal elk ranching! That feat has not been repeated by the Service before or since that date. Tom was open to any suggestion, as long as it was legal, about how he could use the power of his office to enhance Service operations. For example, hiding 275 officers on Fort Carson so we could make final preparations for a massive takedown of commercial-market hunters in the San Luis Valley without being discovered. Without his support, we could not have pulled the operation off so successfully.

During my entire stay as the special agent in charge in the Denver office, I had that big lug to lean on. As a result of his energies, counsel, and assistance, many operations were discussed, thought through more thoroughly, tried, and followed through to successful completion. Many hundreds of the most serious wildlife outlaws fell due to the great work of my officers and Tom's steady hands directing the needed manpower or supplies (through the system) to our battlegrounds.

Having that quality of an earthly guardian angel at my side allowed me to reach further and to shoot cleaner than most of my counterparts. Bad guys were stacked up and prosecuted as a result of that support, and the illegal killing in many of my areas of responsibility began to diminish. Tom was dedicated to protecting, preserving, and defending the world of wildlife and assisted the Service in successfully taking on some of the biggest investigative projects in the history of the agency.

Without Tom and his always quiet, quality support and gifted counsel, many more critters would have been illegally stacked up and removed from Mother Nature's rich but diminishing storehouse. The American people and I owe him big time ... not only for his service then but for his continuing service to our country in foreign lands.

Neill Hartman

Last, but certainly not least in my list of characters who influenced my life and the well-being of the world of wildlife is Neill Hartman, Region 6 assistant special agent in charge at the time of this writing. Neill came to the agent core from the Division of Wildlife Refuges and served commendably under me as a special agent when I was the assistant special agent in charge in Minneapolis. Even then, I could see that he was an officer of exceptional abilities. He was fearless, was a quick and sound thinker, had a driven work ethic and a nose for rooting out those needing an officer's attention at any level.

Years later, as special agent in charge in Denver, I selected Neill as my assistant special agent in charge because of his previous outstanding service. What a fortuitous move that proved to be! As expected, Neill brought a whirlwind of assets and values to my operation, not to mention a profound friendship and loyalty that exists to this day. He is just about without equal in his work ethic. To say that he is driven is an understatement! The man has more energy than a bag full of shrews. He constantly worked on bettering not only himself but the Service and its mission as well. Like other notables in the Service, he was a great teacher; was skilled in the legal arena almost to the point of being equal to the federal attorneys; and had a survival eye that was exceptional, a towering intellect, and loyalty above reproach. He also had a total dedication to his staff, fellow officers, mission, and supervisors. I was blessed to have him over the years as my deputy for a sounding board, teacher, instructor, counselor, leader, commander, and true friend. Nothing seemed impossible with Neill at my side. We did things years ago that the Service is just now discovering it should have been doing all along. We successfully ran grizzly bear backcountry programs with fellow officers such as not only Joel Scrafford, Richard Branzell, Tim "The Lawman" Eicher, and George Domenici; initiated complex covert operations with George Morrison; cooperated with eight states in setting up and operating numerous successful major interstate road blocks; initiated work on the oil field pollution problems with then Agent Gary Mowad; investigated issues of power line mortalities with Agent Leo Suazo; supported wetland easement enforcement programs with Agents Dave Kraft, Jim Klett, and John Cooper; settled cattle trespass problems on Service lands; enforced Service laws along the international borders in the region; set up and ran a wildlife repository with Grace Englund and Bernadette Atencio; and initiated outstanding teaching programs at numerous state and federal levels. None of this would have been possible without the support, guiding hand, intellect, and tremendous energies of my deputy.

If I came up with an idea, I would first run it by Neill. If I sold him, we were off to the races because I knew his quick, bear-trap-like mind had already computed its legality and chances for success. From then on, my trusty partner would take over the reins, and soon the project would be completed or ready for execution. Nothing seemed impossible as we ran along the very edge of the profession, many times picking off some of the worst outlaws in Mother Nature's pantry. Those were great, energy-charged years, and we accomplished a lot with the addition of this man to our region for the Service and the critters. Such accomplishments are not as common as they should be in the Service because of today's stifling politics and a decided lack of experienced leadership.

Neill's overall performance in his many years of service with the agency was exceptional, to say the least. His enlightened work with the various states in the region was brilliant. His work in seeing that the critters had a safe place to live showed that he was a visionary before his time. As a criminal investigator, he was without equal, and as an ethics-driven professional, there was none finer. As my deputy, he was without peer in the Division of Law Enforcement! Every senior-level supervisor should be blessed at least once in his or her career in having a Neill Hartman at his or her side. And as for a friend, a man could ask for none better.

Neill retired in 2005, and when he did, the critters lost a one-of-a-kind friend and protector.

I know I have left out dozens of others deserving to be mentioned in this minor work by a minor author. To those I have unintentionally slighted, I sincerely apologize. I know you are out there, but for some reason, I have slipped a cog and forgotten you and your service.

I wanted to let the American people know that there are folks out there who deserve their recognition and respect for doing an outstanding job on a little-known battlefield. Those fighting such a lopsided fight deserve some form of recognition, thanks, or even just a tip of the cap. They come from all walks of life, be they citizen, county, state, federal, tribal, or provincial officers. And they are giving their all for you, the critters, and generations yet to come. After all, it is a good fight that must be fought.